ROBERT BROWNING

Selected Poems

Edited with an Introduction and Notes by
DANIEL KARLIN

PENGUIN BOOKS

PENGUIN BOOKS

Published by the Penguin Group
Penguin Books Ltd, 80 Strand, London WC2R 0RL, England
Penguin Group (USA) Inc., 375 Hudson Street, New York, New York 10014, USA
Penguin Books Australia Ltd, 250 Camberwell Road, Camberwell, Victoria 3124, Australia
Penguin Books Canada Ltd, 10 Alcorn Avenue, Toronto, Ontario, Canada M4V 3B2
Penguin Books India (P) Ltd, 11 Community Centre, Panchsheel Park, New Delhi – 110 017, India
Penguin Books (NZ) Ltd, Cnr Rosedale and Airborne Roads, Albany, Auckland, New Zealand
Penguin Books (South Africa) (Pty) Ltd, 24 Sturdee Avenue, Rosebank 2196, South Africa

Penguin Books Ltd, Registered Offices: 80 Strand, London WC2R 0RL, England

www.penguin.com

This selection first published in Penguin Books 1989
Reprinted with new Chronology and Further Reading 2004
9

Introduction, Notes, Chronology and Further Reading copyright © Daniel Karlin, 1989, 2004
All rights reserved

Printed in England by Clays Ltd, St Ives plc
Filmset in 9 on 11pt Linotron Ehrhardt

Contents

CONTENTS

6

ROBERT BROWNING was born in Camberwell, in south-east London, in 1812. The major influences on his early development came from his father's large and eccentric library, his mother's deep Nonconformist piety, and his adolescent encounter with Romantic poetry (especially Shelley). After education at local schools and at home, he enrolled at the newly founded University of London in 1828, but left the following year. He travelled widely on the Continent in the 1830s and 1840s. He published *Pauline* anonymously and without success in 1833; *Paracelsus* (1835) made him known to London literary society. However, *Sordello* (1840), derided for its obscurity, blighted his career for over twenty years. He published a series of plays and collections of shorter poems, *Bells and Pomegranates* (1841–6). In January 1845 he began corresponding with Elizabeth Barrett; he met her in May 1845, and they were married in September 1846 after a clandestine courtship (because of Mr Barrett's implacable opposition to the idea of any of his children marrying). The Brownings lived in Italy until Elizabeth Barrett Browning's death in 1861. Browning published *Men and Women* (1855), which contains some of his finest poems, but still did not restore his reputation (or his sales). After his wife's death, Browning returned to England with their only son, and settled in London. He published *Dramatis Personae* (1864), a collection which began to repair his critical fortunes; this process was accomplished by the appearance of *The Ring and the Book* (1868–9). Among the works of his later years, *Fifine at the Fair* (1872), *Aristophanes' Apology* (1875), *La Saisiaz* (1878), *Dramatic Idyls* (1879), *Parleyings with Certain People of Importance in Their Day* (1887) and *Asolando* (1889) are outstanding. Browning died in Venice on 12 December 1889, and was buried in Poets' Corner in Westminster Abbey.

DANIEL KARLIN is Professor of English Literature at University College London. He has published extensively on Browning (both editions and critical books) and has edited *The Penguin Book of Victorian Verse* for Penguin Classics. He has also edited Rudyard Kipling's *The Jungle Books* for Penguin.

CONTENTS

INTRODUCTION

Robert Browning was born in Camberwell, in south-east London, on 7 May 1812. He was the son of Robert Browning, a clerk in the Bank of England, a mild, diffident man who was also an ardent book-lover and collector, and Sarah Anna Wiedemann, a woman of stronger character than her husband, and whose fervent Nonconformist piety was one of the abiding influences on her son's development. What we know of Browning in his early years suggests intellectual precocity, an excess of nervous energy (he is recorded as gnawing the edge of his pew during a long sermon) and a passionate attachment to home. He was not to leave until his marriage at the age of thirty-four, and remained until then financially dependent on his father, who paid for the publication of his poems. He was educated at home, mainly through the resources of his father's vast library. As a dissenter Browning could not go to Oxford or Cambridge; in 1828 he enrolled in London's new University College, but after a year became its most distinguished drop-out. He consistently refused to take up a career, and, overcoming his parents' opposition, formally dedicated himself to becoming a poet. As a young man he travelled extensively: in 1834 to Russia with a British diplomatic mission, in 1838 to Italy, returning through Germany and the Low Countries, in 1844, to Italy again. His literary career began in 1833 with the publication of *Pauline*, an anonymous poem which sank without trace and left Browning so ashamed of having written it that he suppressed it for over thirty years until the threat of piracy forced him to acknowledge it. Then came critical success with the appearance of *Paracelsus*, a long poem ostensibly about the sixteenth-century physician and alchemist, but in reality about the splendours and miseries of (Browning's) genius. *Paracelsus* established Browning on the London literary scene (friendships followed with John Forster, Harriet Martineau, Carlyle, Landor, Dickens) and brought him to the attention of the actor-manager William Charles Macready, at whose prompting he wrote his

9

first play, *Strafford*, produced at Covent Garden in 1837. It did not flop, and Browning was encouraged to try again. He wrote eight plays in all, of which only *Pippa Passes* (1841) and *A Soul's Tragedy* (1846) are other than mediocre. A disastrous production of *A Blot in the 'Scutcheon* (1843), during which Browning broke with Macready, and the subsequent failure of his negotiations with Macready's great rival, Charles Kean, put an end to Browning's theatrical ambitions. In the meantime a failure of a longer-lasting kind had afflicted his career with the publication of *Sordello* in 1840. This great poem, one of the most daring experiments with narrative structure since *Paradise Lost*, and the most radical (in politics and aesthetics) since *Prometheus Unbound*, was received with universal derision for its sublime difficulties of form and language. Tennyson said that there were only two lines in it that he understood, the first – 'Who will, may hear Sordello's story told' – and the last – 'Who would, has heard Sordello's story told' – and that both were lies. Carlyle claimed that his wife had read through the poem without being able to discover whether Sordello was a man, a city, or a book. Browning's reputation was not to recover for a quarter of a century; the publication of two collections of shorter poems, *Dramatic Lyrics* (1842) and *Dramatic Romances and Lyrics* (1845), which between them contain some of his finest poems in the genre he was to make his own, the dramatic monologue, raised barely a whisper of recognition. Frustration with London literary life was at its height when he began his correspondence with the reclusive invalid, Elizabeth Barrett, prompted by a complimentary allusion to him in one of her recently published *Poems* (1844). She, six years older than he, had given herself up for lost in human and social terms; whatever the exaggerations and distortions of the legend, there is no doubt that Browning did, as she said, 'lift me from the ground and carry me into life and the sunshine'. In September 1846, after a clandestine courtship in the shadow of Elizabeth Barrett's domineering and disagreeable (rather than monstrous) father, they married and left England for Italy. There, first at Pisa and then at Florence, and with occasional trips to France and England, they remained until Elizabeth Barrett Browning's death in 1861. Their only child, Robert Wiedemann Barrett Browning ('Pen') was born in 1849. Italy was congenial to Browning's poetry; he was not spared the rebuke of English critics (among them Charles Kingsley) for his unpatriotic liking for the landscapes and characters of 'abroad' (so different from the home life of their own dear Tennyson). *Christmas-Eve and Easter-Day* (1850), a pair of poems on religious subjects, is of interest to Browning specialists; of interest to everyone is *Men and Women* (1855), the collection generally held to be his masterpiece. I would personally prefer the claim of his next volume, *Dramatis Personae* (1864), the first to be published after his wife's death, but there is no doubt that together, and with the addition of *The Ring and the Book* (1868–9), they make up the core of Browning's enduring presence in the canon of English poetry. *The Ring and the Book*, twenty-one thousand lines long, consists of a series of interlocking dramatic monologues all telling the same story, that of an obscure seventeenth-century *cause célèbre*, the murder by Count Guido Franceschini of his wife, Pompilia, and his subsequent trial and execution. The element of sensation and melodrama is mixed with social satire, religious and philosophical meditation, and acute psychological probing: the whole represents Browning's heroic attempt to fuse Milton with Dickens, the modern novel with the epic poem. *The Ring and the Book* also marked the decisive advent of critical and popular acclaim: living in London, Browning re-entered the literary and social scene from which he had been an exile; he was lionized, and eventually canonized with the formation of the Browning Society in 1881. (His attitude to the Society was one of guarded appreciation.) A long overdue re-assessment of his writings after *The Ring and the Book* has taken place in recent years, though it must be accepted that, because of the established fame of the earlier works and the fact that many of the later ones are lengthy and recondite, they are unlikely to achieve the same standing in the tradition. Among the finest of the later works are *Fifine at the Fair* (1872), whose central character is Don Juan; *Aristophanes' Apology* (1875); *La Saisiaz* (1878), a philosophical elegy; the two volumes of *Dramatic Idyls* (1879, 1880; the spelling was chosen to differentiate them from Tennyson's 'English Idylls' and *Idylls of the King*); *Parleyings with Certain People of Importance in Their Day* (1887), an oblique intellectual autobiography; and his last volume, *Asolando*, published on the day of his death. Browning died in Venice on 12 December 1889. He is buried in Westminster Abbey. 'A good many oddities and a good many great writers have been entombed in the Abbey,' wrote Henry James, 'but none of the odd ones have been so great and none of the great ones so odd.'

In the same piece ('Browning in Westminster Abbey', later included in *English Hours*) James gave the best summary critical judgement of Browning when he called him 'a tremendous and incomparable modern'. James, of course, meant by 'modern' what we now call 'Victorian'; but the 'all-touching, all-trying spirit of his work, permeated with accumulations and playing with knowledge' connects Browning as much with our century as with his own. It is as a contemporary that Browning strikes us, not as the funereal grammarian of a past culture. I do not deny that Browning is a poet of his period, but I do deny that he is a period poet. The author of the lines 'God's in his heaven / All's right with the world' has been praised and blamed for being a breezy Victorian optimist, even though the lines are spoken by a young girl outside a house where an adulterous couple are quarrelling over the recent murder of the lady's husband. Such misconceptions haunt Browning's work – ironically perhaps, for he was a poet of misconceptions (the title of one of his poems), of failures, of abortive lives and loves, of the just-missed and the nearly fulfilled: a poet, in other words, of desire, perhaps the greatest in our language. The rapid colloquial energy of his style, his gift for the memorable phrase (especially in the vivid openings of poems: 'Just for a handful of silver he left us', 'It was roses, roses, all the way', 'Stop! Let me have the truth of that'), are not the concomitants of uplift and robust optimism: the three poems I have just cited are all about disillusion and disenchantment. The experience of reading Browning's poems is far from depressing, yet fall and loss are closely woven into their design. They witness to a double vision, famously put in the closing lines of 'Two in the Campagna': 'The old trick! Only I discern / Infinite passion, and the pain / Of finite hearts that yearn.' The poems dramatize the recognition that fulfilment lies beyond reach (as in Fra Lippo Lippi's anticipation that the painters who *succeed* him will also *succeed* where he has failed), but this aftermath is never represented, only gestured towards, and sometimes not even then: 'Childe Roland to the Dark Tower Came' is absolutely *stopped* by the indecipherable enigma of its last line, which repeats the title and, disallowing the question 'what happened next', throws the poem back on itself.

Desire, then, is the keynote of Browning's poetry, its ruling spirit, that which rescues it from Matthew Arnold's charge of 'confused multitudinousness'. Yet the impression of multitudinousness is undeniably there, seized in this early tribute from Walter Savage Landor:

> Since Chaucer was alive and hale,
> No man hath walked along our road with step
> So active, so inquiring eye, or tongue
> So varied in discourse.
>
> ('To Robert Browning', 1845)

The varied discourse of Browning's poetry is perhaps its most immediate attraction; the title of *Men and Women*, as democratic in its way as Whitman's *Leaves of Grass* (published the same year), opens the gates of poetry to the common people and to everyday things. High and low rub shoulders; the landscape is as likely to be suburban as sublime; Browning's kingdom, like the kingdom of heaven, is a homely as well as a glorious place. In part we can see here the influence of both drama (especially Shakespeare) and the contemporary novel on Browning's conception of poetry; but it is also a matter of temperament, of native wit. Writing to Elizabeth Barrett in 1845, Browning expressed his dislike of Mary Shelley's *Rambles in Germany and Italy*, and in doing so revealed the focus and bent of his own imagination:

> And then that way, when she and the like of her are put in a new place, with new flowers, new stones, faces, walls, all new – of looking wisely up at the sun, clouds, evening star, or mountain top and wisely saying 'who shall describe *that* sight!' – Not *you*, we very well see – but why dont you tell us that at Rome they eat roasted chestnuts, and put the shells into their aprons, the women do, and calmly empty the whole on the heads of the passengers in the street below; and that at Padua when a man drives his waggon up to a house and stops, all the mouse-coloured oxen that pull it from a beam against their foreheads sit down in a heap and rest ... Her remarks on art ... are amazing. Fra Angelico, for instance, only painted Martyrs, Virgins &c – she had no eyes for the divine *bon-bourgeoisie* of his pictures; the dear common folk of his crowds, those who sit and listen (spectacle at nose and bent into a comfortable heap to

hear better) at the sermon of the Saint – and the children, and women, – divinely pure they all are, but fresh from the streets & market place . . .

Sun, clouds, evening star, mountain top: these are the traditional props of Romantic lyric, beloved of Browning's early idol, Shelley, now rejected in the prose of Shelley's widow – rejected in favour of the 'streets & market place', closely observed and concretely rendered. The passage brings us close to the aesthetic of 'Fra Lippo Lippi', but it would be a mistake to assume that Browning is advocating, or practised himself, a naïve, literal-minded realism. For one thing, the style is too sophisticated, the detail too ordered: the oxen sitting down in a heap to rest are echoed by the people 'bent into a comfortable heap to hear better'; Mary Shelley has no *eyes* for those who sit 'spectacle at nose'; the 'common folk' are 'fresh from the streets & market place' in the sense that they have just come from there, and also because they have the freshness, the immediacy of the actual life from which they are drawn. Still they are there for 'the sermon of the Saint'; the transcendental is shifted from its unreal, ineffable plane ('who shall describe *that* sight!') to the plane of the human. You have to look *up* in order to see clouds and mountain tops; you look directly *at* flowers, stones, and above all faces – they are on your level.

Just as Browning's observation takes in the 'common folk' as well as the 'Saint', so his style insists on the full human scale, on the demotic as well as the learned, the prosaic as well as the lyric. 'You have taken a great range,' Elizabeth Barrett wrote to him, '– from those high faint notes of the mystics which are beyond personality . .* to dramatic impersonations, gruff with nature.' She goes on to cite, as one of these gruffnesses, the last words of *Soliloquy of the Spanish Cloister*, 'Gr–r–r – you swine!' Browning was to scandalize the gentleman's club atmosphere of English poetry with other snorts, coughs, grunts, and onomatopoeic noises. '*Bang, whang, whang,* goes the drum, *tootle-te-tootle* the fife,' says the speaker of 'Up at a Villa – Down in the City' (and he 'an Italian person of quality'!). 'Fol-lol-the-rido-liddle-iddle-ol!' sings Mr Sludge, embarking on the story of his impudent and irrepressible life. But here again we should not forget the artistry with which such effects are created and controlled. Browning's speakers,

* The two point ellipsis is a nineteenth-century convention for a dash.

from the racy, chatty Fra Lippo Lippi to the melancholy Andrea del Sarto, from Caliban's grotesque primitivism to Cleon's over-refined eloquence, from the colloquial urbanity of the speaker in 'How It Strikes a Contemporary' to the grave plainsong of St John in 'A Death in the Desert', never miss a step in the metrical dance which Browning has choreographed for them. That exclamation of Mr Sludge is, at second glance, a perfectly allowable iambic pentameter. The Duke in 'My Last Duchess', that arch manipulator, is manipulated by the couplets into which his lofty and condescending cadences unknowingly fall. The 'speaking subject' whom the dramatic monologue evokes is also, inevitably, subjected to the poem's imaginative design.

A brief word about the selection and order of poems for this volume. I have tried to strike a balance between the poems for which Browning is best known (but which are not always his best) and those my own taste leads me to recommend; at times the choice has been hard, nowhere more so than in the exclusion of 'Bishop Blougram's Apology' to make way for 'A Death in the Desert'. With two exceptions I have chosen only complete poems; Browning's long poems are not easily broken up, and they are too long to print in their entirety. Readers should be aware of the imbalance this will cause in their impressions of Browning's work; I can only urge them to try the long poems (especially *The Ring and the Book*) for themselves. The two exceptions are the song from *Pippa Passes* containing Browning's best-known lines, which it seemed perverse to omit; and (prompted by Kenneth Allott's inclusion of it in his selection, Oxford University Press, 1967) a scene from the same work which does stand up on its own, and is interesting as a rare example of successful dramatic dialogue in Browning. The poems are printed in the order of their first publication, except for 'Spring Song', which seemed to me the right note (of elegy, of triumph) on which to end.

DANIEL KARLIN

NOTE ON THE TEXT

The text is that of the two-volume edition of Browning's poems edited by John Pettigrew and Thomas J. Collins in the Penguin English Poets series (Harmondsworth, 1981). The copy-text used (with minor emendations and corrections) by Pettigrew and Collins is that of the last collected edition which appeared in Browning's lifetime, the *Poetical Works* of 1888–9. The poems (except for the last one) are printed in order of publication; the volumes in which they first appeared are identified in the Notes.

Porphyria's Lover

The rain set early in tonight,
    The sullen wind was soon awake,
It tore the elm-tops down for spite,
    And did its worst to vex the lake:
    I listened with heart fit to break.
When glided in Porphyria; straight
    She shut the cold out and the storm,
And kneeled and made the cheerless grate
    Blaze up, and all the cottage warm;
    Which done, she rose, and from her form   10
Withdrew the dripping cloak and shawl,
    And laid her soiled gloves by, untied
Her hat and let the damp hair fall,
    And, last, she sat down by my side
    And called me. When no voice replied,
She put my arm about her waist,
    And made her smooth white shoulder bare,
And all her yellow hair displaced,
    And, stooping, made my cheek lie there,
    And spread, o'er all, her yellow hair,   20
Murmuring how she loved me – she
    Too weak, for all her heart's endeavour,
To set its struggling passion free
    From pride, and vainer ties dissever,
    And give herself to me for ever.
But passion sometimes would prevail,
    Nor could tonight's gay feast restrain
A sudden thought of one so pale
    For love of her, and all in vain:
    So, she was come through wind and rain.   30
Be sure I looked up at her eyes

Happy and proud; at last I knew
Porphyria worshipped me; surprise
   Made my heart swell, and still it grew
   While I debated what to do.
That moment she was mine, mine, fair,
   Perfectly pure and good: I found
A thing to do, and all her hair
   In one long yellow string I wound
40   Three times her little throat around,
And strangled her. No pain felt she;
   I am quite sure she felt no pain.
As a shut bud that holds a bee,
   I warily oped her lids: again
   Laughed the blue eyes without a stain.
And I untightened next the tress
   About her neck; her cheek once more
Blushed bright beneath my burning kiss:
   I propped her head up as before,
50   Only, this time my shoulder bore
Her head, which droops upon it still:
   The smiling rosy little head,
So glad it has its utmost will,
   That all it scorned at once is fled,
   And I, its love, am gained instead!
Porphyria's love: she guessed not how
   Her darling one wish would be heard.
And thus we sit together now,
   And all night long we have not stirred,
60   And yet God has not said a word!

Johannes Agricola in Meditation

There's heaven above, and night by night
   I look right through its gorgeous roof;
No suns and moons though e'er so bright
   Avail to stop me; splendour-proof
   I keep the broods of stars aloof:
For I intend to get to God,
   For 'tis to God I speed so fast,
For in God's breast, my own abode,
   Those shoals of dazzling glory passed,
   I lay my spirit down at last.   10
I lie where I have always lain,
   God smiles as he has always smiled;
Ere suns and moons could wax and wane,
   Ere stars were thundergirt, or piled
   The heavens, God thought on me his child;
Ordained a life for me, arrayed
   Its circumstances every one
To the minutest; ay, God said
   This head this hand should rest upon
   Thus, ere he fashioned star or sun.   20
And having thus created me,
   Thus rooted me, he bade me grow,
Guiltless for ever, like a tree
   That buds and blooms, nor seeks to know
   The law by which it prospers so:
But sure that thought and word and deed
   All go to swell his love for me,
Me, made because that love had need
   Of something irreversibly
   Pledged solely its content to be.   30
Yes, yes, a tree which must ascend,

No poison-gourd foredoomed to stoop!
I have God's warrant, could I blend
    All hideous sins, as in a cup,
    To drink the mingled venoms up;
Secure my nature will convert
    The draught to blossoming gladness fast:
While sweet dews turn to the gourd's hurt,
    And bloat, and while they bloat it, blast,
40   As from the first its lot was cast.
For as I lie, smiled on, full-fed
    By unexhausted power to bless,
I gaze below on hell's fierce bed,
    And those its waves of flame oppress,
    Swarming in ghastly wretchedness;
Whose life on earth aspired to be
    One altar-smoke, so pure! – to win
If not love like God's love for me,
    At least to keep his anger in;
50   And all their striving turned to sin.
Priest, doctor, hermit, monk grown white
    With prayer, the broken-hearted nun,
The martyr, the wan acolyte,
    The incense-swinging child, – undone
    Before God fashioned star or sun!
God, whom I praise; how could I praise,
    If such as I might understand,
Make out and reckon on his ways,
    And bargain for his love, and stand,
60   Paying a price, at his right hand?

Song from Pippa Passes

The year's at the spring
And day's at the morn;
Morning's at seven;
The hill-side's dew-pearled;
The lark's on the wing;
The snail's on the thorn:
God's in his heaven –
All's right with the world!

Scene from Pippa Passes

FIRST GIRL: There goes a swallow to Venice – the stout
    seafarer!
  Seeing those birds fly, makes one wish for wings.
  Let us all wish; you wish first!
SECOND GIRL: I? This sunset
  To finish.
THIRD GIRL: That old – somebody I know,
  Greyer and older than my grandfather,
  To give me the same treat he gave last week –
  Feeding me on his knee with fig-peckers,
  Lampreys and red Breganze-wine, and mumbling
  The while some folly about how well I fare,
10 Let sit and eat my supper quietly:
  Since had he not himself been late this morning
  Detained at – never mind where, – had he not . . .
  'Eh, baggage, had I not!' –
SECOND GIRL: How she can lie!
THIRD GIRL: Look there – by the nails!
SECOND GIRL: What makes your fingers
  red?
THIRD GIRL: Dipping them into wine to write bad words with
  On the bright table: how he laughed!
FIRST GIRL: My turn.
  Spring's come and summer's coming. I would wear
  A long loose gown, down to the feet and hands,
  With plaits here, close about the throat, all day;
20 And all night lie, the cool long nights, in bed;
  And have new milk to drink, apples to eat,
  Deuzans and junetings, leather-coats . . . ah, I should say,
  This is away in the fields – miles!
THIRD GIRL: Say at once

You'd be at home: she'd always be at home!
Now comes the story of the farm among
The cherry orchards, and how April snowed
White blossoms on her as she ran. Why, fool,
They've rubbed the chalk-mark out, how tall you were,
Twisted your starling's neck, broken his cage,
Made a dung-hill of your garden!

FIRST GIRL: They, destroy   30
  My garden since I left them? well – perhaps!
  I would have done so: so I hope they have!
  A fig-tree curled out of our cottage wall;
  They called it mine, I have forgotten why,
  It must have been there long ere I was born:
  Cric – cric – I think I hear the wasps o'erhead
  Pricking the papers strung to flutter there
  And keep off birds in fruit-time – coarse long papers,
  And the wasps eat them, prick them through and through.

THIRD GIRL: How her mouth twitches! Where was I? – before 40
  She broke in with her wishes and long gowns
  And wasps – would I be such a fool! – Oh, here!
  This is my way: I answer every one
  Who asks me why I make so much of him –
  (If you say, 'you love him' – straight 'he'll not be gulled!')
  'He that seduced me when I was a girl
  Thus high – had eyes like yours, or hair like yours,
  Brown, red, white,' – as the case may be: that pleases!
  See how that beetle burnishes in the path!
  There sparkles he along the dust: and, there – 50
  Your journey to that maize-tuft spoiled at least!

FIRST GIRL: When I was young, they said if you killed one
  Of those sunshiny beetles, that his friend
  Up there, would shine no more that day nor next.

SECOND GIRL: When you were young? Nor are you young,
    that's true.
  How your plump arms, that were, have dropped away!
  Why, I can span them. Cecco beats you still?
  No matter, so you keep your curious hair.
  I wish they'd find a way to dye our hair

60   Your colour – any lighter tint, indeed,
       Than black: the men say they are sick of black,
       Black eyes, black hair!

My Last Duchess

Ferrara

That's my last Duchess painted on the wall,
Looking as if she were alive. I call
That piece a wonder, now: Frà Pandolf's hands
Worked busily a day, and there she stands.
Will't please you sit and look at her? I said
'Frà Pandolf' by design, for never read
Strangers like you that pictured countenance,
The depth and passion of its earnest glance,
But to myself they turned (since none puts by
The curtain I have drawn for you, but I)   10
And seemed as they would ask me, if they durst,
How such a glance came there; so, not the first
Are you to turn and ask thus. Sir, 'twas not
Her husband's presence only, called that spot
Of joy into the Duchess' cheek: perhaps
Frà Pandolf chanced to say 'Her mantle laps
Over my lady's wrist too much,' or 'Paint
Must never hope to reproduce the faint
Half-flush that dies along her throat': such stuff
Was courtesy, she thought, and cause enough   20
For calling up that spot of joy. She had
A heart — how shall I say? — too soon made glad,
Too easily impressed; she liked whate'er
She looked on, and her looks went everywhere.
Sir, 'twas all one! My favour at her breast,
The dropping of the daylight in the West,
The bough of cherries some officious fool
Broke in the orchard for her, the white mule
She rode with round the terrace — all and each

30 Would draw from her alike the approving speech,
  Or blush, at least. She thanked men, – good! but thanked
  Somehow – I know not how – as if she ranked
  My gift of a nine-hundred-years-old name
  With anybody's gift. Who'd stoop to blame
  This sort of trifling? Even had you skill
  In speech – (which I have not) – to make your will
  Quite clear to such an one, and say, 'Just this
  Or that in you disgusts me; here you miss,
  Or there exceed the mark' – and if she let
40 Herself be lessoned so, nor plainly set
  Her wits to yours, forsooth, and made excuse,
  – E'en then would be some stooping; and I choose
  Never to stoop. Oh sir, she smiled, no doubt,
  Whene'er I passed her; but who passed without
  Much the same smile? This grew; I gave commands;
  Then all smiles stopped together. There she stands
  As if alive. Will't please you rise? We'll meet
  The company below, then. I repeat,
  The Count your master's known munificence
50 Is ample warrant that no just pretence
  Of mine for dowry will be disallowed;
  Though his fair daughter's self, as I avowed
  At starting, is my object. Nay, we'll go
  Together down, sir. Notice Neptune, though,
  Taming a sea-horse, thought a rarity,
  Which Claus of Innsbruck cast in bronze for me!

Soliloquy of the Spanish Cloister

I

Gr-r-r – there go, my heart's abhorrence!
　　Water your damned flower-pots, do!
If hate killed men, Brother Lawrence,
　　God's blood, would not mine kill you!
What? your myrtle-bush wants trimming?
　　Oh, that rose has prior claims –
Needs its leaden vase filled brimming?
　　Hell dry you up with its flames!

II

At the meal we sit together:
　　Salve tibi! I must hear　　　　　　　　　　10
Wise talk of the kind of weather,
　　Sort of season, time of year:
Not a plenteous cork-crop: scarcely
　　Dare we hope oak-galls, I doubt:
What's the Latin name for 'parsley'?
　　What's the Greek name for Swine's Snout?

III

Whew! We'll have our platter burnished,
　　Laid with care on our own shelf!
With a fire-new spoon we're furnished,
　　And a goblet for ourself,　　　　　　　　　　20
Rinsed like something sacrificial
　　Ere 'tis fit to touch our chaps –
Marked with L. for our initial!
　　(He-he! There his lily snaps!)

IV

Saint, forsooth! While brown Dolores
    Squats outside the Convent bank
With Sanchicha, telling stories,
    Steeping tresses in the tank,
Blue-black, lustrous, thick like horsehairs,
30   – Can't I see his dead eye glow,
Bright as 'twere a Barbary corsair's?
    (That is, if he'd let it show!)

V

When he finishes refection,
    Knife and fork he never lays
Cross-wise, to my recollection,
    As do I, in Jesu's praise.
I the Trinity illustrate,
    Drinking watered orange-pulp –
In three sips the Arian frustrate;
40   While he drains his at one gulp.

VI

Oh, those melons? If he's able
    We're to have a feast! so nice!
One goes to the Abbot's table,
    All of us get each a slice.
How go on your flowers? None double?
    Not one fruit-sort can you spy?
Strange! – And I, too, at such trouble,
    Keep them close-nipped on the sly!

VII

There's a great text in Galatians,
50   Once you trip on it, entails
Twenty-nine distinct damnations,
    One sure, if another fails:
If I trip him just a-dying,
    Sure of heaven as sure can be,
Spin him round and send him flying
    Off to hell, a Manichee?

VIII

Or, my scrofulous French novel
   On grey paper with blunt type!
Simply glance at it, you grovel
   Hand and foot in Belial's gripe: 60
If I double down its pages
   At the woeful sixteenth print,
When he gathers his greengages,
   Ope a sieve and slip it in't?

IX

Or, there's Satan! – one might venture
   Pledge one's soul to him, yet leave
Such a flaw in the indenture
   As he'd miss till, past retrieve,
Blasted lay that rose-acacia
   We're so proud of! *Hy, Zy, Hine* . . .   70
'St, there's Vespers! *Plena gratiâ*
   Ave, Virgo! Gr-r-r – you swine!

The Pied Piper of Hamelin;
A Child's Story

(Written for, and inscribed to, W.M. the Younger)

I

Hamelin Town's in Brunswick,
   By famous Hanover city;
The river Weser, deep and wide,
Washes its wall on the southern side;
A pleasanter spot you never spied;
   But, when begins my ditty,
Almost five hundred years ago,
To see the townsfolk suffer so
   From vermin, was a pity.

II

10   Rats!
They fought the dogs and killed the cats,
   And bit the babies in the cradles,
And ate the cheeses out of the vats,
   And licked the soup from the cooks' own ladles,
Split open the kegs of salted sprats,
Made nests inside men's Sunday hats,
And even spoiled the women's chats
    By drowning their speaking
    With shrieking and squeaking
20 In fifty different sharps and flats.

III

At last the people in a body
    To the Town Hall came flocking:
' 'Tis clear,' cried they, 'our Mayor's a noddy;
    And as for our Corporation – shocking
To think we buy gowns lined with ermine

For dolts that can't or won't determine
What's best to rid us of our vermin!
You hope, because you're old and obese,
To find in the furry civic robe ease?
Rouse up, sirs! Give your brains a racking   30
To find the remedy we're lacking,
Or, sure as fate, we'll send you packing!'
At this the Mayor and Corporation
Quaked with a mighty consternation.

IV
An hour they sat in council,
   At length the Mayor broke silence:
'For a guilder I'd my ermine gown sell,
   I wish I were a mile hence!
It's easy to bid one rack one's brain –
I'm sure my poor head aches again,   40
I've scratched it so, and all in vain.
Oh for a trap, a trap, a trap!'
Just as he said this, what should hap
At the chamber door but a gentle tap?
'Bless us,' cried the Mayor, 'what's that?'
(With the Corporation as he sat,
Looking little though wondrous fat;
Nor brighter was his eye, nor moister
Than a too-long-opened oyster,
Save when at noon his paunch grew mutinous   50
For a plate of turtle green and glutinous)
'Only a scraping of shoes on the mat?
Anything like the sound of a rat
Makes my heart go pit-a-pat!'

V
'Come in!' – the Mayor cried, looking bigger:
And in did come the strangest figure!
His queer long coat from heel to head
Was half of yellow and half of red,
And he himself was tall and thin,
With sharp blue eyes, each like a pin,   60

And light loose hair, yet swarthy skin,
No tuft on cheek nor beard on chin,
But lips where smiles went out and in;
There was no guessing his kith and kin:
And nobody could enough admire
The tall man and his quaint attire.
Quoth one: 'It's as my great-grandsire,
Starting up at the Trump of Doom's tone,
Had walked this way from his painted tombstone!'

VI

70 He advanced to the council-table:
And, 'Please your honours,' said he, 'I'm able,
By means of a secret charm, to draw
   All creatures living beneath the sun,
   That creep or swim or fly or run,
After me so as you never saw!
And I chiefly use my charm
On creatures that do people harm,
The mole and toad and newt and viper;
And people call me the Pied Piper.'
80 (And here they noticed round his neck,
   A scarf of red and yellow stripe,
To match with his coat of the self-same check;
   And at the scarf's end hung a pipe;
And his fingers, they noticed, were ever straying
As if impatient to be playing
Upon this pipe, as low it dangled
Over his vesture so old-fangled.)
'Yet,' said he, 'poor piper as I am,
In Tartary I freed the Cham,
90   Last June, from his huge swarms of gnats;
I eased in Asia the Nizam
   Of a monstrous brood of vampire-bats:
And as for what your brain bewilders,
   If I can rid your town of rats
Will you give me a thousand guilders?'

'One? fifty thousand!' – was the exclamation
Of the astonished Mayor and Corporation.

VII

Into the street the Piper stept,
   Smiling first a little smile,
As if he knew what magic slept   100
   In his quiet pipe the while;
Then, like a musical adept,
To blow the pipe his lips he wrinkled,
And green and blue his sharp eyes twinkled,
Like a candle-flame where salt is sprinkled;
And ere three shrill notes the pipe uttered,
You heard as if an army muttered;
And the muttering grew to a grumbling;
And the grumbling grew to a mighty rumbling;
And out of the houses the rats came tumbling. 110
Great rats, small rats, lean rats, brawny rats,
Brown rats, black rats, grey rats, tawny rats,
Grave old plodders, gay young friskers,
   Fathers, mothers, uncles, cousins,
Cocking tails and pricking whiskers,
   Families by tens and dozens,
Brothers, sisters, husbands, wives –
Followed the Piper for their lives.
From street to street he piped advancing,
And step for step they followed dancing,   120
Until they came to the river Weser,
   Wherein all plunged and perished!
– Save one who, stout as Julius Caesar,
Swam across and lived to carry
   (As he, the manuscript he cherished)
To Rat-land home his commentary:
Which was, 'At the first shrill notes of the pipe,
I heard a sound as of scraping tripe,
And putting apples, wondrous ripe,
Into a cider-press's gripe: 130
And a moving away of pickle-tub-boards,

And a leaving ajar of conserve-cupboards,
And a drawing the corks of train-oil-flasks,
And a breaking the hoops of butter-casks:
And it seemed as if a voice
   (Sweeter far than bý harp or bý psaltery
Is breathed) called out, "Oh rats, rejoice!
   The world is grown to one vast drysaltery!
So munch on, crunch on, take your nuncheon,
140   Breakfast, supper, dinner, luncheon!"
And just as a bulky sugar-puncheon,
All ready staved, like a great sun shone
Glorious scarce an inch before me,
Just as methought it said, "Come, bore me!"
– I found the Weser rolling o'er me.'

VIII

You should have heard the Hamelin people
Ringing the bells till they rocked the steeple.
'Go,' cried the Mayor, 'and get long poles,
Poke out the nests and block up the holes!
150   Consult with carpenters and builders,
And leave in our town not even a trace
Of the rats!' – when suddenly, up the face
Of the Piper perked in the market-place,
With a, 'First, if you please, my thousand guilders!'

IX

A thousand guilders! The Mayor looked blue;
So did the Corporation too.
For council dinners made rare havoc
With Claret, Moselle, Vin-de-Grave, Hock;
And half the money would replenish
160   Their cellar's biggest butt with Rhenish.
To pay this sum to a wandering fellow
With a gypsy coat of red and yellow!
'Beside,' quoth the Mayor with a knowing wink,
'Our business was done at the river's brink;
We saw with our eyes the vermin sink,
And what's dead can't come to life, I think.

So, friend, we're not the folks to shrink
From the duty of giving you something for drink,
And a matter of money to put in your poke;
But as for the guilders, what we spoke   170
Of them, as you very well know, was in joke.
Beside, our losses have made us thrifty.
A thousand guilders! Come, take fifty!'

X

The Piper's face fell, and he cried
'No trifling! I can't wait, beside!
I've promised to visit by dinner-time
Bagdat, and accept the prime
Of the Head-Cook's pottage, all he's rich in,
For having left, in the Caliph's kitchen,
Of a nest of scorpions no survivor: 180
With him I proved no bargain-driver,
With you, don't think I'll bate a stiver!
And folks who put me in a passion
May find me pipe after another fashion.'

XI

'How?' cried the Mayor, 'd'ye think I brook
Being worse treated than a Cook?
Insulted by a lazy ribald
With idle pipe and vesture piebald?
You threaten us, fellow? Do your worst,
Blow your pipe there till you burst!'   190

XII

Once more he stept into the street
    And to his lips again
    Laid his long pipe of smooth straight cane;
And ere he blew three notes (such sweet
Soft notes as yet musician's cunning
    Never gave the enraptured air)
There was a rustling that seemed like a bustling
Of merry crowds justling at pitching and hustling,
Small feet were pattering, wooden shoes clattering,

200   Little hands clapping and little tongues chattering,
       And, like fowls in a farm-yard when barley is scattering,
       Out came the children running.
       All the little boys and girls,
       With rosy cheeks and flaxen curls,
       And sparkling eyes and teeth like pearls,
       Tripping and skipping, ran merrily after
       The wonderful music with shouting and laughter.

XIII

       The Mayor was dumb, and the Council stood
       As if they were changed into blocks of wood.
210   Unable to move a step, or cry
       To the children merrily skipping by,
       – Could only follow with the eye
       That joyous crowd at the Piper's back.
       But how the Major was on the rack,
       And the wretched Council's bosoms beat,
       As the Piper turned from the High Street
       To where the Weser rolled its waters
       Right in the way of their sons and daughters!
       However he turned from South to West,
220   And to Koppelberg Hill his steps addressed,
       And after him the children pressed;
       Great was the joy in every breast.
       'He never can cross that mighty top!
       He's forced to let the piping drop,
       And we shall see our children stop!'
       When, lo, as they reached the mountain-side,
       A wondrous portal opened wide,
       As if a cavern was suddenly hollowed;
       And the Piper advanced and the children followed,
230   And when all were in to the very last,
       The door in the mountain-side shut fast.
       Did I say, all? No! One was lame,
         And could not dance the whole of the way;
       And in after years, if you would blame
         His sadness, he was used to say, –

'It's dull in our town since my playmates left!
I can't forget that I'm bereft
Of all the pleasant sights they see,
Which the Piper also promised me.
For he led us, he said, to a joyous land,   240
Joining the town and just at hand,
Where waters gushed and fruit-trees grew
And flowers put forth a fairer hue,
And everything was strange and new;
The sparrows were brighter than peacocks here,
And their dogs outran our fallow deer,
And honey-bees had lost their stings,
And horses were born with eagles' wings:
And just as I became assured
My lame foot would be speedily cured,   250
The music stopped and I stood still,
And found myself outside the hill,
Left alone against my will,
To go now limping as before,
And never hear of the country more!'

XIV
Alas, alas for Hamelin!
     There came into many a burgher's pate
     A text which says that heaven's gate
     Opes to the rich at as easy rate
As the needle's eye takes a camel in!   260
The mayor sent East, West, North and South,
To offer the Piper, by word of mouth,
     Wherever it was men's lot to find him,
Silver and gold to his heart's content,
If he'd only return the way he went,
     And bring the children behind him.
But when they saw 'twas a lost endeavour,
And Piper and dancers were gone for ever,
They made a decree that lawyers never
     Should think their records dated duly   270
If, after the day of the month and year,

These words did not as well appear,
'And so long after what happened here
  On the Twenty-second of July,
Thirteen hundred and seventy-six':
And the better in memory to fix
The place of the children's last retreat,
They called it, the Pied Piper's Street –
Where any one playing on pipe or tabor
280 Was sure for the future to lose his labour.
Nor suffered they hostelry or tavern
  To shock with mirth a street so solemn;
But opposite the place of the cavern
  They wrote the story on a column,
And on the great church-window painted
The same, to make the world acquainted
How their children were stolen away,
And there it stands to this very day.
And I must not omit to say
290 That in Transylvania there's a tribe
Of alien people who ascribe
The outlandish ways and dress
On which their neighbours lay such stress,
To their fathers and mothers having risen
Out of some subterraneous prison
Into which they were trepanned
Long time ago in a mighty band
Out of Hamelin town in Bruswick land,
But how or why, they don't understand.

XV

300 So, Willy, let me and you be wipers
Of scores out with all men – especially pipers!
And, whether they pipe us free fróm rats or fróm mice,
If we've promised them aught, let us keep our promise!

'How They Brought the Good News from Ghent to Aix'

[16—]

I

I sprang to the stirrup, and Joris, and he;
I galloped, Dirck galloped, we galloped all three;
'Good speed!' cried the watch, as the gate-bolts undrew;
'Speed!' echoed the wall to us galloping through;
Behind shut the postern, the lights sank to rest,
And into the midnight we galloped abreast.

II

Not a word to each other; we kept the great pace
Neck by neck, stride by stride, never changing our place;
I turned in my saddle and made its girths tight,
Then shortened each stirrup, and set the pique right,   10
Rebuckled the cheek-strap, chained slacker the bit,
Nor galloped less steadily Roland a whit.

III

'Twas moonset at starting; but while we drew near
Lokeren, the cocks crew and twilight dawned clear;
At Boom, a great yellow star came out to see;
At Düffeld, 'twas morning as plain as could be;
And from Mecheln church-steeple we heard the half-chime,
So, Joris broke silence with, 'Yet there is time!'

IV

At Aershot, up leaped of a sudden the sun,
And against him the cattle stood black every one,   20
To stare through the mist at us galloping past,
And I saw my stout galloper Roland at last,
With resolute shoulders, each butting away
The haze, as some bluff river headland its spray:

39

V

And his low head and crest, just one sharp ear bent back
For my voice, and the other pricked out on his track;
And one eye's black intelligence, – ever that glance
O'er its white edge at me, his own master, askance!
And the thick heavy spume-flakes which aye and anon
30   His fierce lips shook upwards in galloping on.

VI

By Hasselt, Dirck groaned; and cried Joris, 'Stay spur!
Your Roos galloped bravely, the fault's not in her,
We'll remember at Aix' – for one heard the quick wheeze
Of her chest, saw the stretched neck and staggering knees,
And sunk tail, and horrible heave of the flank,
As down on her haunches she shuddered and sank.

VII

So, we were left galloping, Joris and I,
Past Looz and past Tongres, no cloud in the sky;
The broad sun above laughed a pitiless laugh,
40   'Neath our feet broke the brittle bright stubble like chaff;
Till over by Dalhem a dome-spire sprang white,
And 'Gallop,' gasped Joris, 'for Aix is in sight!'

VIII

'How they'll greet us!' – and all in a moment his roan
Rolled neck and croup over, lay dead as a stone;
And there was my Roland to bear the whole weight
Of the news which alone could save Aix from her fate,
With his nostrils like pits full of blood to the brim,
And with circles of red for his eye-sockets' rim.

IX

Then I cast loose my buffcoat, each holster let fall,
50   Shook off both my jack-boots, let go belt and all,
Stood up in the stirrup, leaned, patted his ear,
Called my Roland his pet-name, my horse without peer;
Clapped my hands, laughed and sang, any noise, bad or good,
Till at length into Aix Roland galloped and stood.

X
And all I remember is – friends flocking round
As I sat with his head 'twixt my knees on the ground;
And no voice but was praising this Roland of mine,
As I poured down his throat our last measure of wine,
Which (the burgesses voted by common consent)
Was no more than his due who brought good news from Ghent. 60

The Lost Leader

I

Just for a handful of silver he left us,
  Just for a riband to stick in his coat –
Found the one gift of which fortune bereft us,
  Lost all the others she lets us devote;
They, with the gold to give, doled him out silver,
  So much was theirs who so little allowed:
How all our copper had gone for his service!
  Rags – were they purple, his heart had been proud!
We that had loved him so, followed him, honoured him,
10   Lived in his mild and magnificent eye,
Learned his great language, caught his clear accents,
  Made him our pattern to live and to die!
Shakespeare was of us, Milton was for us,
  Burns, Shelley, were with us, – they watch from their graves!
He alone breaks from the van and the freemen,
  – He alone sinks to the rear and the slaves!

II

We shall march prospering, – not through his presence;
  Songs may inspirit us, – not from his lyre;
Deeds will be done, – while he boasts his quiescence,
20   Still bidding crouch whom the rest bade aspire:
Blot out his name, then, record one lost soul more,
  One task more declined, one more footpath untrod,
One more devils'-triumph and sorrow for angels,
  One wrong more to man, one more insult to God!
Life's night begins: let him never come back to us!
  There would be doubt, hesitation and pain,
Forced praise on our part – the glimmer of twilight,
  Never glad confident morning again!

Best fight on well, for we taught him – strike gallantly,
   Menace our heart ere we master his own;   30
Then let him receive the new knowledge and wait us,
   Pardoned in heaven, the first by the throne!

Meeting at Night

I

The grey sea and the long black land;
And the yellow half-moon large and low;
And the startled little waves that leap
In fiery ringlets from their sleep,
As I gain the cove with pushing prow,
And quench its speed i' the slushy sand.

II

Then a mile of warm sea-scented beach;
Three fields to cross till a farm appears;
A tap at the pane, the quick sharp scratch
10 And blue spurt of a lighted match,
And a voice less loud, through its joys and fears,
Than the two hearts beating each to each!

Parting at Morning

Round the cape of a sudden came the sea,
And the sun looked over the mountain's rim:
And straight was a path of gold for him,
And the need of a world of men for me.

Home-Thoughts, from Abroad

I
Oh, to be in England
Now that April's there,
And whoever wakes in England
Sees, some morning, unaware,
That the lowest boughs and the brushwood sheaf
Round the elm-tree bole are in tiny leaf,
While the chaffinch sings on the orchard bough
In England – now!

II
And after April, when May follows,
And the whitethroat builds, and all the swallows!
Hark, where my blossomed pear-tree in the hedge
Leans to the field and scatters on the clover
Blossoms and dewdrops – at the bent spray's edge –
That's the wise thrush; he sings each song twice over,
Lest you should think he never could recapture
The first fine careless rapture!
And though the fields look rough with hoary dew,
All will be gay when noontide wakes anew
The buttercups, the little children's dower
– Far brighter than this gaudy melon-flower!

44

The Bishop Orders His Tomb at Saint Praxed's Church

Rome, 15—

Vanity, saith the preacher, vanity!
Draw round my bed: is Anselm keeping back?
Nephews – sons mine . . . ah God, I know not! Well –
She, men would have to be your mother once,
Old Gandolf envied me, so fair she was!
What's done is done, and she is dead beside,
Dead long ago, and I am Bishop since,
And as she died so must we die ourselves,
And thence ye may perceive the world's a dream.
Life, how and what is it? As here I lie   10
In this state-chamber, dying by degrees,
Hours and long hours in the dead night, I ask
'Do I live, am I dead?' Peace, peace seems all.
Saint Praxed's ever was the church for peace;
And so, about this tomb of mine. I fought
With tooth and nail to save my niche, ye know:
– Old Gandolf cozened me, despite my care;
Shrewd was that snatch from out the corner South
He graced his carrion with, God curse the same!
Yet still my niche is not so cramped but thence   20
One sees the pulpit o' the epistle-side,
And somewhat of the choir, those silent seats,
And up into the airy dome where live
The angels, and a sunbeam's sure to lurk:
And I shall fill my slab of basalt there,
And 'neath my tabernacle take my rest,
With those nine columns round me, two and two,
The odd one at my feet where Anselm stands:
Peach-blossom marble all, the rare, the ripe

45

30 As fresh-poured red wine of a mighty pulse.
    – Old Gandolf with his paltry onion-stone,
    Put me where I may look at him! True peach,
    Rosy and flawless: how I earned the prize!
    Draw close: that conflagration of my church
    – What then? So much was saved if aught were missed!
    My sons, ye would not be my death? Go dig
    The white-grape vineyard where the oil-press stood,
    Drop water gently till the surface sink,
    And if ye find . . . Ah God, I know not, I! . . .
40 Bedded in store of rotten fig-leaves soft,
    And corded up in a tight olive-frail,
    Some lump, ah God, of *lapis lazuli*,
    Big as a Jew's head cut off at the nape,
    Blue as a vein o'er the Madonna's breast . . .
    Sons, all have I bequeathed you, villas, all,
    That brave Frascati villa with its bath,
    So, let the blue lump poise between my knees,
    Like God the Father's globe on both his hands
    Ye worship in the Jesu Church so gay,
50 For Gandolf shall not choose but see and burst!
    Swift as a weaver's shuttle fleet our years:
    Man goeth to the grave, and where is he?
    Did I say basalt for my slab, sons? Black –
    'Twas ever antique-black I meant! How else
    Shall ye contrast my frieze to come beneath?
    The bas-relief in bronze ye promised me,
    Those Pans and Nymphs ye wot of, and perchance
    Some tripod, thyrsus, with a vase or so,
    The Saviour at his sermon on the mount,
60 Saint Praxed in a glory, and one Pan
    Ready to twitch the Nymph's last garment off,
    And Moses with the tables . . . but I know
    Ye mark me not! What do they whisper thee,
    Child of my bowels, Anselm? Ah, ye hope
    To revel down my villas while I gasp
    Bricked o'er with beggar's mouldy travertine
    Which Gandolf from his tomb-top chuckles at!

Nay, boys, ye love me – all of jasper, then!
'Tis jasper ye stand pledged to, lest I grieve
My bath must needs be left behind, alas!   70
One block, pure green as a pistachio-nut,
There's plenty jasper somewhere in the world –
And have I not Saint Praxed's ear to pray
Horses for ye, and brown Greek manuscripts,
And mistresses with great smooth marbly limbs?
– That's if ye carve my epitaph aright,
Choice Latin, picked phrase, Tully's every word,
No gaudy ware like Gandolf's second line –
Tully, my masters? Ulpian serves his need!
And then how I shall lie through centuries,   80
And hear the blessed mutter of the mass,
And see God made and eaten all day long,
And feel the steady candle-flame, and taste
Good strong thick stupefying incense-smoke!
For as I lie here, hours of the dead night,
Dying in state and by such slow degrees,
I fold my arms as if they clasped a crook,
And stretch my feet forth straight as stone can point,
And let the bedclothes, for a mortcloth, drop
Into great laps and folds of sculptor's-work: 90
And as yon tapers dwindle, and strange thoughts
Grow, with a certain humming in my ears,
About the life before I lived this life,
And this life too, popes, cardinals and priests,
Saint Praxed at his sermon on the mount,
Your tall pale mother with her talking eyes,
And new-found agate urns as fresh as day,
And marble's language, Latin pure, discreet,
– Aha, ELUCESCEBAT quoth our friend?
No Tully, said I, Ulpian at the best!   100
Evil and brief hath been my pilgrimage.
All *lapis*, all, sons! Else I give the Pope
My villas! Will ye ever eat my heart?
Ever your eyes were as a lizard's quick,
They glitter like your mother's for my soul,

Or ye would heighten my impoverished frieze,
Piece out its starved design, and fill my vase
With grapes, and add a vizor and a Term,
And to the tripod ye would tie a lynx
110 That in his struggle throws the thyrsus down,
To comfort me on my entablature
Whereon I am to lie till I must ask
'Do I live, am I dead?' There, leave me, there!
For ye have stabbed me with ingratitude
To death – ye wish it – God, ye wish it! Stone –
Gritstone, a-crumble! Clammy squares which sweat
As if the corpse they keep were oozing through –
And no more *lapis* to delight the world!
Well go! I bless ye. Fewer tapers there,
120 But in a row: and, going, turn your backs
– Ay, like departing altar-ministrants,
And leave me in my church, the church for peace,
That I may watch at leisure if he leers –
Old Gandolf, at me, from his onion-stone,
As still he envied me, so fair she was!

Love Among the Ruins

I

Where the quiet-coloured end of evening smiles,
  Miles and miles
On the solitary pastures where our sheep
  Half-asleep
Tinkle homeward through the twilight, stray or stop
  As they crop –
Was the site once of a city great and gay,
  (So they say)
Of our country's very capital, its prince
  Ages since   10
Held his court in, gathered councils, wielding far
  Peace or war.

II

Now, – the country does not even boast a tree,
  As you see,
To distinguish slopes of verdure, certain rills
  From the hills
Intersect and give a name to, (else they run
  Into one)
Where the domed and daring palace shot its spires
  Up like fires   20
O'er the hundred-gated circuit of a wall
  Bounding all,
Made of marble, men might march on nor be pressed,
  Twelve abreast.

III

And such plenty and perfection, see, of grass
  Never was!

Such a carpet as, this summer-time, o'erspreads
    And embeds
Every vestige of the city, guessed alone,
30   Stock or stone –
Where a multitude of men breathed joy and woe
    Long ago;
Lust of glory pricked their hearts up, dread of shame
    Struck them tame;
And that glory and that shame alike, the gold
    Bought and sold.

IV
Now, – the single little turret that remains
    On the plains,
By the caper over-rooted, by the gourd
40   Overscored,
While the patching houseleek's head of blossom winks
    Through the chinks –
Marks the basement whence a tower in ancient time
    Sprang sublime,
And a burning ring, all round, the chariots traced
    As they raced,
And the monarch and his minions and his dames
    Viewed the games.

V
And I know, while thus the quiet-coloured eve
50   Smiles to leave
To their folding, all our many-tinkling fleece
    In such peace,
And the slopes and rills in undistinguished grey
    Melt away –
That a girl with eager eyes and yellow hair
    Waits me there
In the turret whence the charioteers caught soul
    For the goal,
When the king looked, where she looks now, breathless, dumb
60   Till I come.

VI

But he looked upon the city, every side,
    Far and wide,
All the mountains topped with temples, all the glades'
    Colonnades,
All the causeys, bridges, aqueducts, – and then,
    All the men!
When I do come, she will speak not, she will stand,
    Either hand
On my shoulder, give her eyes the first embrace
    Of my face,   70
Ere we rush, ere we extinguish sight and speech
    Each on each.

VII

In one year they sent a million fighters forth
    South and North,
And they built their gods a brazen pillar high
    As the sky,
Yet reserved a thousand chariots in full force –
    Gold, of course.
Oh heart! oh blood that freezes, blood that burns!
    Earth's returns   80
For whole centuries of folly, noise and sin!
    Shut them in,
With their triumphs and their glories and the rest!
    Love is best.

A Lovers' Quarrel

I

Oh, what a dawn of day!
How the March sun feels like May!
   All is blue again
   After last night's rain,
And the South dries the hawthorn-spray.
   Only, my Love's away!
I'd as lief that the blue were grey.

II

Runnels, which rillets swell,
Must be dancing down the dell,
   With a foaming head
   On the beryl bed
Paven smooth as a hermit's cell;
   Each with a tale to tell,
Could my Love but attend as well.

III

Dearest, three months ago!
When we lived blocked-up with snow, –
   When the wind would edge
   In and in his wedge,
In, as far as the point could go –
   Not to our ingle, though,
Where we loved each the other so!

IV

Laughs with so little cause!
We devised games out of straws.
   We would try and trace
   One another's face

In the ash, as an artist draws;
   Free on each other's flaws,
How we chattered like two church daws!

V

What's in the 'Times'? – a scold
At the Emperor deep and cold;   30
   He has taken a bride
   To his gruesome side,
That's as fair as himself is bold:
   There they sit ermine-stoled,
And she powders her hair with gold.

VI

Fancy the Pampas' sheen!
Miles and miles of gold and green
   Where the sunflowers blow
   In a solid glow,
And – to break now and then the screen – 40
   Black neck and eyeballs keen,
Up a wild horse leaps between!

VII

Try, will our table turn?
Lay your hands there light, and yearn
   Till the yearning slips
   Through the finger-tips
In a fire which a few discern,
   And a very few feel burn,
And the rest, they may live and learn!

VIII

Then we would up and pace,   50
For a change, about the place,
   Each with arm o'er neck:
   'Tis our quarter-deck,
We are seamen in woeful case.
   Help in the ocean-space!
Or, if no help, we'll embrace.

IX

See, how she looks now, dressed
In a sledging-cap and vest!
　'Tis a huge fur cloak –
60　　Like a reindeer's yoke
Falls the lappet along the breast:
　Sleeves for her arms to rest,
Or to hang, as my Love likes best.

X

Teach me to flirt a fan
As the Spanish ladies can,
　Or I tint your lip
　With a burnt stick's tip
And you turn into such a man!
　Just the two spots that span
70　Half the bill of the young male swan.

XI

Dearest, three months ago
When the mesmerizer Snow
　With his hand's first sweep
　Put the earth to sleep:
'Twas a time when the heart could show
　All – how was earth to know,
'Neath the mute hand's to-and-fro?

XII

Dearest, three months ago
When we loved each other so,
80　　Lived and loved the same
　　Till an evening came
When a shaft from the devil's bow
　Pierced to our ingle-glow,
And the friends were friend and foe!

XIII

Not from the heart beneath –
'Twas a bubble born of breath,
　Neither sneer nor vaunt,

Nor reproach nor taunt.
See a word, how it severeth!
    Oh, power of life and death   90
In the tongue, as the Preacher saith!

XIV

Woman, and will you cast
For a word, quite off at last
    Me, your own, your You, –
    Since, as truth is true,
I was You all the happy past –
    Me do you leave aghast
With the memories We amassed?

XV

Love, if you knew the light
That your soul casts in my sight,   100
    How I look to you
    For the pure and true
And the beauteous and the right, –
    Bear with a moment's spite
When a mere mote threats the white!

XVI

What of a hasty word?
Is the fleshly heart not stirred
    By a worm's pin-prick
    Where its roots are quick?
See the eye, by a fly's foot blurred –   110
    Ear, when a straw is heard
Scratch the brain's coat of curd!

XVII

Foul be the world or fair
More or less, how can I care?
    'Tis the world the same
    For my praise or blame,
And endurance is easy there.
    Wrong in the one thing rare –
Oh, it is hard to bear!

XVIII

120 Here's the spring back or close,
When the almond-blossom blows:
    We shall have the word
    In a minor third
There is none but the cuckoo knows:
    Heaps of the guelder-rose!
I must bear with it, I suppose.

XIX

Could but November come,
Were the noisy birds struck dumb
    At the warning slash
130   Of his driver's-lash –
I would laugh like the valiant Thumb
    Facing the castle glum
And the giant's fee-faw-fum!

XX

Then, were the world well stripped
Of the gear wherein equipped
    We can stand apart,
    Heart dispense with heart
In the sun, with the flowers unnipped, –
    Oh, the world's hangings ripped,
140 We were both in a bare-walled crypt!

XXI

Each in the crypt would cry
'But one freezes here! and why?
    When a heart, as chill,
    At my own would thrill
Back to life, and its fires out-fly?
    Heart, shall we live or die?
The rest, . . . settle by-and-by!'

XXII

So, she'd efface the score,
And forgive me as before.
150   It is twelve o'clock:

I shall hear her knock
In the worst of a storm's uproar,
I shall pull her through the door,
I shall have her for evermore!

Up at a Villa – Down in the City

(As Distinguished by
an Italian Person of Quality)

I

Had I but plenty of money, money enough and to spare,
The house for me, no doubt, were a house in the city-square;
Ah, such a life, such a life, as one leads at the window there!

II

Something to see, by Bacchus, something to hear, at least!
There, the whole day long, one's life is a perfect feast;
While up at a villa one lives, I maintain it, no more than a beast.

III

Well now, look at our villa! stuck like the horn of a bull
Just on a mountain-edge as bare as the creature's skull,
Save a mere shag of a bush with hardly a leaf to pull!
10   – I scratch my own, sometimes, to see if the hair's turned wool.

IV

But the city, oh the city – the square with the houses! Why?
They are stone-faced, white as a curd, there's something to take
    the eye!
Houses in four straight lines, not a single front awry;
You watch who crosses and gossips, who saunters, who hurries
    by;
Green blinds, as a matter of course, to draw when the sun gets
    high;
And the shops with fanciful signs which are painted properly.

V

What of a villa? Though winter be over in March by rights,
'Tis May perhaps ere the snow shall have withered well off the
    heights:

You've the brown ploughed land before, where the oxen steam
and wheeze,
And the hills over-smoked behind by the faint grey olive-trees.   20

VI

Is it better in May, I ask you? You've summer all at once;
In a day he leaps complete with a few strong April suns.
'Mid the sharp short emerald wheat, scarce risen three fingers
well,
The wild tulip, at end of its tube, blows out its great red bell
Like a thin clear bubble of blood, for the children to pick and
sell.

VII

Is it ever hot in the square? There's a fountain to spout and
splash!
In the shade it sings and springs; in the shine such foam-bows
flash
On the horses with curling fish-tails, that prance and paddle
and pash
Round the lady atop in her conch – fifty gazers do not abash,
Though all that she wears is some weeds round her waist in a   30
sort of sash.

VIII

All the year long at the villa, nothing to see though you linger,
Except yon cypress that points like death's lean lifted forefinger.
Some think fireflies pretty, when they mix i' the corn and
mingle,
Or thrid the stinking hemp till the stalks of it seem a-tingle.
Late August or early September, the stunning cicala is shrill,
And the bees keep their tiresome whine round the resinous firs
on the hill.
Enough of the seasons, – I spare you the months of the fever
and chill.

IX

Ere you open your eyes in the city, the blessed church-bells
begin:
No sooner the bells leave off than the diligence rattles in:

40 You get the pick of the news, and it costs you never a pin.
By-and-by there's the travelling doctor gives pills, lets blood,
    draws teeth;
Or the Pulcinello-trumpet breaks up the market beneath.
At the post-office such a scene-picture – the new play, piping
    hot!
And a notice how, only this morning, three liberal thieves were
    shot.
Above it, behold the Archbishop's most fatherly of rebukes,
And beneath, with his crown and his lion, some little new law of
    the Duke's!
Or a sonnet with flowery marge, to the Reverend Don
    So-and-so
Who is Dante, Boccaccio, Petrarca, Saint Jerome and Cicero,
'And moreover,' (the sonnet goes rhyming,) 'the skirts of Saint
    Paul has reached,
50 Having preached us those six Lent-lectures more unctuous
    than ever he preached.'
Noon strikes, – here sweeps the procession! our Lady borne
    smiling and smart
With a pink gauze gown all spangles, and seven swords stuck in
    her heart!
Bang-whang-whang goes the drum, *tootle-te-tootle* the fife;
No keeping one's haunches still: it's the greatest pleasure in
    life.

X

But bless you, it's dear – it's dear! fowls, wine, at double the
    rate.
They have clapped a new tax upon salt, and what oil pays
    passing the gate
It's a horror to think of. And so, the villa for me, not the city!
Beggars can scarcely be choosers: but still – ah, the pity, the
    pity!
Look, two and two go the priests, then the monks with cowls
    and sandals,
60 And the penitents dressed in white shirts, a-holding the yellow
    candles;

One, he carries a flag up straight, and another a cross with
    handles,
And the Duke's guard brings up the rear, for the better
    prevention of scandals:
Bang-whang-whang goes the drum, *tootle-te-tootle* the fife.
Oh, a day in the city-square, there is no such pleasure in life!

Fra Lippo Lippi

I am poor brother Lippo, by your leave!
You need not clap your torches to my face.
Zooks, what's to blame? you think you see a monk!
What, 'tis past midnight, and you go the rounds,
And here you catch me at an alley's end
Where sportive ladies leave their doors ajar?
The Carmine's my cloister: hunt it up,
Do, – harry out, if you must show your zeal,
Whatever rat, there, haps on his wrong hole,
And nip each softling of a wee white mouse,
Weke, weke, that's crept to keep him company!
Aha, you know your betters! Then, you'll take
Your hand away that's fiddling on my throat,
And please to know me likewise. Who am I?
Why, one, sir, who is lodging with a friend
Three streets off – he's a certain . . . how d'ye call?
Master – a . . . Cosimo of the Medici,
I' the house that caps the corner. Boh! you were best!
Remember and tell me, the day you're hanged,
How you affected such a gullet's-gripe!
But you, sir, it concerns you that your knaves
Pick up a manner nor discredit you:
Zooks, are we pilchards, that they sweep the streets
And count fair prize what comes into their net?
He's Judas to a tittle, that man is!
Just such a face! Why, sir, you make amends.
Lord, I'm not angry! Bid your hangdogs go
Drink out this quarter-florin to the health
Of the munificent House that harbours me
(And many more beside, lads! more beside!)
And all's come square again. I'd like his face –

His, elbowing on his comrade in the door
With the pike and lantern, – for the slave that holds
John Baptist's head a-dangle by the hair
With one hand ('Look you, now,' as who should say)
And his weapon in the other, yet unwiped!
It's not your chance to have a bit of chalk,
A wood-coal or the like? or you should see!
Yes, I'm the painter, since you style me so.
What, brother Lippo's doings, up and down,   40
You know them and they take you? like enough!
I saw the proper twinkle in your eye –
'Tell you, I liked your looks at very first.
Let's sit and set things straight now, hip to haunch.
Here's spring come, and the nights one makes up bands
To roam the town and sing out carnival,
And I've been three weeks shut within my mew,
A-painting for the great man, saints and saints
And saints again. I could not paint all night –
Ouf! I leaned out of window for fresh air.   50
There came a hurry of feet and little feet,
A sweep of lute-strings, laughs, and whifts of song, –
Flower o' the broom,
Take away love, and our earth is a tomb!
Flower o' the quince,
I let Lisa go, and what good in life since?
Flower o' the thyme – and so on. Round they went.
Scarce had they turned the corner when a titter
Like the skipping of rabbits by moonlight, – three slim shapes,
And a face that looked up . . . zooks, sir, flesh and blood,   60
That's all I'm made of! Into shreds it went,
Curtain and counterpane and coverlet,
All the bed-furniture – a dozen knots,
There was a ladder! Down I let myself,
Hands and feet, scrambling somehow, and so dropped,
And after them. I came up with the fun
Hard by Saint Laurence, hail fellow, well met, –
Flower o' the rose,
If I've been merry, what matter who knows?

63

70 And so as I was stealing back again
To get to bed and have a bit of sleep
Ere I rise up tomorrow and go work
On Jerome knocking at his poor old breast
With his great round stone to subdue the flesh,
You snap me of the sudden. Ah, I see!
Though your eye twinkles still, you shake your head –
Mine's shaved – a monk, you say – the sting's in that!
If Master Cosimo announced himself,
Mum's the word naturally; but a monk!

80 Come, what am I a beast for? tell us, now!
I was a baby when my mother died
And father died and left me in the street.
I starved there, God knows how, a year or two
On fig-skins, melon-parings, rinds and shucks,
Refuse and rubbish. One fine frosty day,
My stomach being empty as your hat,
The wind doubled me up and down I went.
Old Aunt Lapaccia trussed me with one hand,
(Its fellow was a stinger as I knew)

90 And so along the wall, over the bridge,
By the straight cut to the convent. Six words there,
While I stood munching my first bread that month:
'So, boy, you're minded,' quoth the good fat father
Wiping his own mouth, 'twas refection-time, –
'To quit this very miserable world?
Will you renounce' . . . 'the mouthful of bread?' thought I;
By no means! Brief, they made a monk of me;
I did renounce the world, its pride and greed,
Palace, farm, villa, shop and banking-house,

100 Trash, such as these poor devils of Medici
Have given their hearts to – all at eight years old.
Well, sir, I found in time, you may be sure,
'Twas not for nothing – the good bellyful,
The warm serge and the rope that goes all round,
And day-long blessed idleness beside!
'Let's see what the urchin's fit for' – that came next.
Not overmuch their way, I must confess.

Such a to-do! They tried me with their books:
Lord, they'd have taught me Latin in pure waste!
Flower o' the clove,   110
All the Latin I construe is, 'amo' I love!
But, mind you, when a boy starves in the streets
Eight years together, as my fortune was,
Watching folk's faces to know who will fling
The bit of half-stripped grape-bunch he desires,
And who will curse or kick him for his pains, –
Which gentleman processional and fine,
Holding a candle to the Sacrament,
Will wink and let him lift a plate and catch
The droppings of the wax to sell again,   120
Or holla for the Eight and have him whipped, –
How say I? – nay, which dog bites, which lets drop
His bone from the heap of offal in the street, –
Why, soul and sense of him grow sharp alike,
He learns the look of things, and none the less
For admonition from the hunger-pinch.
I had a store of such remarks, be sure,
Which, after I found leisure, turned to use.
I drew men's faces on my copy-books,
Scrawled them within the antiphonary's marge,   130
Joined legs and arms to the long music-notes,
Found eyes and nose and chin for A's and B's,
And made a string of pictures of the world
Betwixt the ins and outs of verb and noun,
On the wall, the bench, the door. The monks looked black.
'Nay,' quoth the Prior, 'turn him out, d'ye say?
In no wise. Lose a crow and catch a lark.
What if at last we get our man of parts,
We Carmelites, like those Camaldolese
And Preaching Friars, to do our church up fine   140
And put the front on it that ought to be!'
And hereupon he bade me daub away.
Thank you! my head being crammed, the walls a blank,
Never was such prompt disemburdening.
First, every sort of monk, the black and white,

I drew them, fat and lean: then, folk at church,
From good old gossips waiting to confess
Their cribs of barrel-droppings, candle-ends, –
To the breathless fellow at the altar-foot,
150 Fresh from his murder, safe and sitting there
With the little children round him in a row
Of admiration, half for his beard and half
For that white anger of his victim's son
Shaking a fist at him with one fierce arm,
Signing himself with the other because of Christ
(Whose sad face on the cross sees only this
After the passion of a thousand years)
Till some poor girl, her apron o'er her head,
(Which the intense eyes looked through) came at eve
160 On tiptoe, said a word, dropped in a loaf,
Her pair of earrings and a bunch of flowers
(The brute took growling), prayed, and so was gone.
I painted all, then cried ''Tis ask and have;
Choose, for more's ready!' – laid the ladder flat,
And showed my covered bit of cloister-wall.
The monks closed in a circle and praised loud
Till checked, taught what to see and not to see,
Being simple bodies, – 'That's the very man!
Look at the boy who stoops to pat the dog!
170 That woman's like the Prior's niece who comes
To care about his asthma: it's the life!'
But there my triumph's straw-fire flared and funked;
Their betters took their turn to see and say:
The Prior and the learned pulled a face
And stopped all that in no time. 'How? what's here?
Quite from the mark of painting, bless us all!
Faces, arms, legs and bodies like the true
As much as pea and pea! it's devil's-game!
Your business is not to catch men with show,
180 With homage to the perishable clay,
But lift them over it, ignore it all,
Make them forget there's such a thing as flesh.
Your business is to paint the souls of men –

Man's soul, and it's a fire, smoke . . . no, it's not . . .
It's vapour done up like a new-born babe –
(In that shape when you die it leaves your mouth)
It's . . . well, what matters talking, it's the soul!
Give us no more of body than shows soul!
Here's Giotto, with his Saint a-praising God,
That sets us praising, – why not stop with him?   190
Why put all thoughts of praise out of our head
With wonder at lines, colours, and what not?
Paint the soul, never mind the legs and arms!
Rub all out, try at it a second time.
Oh, that white smallish female with the breasts,
She's just my niece . . . Herodias, I would say, –
Who went and danced and got men's heads cut off!
Have it all out!' Now, is this sense, I ask?
A fine way to paint soul, by painting body
So ill, the eye can't stop there, must go further   200
And can't fare worse! Thus, yellow does for white
When what you put for yellow's simply black,
And any sort of meaning looks intense
When all beside itself means and looks naught.
Why can't a painter lift each foot in turn,
Left foot and right foot, go a double step,
Make his flesh liker and his soul more like,
Both in their order? Take the prettiest face,
The Prior's niece . . . patron-saint – is it so pretty
You can't discover if it means hope, fear,   210
Sorrow or joy? won't beauty go with these?
Suppose I've made her eyes all right and blue,
Can't I take breath and try to add life's flash,
And then add soul and heighten them threefold?
Or say there's beauty with no soul at all –
(I never saw it – put the case the same –)
If you get simple beauty and naught else,
You get about the best thing God invents:
That's somewhat: and you'll find the soul you have missed,
Within yourself, when you return him thanks.   220
'Rub all out!' Well, well, there's my life, in short,

And so the thing has gone on ever since.
I'm grown a man no doubt, I've broken bounds:
You should not take a fellow eight years old
And make him swear to never kiss the girls.
I'm my own master, paint now as I please –
Having a friend, you see, in the Corner-house!
Lord, it's fast holding by the rings in front –
Those great rings serve more purposes than just
230 To plant a flag in, or tie up a horse!
And yet the old schooling sticks, the old grave eyes
Are peeping o'er my shoulder as I work,
The heads shake still – 'It's art's decline, my son!
You're not of the true painters, great and old;
Brother Angelico's the man, you'll find;
Brother Lorenzo stands his single peer:
Fag on at flesh, you'll never make the third!'
Flower o' the pine,
You keep your mistr . . . manners, and I'll stick to mine!
240 I'm not the third, then: bless us, they must know!
Don't you think they're the likeliest to know,
They with their Latin? So, I swallow my rage,
Clench my teeth, suck my lips in tight, and paint
To please them – sometimes do and sometimes don't;
For, doing most, there's pretty sure to come
A turn, some warm eve finds me at my saints –
A laugh, a cry, the business of the world –
(*Flower o' the peach,*
Death for us all, and his own life for each!)
250 And my whole soul revolves, the cup runs over,
The world and life's too big to pass for a dream,
And I do these wild things in sheer despite,
And play the fooleries you catch me at,
In pure rage! The old mill-horse, out at grass
After hard years, throws up his stiff heels so,
Although the miller does not preach to him
The only good of grass is to make chaff.
What would men have? Do they like grass or no –
May they or mayn't they? all I want's the thing

Settled for ever one way. As it is,   260
You tell too many lies and hurt yourself:
You don't like what you only like too much,
You do like what, if given you at your word,
You find abundantly detestable.
For me, I think I speak as I was taught;
I always see the garden and God there
A-making man's wife: and, my lesson learned,
The value and significance of flesh,
I can't unlearn ten minutes afterwards.

    You understand me: I'm a beast, I know.   270
But see, now – why, I see as certainly
As that the morning-star's about to shine,
What will hap some day. We've a youngster here
Comes to our convent, studies what I do,
Slouches and stares and lets no atom drop:
His name is Guidi – he'll not mind the monks –
They call him Hulking Tom, he lets them talk –
He picks my practice up – he'll paint apace,
I hope so – though I never live so long,
I know what's sure to follow. You be judge!   280
You speak no Latin more than I, belike;
However, you're my man, you've seen the world
– The beauty and the wonder and the power,
The shapes of things, their colours, lights and shades,
Changes, surprises, – and God made it all!
– For what? Do you feel thankful, ay or no,
For this fair town's face, yonder river's line,
The mountain round it and the sky above,
Much more the figures of man, woman, child,
These are the frame to? What's it all about?   290
To be passed over, despised? or dwelt upon,
Wondered at? oh, this last of course! – you say.
But why not do as well as say, – paint these
Just as they are, careless what comes of it?
God's works – paint anyone, and count it crime
To let a truth slip. Don't object, 'His works

Are here already; nature is complete:
Suppose you reproduce her' – (which you can't)
'There's no advantage! you must beat her, then.'
300 For, don't you mark? we're made so that we love
First when we see them painted, things we have passed
Perhaps a hundred times nor cared to see;
And so they are better, painted – better to us,
Which is the same thing. Art was given for that;
God uses us to help each other so,
Lending our minds out. Have you noticed, now,
Your cullion's hanging face? A bit of chalk,
And trust me but you should, though! How much more,
If I drew higher things with the same truth!
310 That were to take the Prior's pulpit-place,
Interpret God to all of you! Oh, oh,
It makes me mad to see what men shall do
And we in our graves! This world's no blot for us,
Nor blank; it means intensely, and means good:
To find its meaning is my meat and drink.
'Ay, but you don't so instigate to prayer!'
Strikes in the Prior: 'when your meaning's plain
It does not say to folk – remember matins,
Or, mind you fast next Friday!' Why, for this
320 What need of art at all? A skull and bones,
Two bits of stick nailed crosswise, or, what's best,
A bell to chime the hour with, does as well.
I painted a Saint Laurence six months since
At Prato, splashed the fresco in fine style:
'How looks my painting, now the scaffold's down?'
I ask a brother: 'Hugely,' he returns –
'Already not one phiz of your three slaves
Who turn the Deacon off his toasted side,
But's scratched and prodded to our heart's content,
330 The pious people have so eased their own
With coming to say prayers there in a rage:
We get on fast to see the bricks beneath.
Expect another job this time next year,
For pity and religion grow i' the crowd –

Your painting serves its purpose!' Hang the fools!

‒That is ‒ you'll not mistake an idle word
Spoke in a huff by a poor monk, Got wot,
Tasting the air this spicy night which turns
The unaccustomed head like Chianti wine!
Oh, the church knows! don't misreport me, now!   340
It's natural a poor monk out of bounds
Should have his apt word to excuse himself:
And hearken how I plot to make amends.
I have bethought me: I shall paint a piece
. . . There's for you! Give me six months, then go, see
Something in Sant' Ambrogio's! Bless the nuns!
They want a cast o' my office. I shall paint
God in the midst, Madonna and her babe,
Ringed by a bowery flowery angel-brood,
Lilies and vestments and white faces, sweet   350
As puff on puff of grated orris-root
When ladies crowd to Church at midsummer.
And then i' the front, of course a saint or two ‒
Saint John, because he saves the Florentines,
Saint Ambrose, who puts down in black and white
The convent's friends and gives them a long day,
And Job, I must have him there past mistake,
The man of Uz (and Us without the z,
Painters who need his patience). Well, all these
Secured at their devotion, up shall come   360
Out of a corner when you least expect,
As one by a dark stair into a great light,
Music and talking, who but Lippo! I! ‒
Mazed, motionless and moonstruck ‒ I'm the man!
Back I shrink ‒ what is this I see and hear?
I, caught up with my monk's-things by mistake,
My old serge gown and rope that goes all round,
I, in this presence, this pure company!
Where's a hole, where's a corner for escape?
Then steps a sweet angelic slip of a thing   370
Forward, puts out a soft palm ‒ 'Not so fast!'

– Addresses the celestial presence, 'nay –
He made you and devised you, after all,
Though he's none of you! Could Saint John there draw –
His camel-hair make up a painting-brush?
We come to brother Lippo for all that,
Iste perfecit opus!' So, all smile –
I shuffle sideways with my blushing face
Under the cover of a hundred wings

380 Thrown like a spread of kirtles when you're gay
And play hot cockles, all the doors being shut,
Till, wholly unexpected, in there pops
The hothead husband! Thus I scuttle off
To some safe bench behind, not letting go
The palm of her, the little lily thing
That spoke the good word for me in the nick,
Like the Prior's niece . . . Saint Lucy, I would say.
And so all's saved for me, and for the church
A pretty picture gained. Go, six months hence!

390 Your hand, sir, and good-bye: no lights, no lights!
The street's hushed, and I know my own way back,
Don't fear me! There's the grey beginning. Zooks!

A Toccata of Galuppi's

I

Oh Galuppi, Baldassaro, this is very sad to find!
I can hardly misconceive you; it would prove me deaf and blind;
But although I take your meaning, 'tis with such a heavy mind!

II

Here you come with your old music, and here's all the good it
brings.
What, they lived once thus at Venice where the merchants were
the kings,
Where Saint Mark's is, where the Doges used to wed the sea
with rings?

III

Ay, because the sea's the street there; and 'tis arched by . . .
what you call
. . . Shylock's bridge with houses on it, where they kept the
carnival:
I was never out of England – it's as if I saw it all.

IV

Did young people take their pleasure when the sea was warm in
May?
Balls and masks begun at midnight, burning ever to midday,
When they made up fresh adventures for the morrow, do you
say?

V

Was a lady such a lady, cheeks so round and lips so red, –
On her neck the small face buoyant, like a bell-flower on its
bed,
O'er the breast's superb abundance where a man might base his
head?

73

VI

Well, and it was graceful of them – they'd break talk off and
    afford
– She, to bite her mask's black velvet – he, to finger on his
    sword,
While you sat and played Toccatas, stately at the clavichord?

VII

What? Those lesser thirds so plaintive, sixths diminished, sigh
    on sigh,
20 Told them something? Those suspensions, those solutions –
    'Must we die?'
These commiserating sevenths – 'Life might last! we can but
    try!'

VIII

'Were you happy?' – 'Yes.' – 'And are you still as happy?' – 'Yes.
    And you?'
– 'Then, more kisses?' – 'Did *I* stop them, when a million
    seemed so few?'
Hark, the dominant's persistence till it must be answered to!

IX

So, an octave struck the answer. Oh, they praised you, I dare
    say!
'Brave Galuppi! that was music! good alike at grave and gay!
I can always leave off talking when I hear a master play!'

X

Then they left you for their pleasure: till in due time, one by
    one,
Some with lives that came to nothing, some with deeds as well
    undone,
30 Death stepped tacitly and took them where they never see the
    sun.

XI

But when I sit down to reason, think to take my stand nor
    swerve,
While I triumph o'er a secret wrung from nature's close reserve,

In you come with your cold music till I creep through every
    nerve.

XII

Yes, you, like a ghostly cricket, creaking where a house was
    burned:
'Dust and ashes, dead and done with, Venice spent what Venice
    earned.
The soul, doubtless, is immortal – where a soul can be
    discerned.

XIII

'Yours for instance: you know physics, something of geology,
Mathematics are your pastime; souls shall rise in their degree;
Butterflies may dread extinction, – you'll not die, it cannot be!

XIV

'As for Venice and her people, merely born to bloom and drop,   40
Here on earth they bore their fruitage, mirth and folly were the
    crop:
What of soul was left, I wonder, when the kissing had to stop?

XV

'Dust and ashes!' So you creak it, and I want the heart to scold.
Dear dead women, with such hair, too – what's become of all
    the gold
Used to hang and brush their bosoms? I feel chilly and grown
    old.

An Epistle Containing the Strange Medical Experience of Karshish, the Arab Physician

Karshish, the picker-up of learning's crumbs,
The not-incurious in God's handiwork
(This man's-flesh he hath admirably made,
Blown like a bubble, kneaded like a paste,
To coop up and keep down on earth a space
That puff of vapour from his mouth, man's soul)
– To Abib, all-sagacious in our art,
Breeder in me of what poor skill I boast,
Like me inquisitive how pricks and cracks
10 Befall the flesh through too much stress and strain,
Whereby the wily vapour fain would slip
Back and rejoin its source before the term, –
And aptest in contrivance (under God)
To baffle it by deftly stopping such: –
The vagrant Scholar to his Sage at home
Sends greeting (health and knowledge, fame with peace)
Three samples of true snakestone – rarer still,
One of the other sort, the melon-shaped,
(But fitter, pounded fine, for charms than drugs)
20 And writeth now the twenty-second time.

My journeyings were brought to Jericho:
Thus I resume. Who studious in our art
Shall count a little labour unrepaid?
I have shed sweat enough, left flesh and bone
On many a flinty furlong of this land.
Also, the country-side is all on fire
With rumours of a marching hitherward:
Some say Vespasian cometh, some, his son.
A black lynx snarled and pricked a tufted ear;
30 Lust of my blood inflamed his yellow balls:

I cried and threw my staff and he was gone.
Twice have the robbers stripped and beaten me,
And once a town declared me for a spy;
But at the end, I reach Jerusalem,
Since this poor covert where I pass the night,
This Bethany, lies scarce the distance thence
A man with plague-sores at the third degree
Runs till he drops down dead. Thou laughest here!
'Sooth, it elates me, thus reposed and safe,
To void the stuffing of my travel-scrip   40
And share with thee whatever Jewry yields.
A viscid choler is observable
In tertians, I was nearly bold to say;
And falling-sickness hath a happier cure
Than our school wots of: there's a spider here
Weaves no web, watches on the ledge of tombs,
Sprinkled with mottles on an ash-grey back;
Take five and drop them . . . but who knows his mind,
The Syrian runagate I trust this to?
His service payeth me a sublimate   50
Blown up his nose to help the ailing eye.
Best wait: I reach Jerusalem at morn,
There set in order my experiences,
Gather what most deserves, and give thee all –
Or I might add, Judea's gum-tragacanth
Scales off in purer flakes, shines clearer-gained,
Cracks 'twixt the pestle and the porphyry,
In fine exceeds our produce. Scalp-disease
Confounds me, crossing so with leprosy –
Thou hadst admired one sort I gained at Zoar –   60
But zeal outruns discretion. Here I end.

    Yet stay: my Syrian blinketh gratefully,
Protesteth his devotion is my price –
Suppose I write what harms not, though he steal?
I half resolve to tell thee, yet I blush,
What set me off a-writing first of all.
An itch I had, a sting to write, a tang!

For, be it this town's barrenness – or else
The Man had something in the look of him –
70   His case has struck me far more than 'tis worth.
So, pardon if – (lest presently I lose
In the great press of novelty at hand
The care and pains this somehow stole from me)
I bid thee take the thing while fresh in mind,
Almost in sight – for, wilt thou have the truth?
The very man is gone from me but now,
Whose ailment is the subject of discourse.
Thus then, and let thy better wit help all!

    'Tis but a case of mania – subinduced
80   By epilepsy, at the turning-point
Of trance prolonged unduly some three days:
When, by the exhibition of some drug
Or spell, exorcization, stroke of art
Unknown to me and which 'twere well to know,
The evil thing out-breaking all at once
Left the man whole and sound of body indeed, –
But, flinging (so to speak) life's gates too wide,
Making a clear house of it too suddenly,
The first conceit that entered might inscribe
90   Whatever it was minded on the wall
So plainly at that vantage, as it were,
(First come, first served) that nothing subsequent
Attaineth to erase those fancy-scrawls
The just-returned and new-established soul
Hath gotten now so thoroughly by heart
That henceforth she will read or these or none.
And first – the man's own firm conviction rests
That he was dead (in fact they buried him)
– That he was dead and then restored to life
100   By a Nazarene physician of his tribe:
– 'Sayeth, the same bade 'Rise,' and he did rise.
'Such cases are diurnal,' thou wilt cry.
Not so this figment! – not, that such a fume,
Instead of giving way to time and health,

Should eat itself into the life of life,
As saffron tingeth flesh, blood, bones and all!
For see, how he takes up the after-life.
The man – it is one Lazarus a Jew,
Sanguine, proportioned, fifty years of age,
The body's habit wholly laudable,　　　　　110
As much, indeed, beyond the common health
As he were made and put aside to show.
Think, could we penetrate by any drug
And bathe the wearied soul and worried flesh,
And bring it clear and fair, by three days' sleep!
Whence has the man the balm that brightens all?
This grown man eyes the world now like a child.
Some elders of his tribe, I should premise,
Led in their friend, obedient as a sheep,
To bear my inquisition. While they spoke,　　120
Now sharply, now with sorrow, – told the case, –
He listened not except I spoke to him,
But folded his two hands and let them talk,
Watching the flies that buzzed: and yet no fool.
And that's a sample how his years must go.
Look, if a beggar, in fixed middle-life,
Should find a treasure, – can he use the same
With straitened habits and with tastes starved small,
And take at once to his impoverished brain
The sudden element that changes things,　　130
That sets the undreamed-of rapture at his hand
And puts the cheap old joy in the scorned dust?
Is he not such an one as moves to mirth –
Warily parsimonious, when no need,
Wasteful as drunkenness at undue times?
All prudent counsel as to what befits
The golden mean, is lost on such an one:
The man's fantastic will is the man's law.
So here – we call the treasure knowledge, say,
Increased beyond the fleshly faculty –　　　140
Heaven opened to a soul while yet on earth,
Earth forced on a soul's use while seeing heaven:

The man is witless of the size, the sum,
The value in proportion of all things,
Or whether it be little or be much.
Discourse to him of prodigious armaments
Assembled to besiege his city now,
And of the passing of a mule with gourds –
'Tis one! Then take it on the other side,
150 Speak of some trifling fact, – he will gaze rapt
With stupor at its very littleness,
(Far as I see) as if in that indeed
He caught prodigious import, whole results;
And so will turn to us the bystanders
In ever the same stupor (note this point)
That we too see not with his opened eyes.
Wonder and doubt come wrongly into play,
Preposterously, at cross-purposes.
Should his child sicken unto death, – why, look
160 For scarce abatement of his cheerfulness,
Or pretermission of the daily craft!
While a word, gesture, glance from that same child
At play or in the school or laid asleep,
Will startle him to an agony of fear,
Exasperation, just as like. Demand
The reason why – ''tis but a word,' object –
'A gesture' – he regards thee as our lord
Who lived there in the pyramid alone,
Looked at us (dost thou mind?) when, being young,
170 We both would unadvisedly recite
Some charm's beginning, from that book of his,
Able to bid the sun throb wide and burst
All into stars, as suns grown old are wont.
Thou and the child have each a veil alike
Thrown o'er your heads, from under which ye both
Stretch your blind hands and trifle with a match
Over a mine of Greek fire, did ye know!
He holds on firmly to some thread of life –
(It is the life to lead perforcedly)
180 Which runs across some vast distracting orb

Of glory on either side that meagre thread,
Which, conscious of, he must not enter yet –
The spiritual life around the earthly life:
The law of that is known to him as this,
His heart and brain move there, his feet stay here.
So is the man perplext with impulses
Sudden to start off crosswise, not straight on,
Proclaiming what is right and wrong across,
And not along, this black thread through the blaze –
'It should be' balked by 'here it cannot be.'   190
And oft the man's soul springs into his face
As if he saw again and heard again
His sage that bade him 'Rise' and he did rise.
Something, a word, a tick o' the blood within
Admonishes: then back he sinks at once
To ashes, who was very fire before,
In sedulous recurrence to his trade
Whereby he earneth him the daily bread;
And studiously the humbler for that pride,
Professedly the faultier that he knows   200
God's secret, while he holds the thread of life.
Indeed the especial marking of the man
Is prone submission to the heavenly will –
Seeing it, what it is, and why it is.
'Sayeth, he will wait patient to the last
For that same death which must restore his being
To equilibrium, body loosening soul
Divorced even now by premature full growth:
He will live, nay, it pleaseth him to live
So long as God please, and just how God please.   210
He even seeketh not to please God more
(Which meaneth, otherwise) than as God please.
Hence, I perceive not he affects to preach
The doctrine of his sect whate'er it be,
Make proselytes as madmen thirst to do:
How can he give his neighbour the real ground,
His own conviction? Ardent as he is –
Call his great truth a lie, why, still the old

'Be it as God please' reassureth him.
220 I probed the sore as thy disciple should:
'How, beast,' said I, 'this stolid carelessness
Sufficeth thee, when Rome is on her march
To stamp out like a little spark thy town,
Thy tribe, thy crazy tale and thee at once?'
He merely looked with his large eyes on me.
The man is apathetic, you deduce?
Contrariwise, he loves both old and young,
Able and weak, affects the very brutes
And birds – how say I? flowers of the field –
230 As a wise workman recognizes tools
In a master's workshop, loving what they make.
Thus is the man, as harmless as a lamb:
Only impatient, let him do his best,
At ignorance and carelessness and sin –
An indignation which is promptly curbed:
As when in certain travels I have feigned
To be an ignoramus in our art
According to some preconceived design,
And happed to hear the land's practitioners
240 Steeped in conceit sublimed by ignorance,
Prattle fantastically on disease,
Its cause and cure – and I must hold my peace!

Thou wilt object – Why have I not ere this
Sought out the sage himself, the Nazarene
Who wrought this cure, inquiring at the source,
Conferring with the frankness that befits?
Alas! it grieveth me, the learned leech
Perished in a tumult many years ago,
Accused, – our learning's fate, – of wizardry,
250 Rebellion, to the setting up a rule
And creed prodigious as described to me.
His death, which happened when the earthquake fell
(Prefiguring, as soon appeared, the loss
To occult learning in our lord the sage
Who lived there in the pyramid alone)

Was wrought by the mad people – that's their wont!
On vain recourse, as I conjecture it,
To his tried virtue, for miraculous help –
How could he stop the earthquake? That's their way!
The other imputations must be lies: 260
But take one, though I loathe to give it thee,
In mere respect for any good man's fame.
(And after all, our patient Lazarus
Is stark mad; should we count on what he says?
Perhaps not: though in writing to a leech
'Tis well to keep back nothing of a case.)
This man so cured regards the curer, then,
As – God forgive me! who but God himself,
Creator and sustainer of the world,
That came and dwelt in flesh on it awhile!   270
– 'Sayeth that such an one was born and lived,
Taught, healed the sick, broke bread at his own house,
Then died, with Lazarus by, for aught I know,
And yet was . . . what I said nor choose repeat,
And must have so avouched himself, in fact,
In hearing of this very Lazarus
Who saith – but why all this of what he saith?
Why write of trivial matters, things of price
Calling at every moment for remark?
I noticed on the margin of a pool   280
Blue-flowering borage, the Aleppo sort,
Aboundeth, very nitrous. It is strange!

    Thy pardon for this long and tedious case,
Which, now that I review it, needs must seem
Unduly dwelt on, prolixly set forth!
Nor I myself discern in what is writ
Good cause for the peculiar interest
And awe indeed this man has touched me with.
Perhaps the journey's end, the weariness
Had wrought upon me first. I met him thus: 290
I crossed a ridge of short sharp broken hills
Like an old lion's cheek teeth. Out there came

A moon made like a face with certain spots
Multiform, manifold and menacing:
Then a wind rose behind me. So we met
In this old sleepy town at unaware,
The man and I. I send thee what is writ.
Regard it as a chance, a matter risked
To this ambiguous Syrian – he may lose,
300   Or steal, or give it thee with equal good.
Jerusalem's repose shall make amends
For time this letter wastes, thy time and mine;
Till when, once more thy pardon and farewell!

    The very God! think, Abib; dost thou think?
So, the All-Great, were the All-Loving too –
So, through the thunder comes a human voice
Saying, 'O heart I made, a heart beats here!
Face, my hands fashioned, see it in myself!
Thou hast no power nor mayst conceive of mine,
310   But love I gave thee, with myself to love,
And thou must love me who have died for thee!'
The madman saith He said so: it is strange.

Mesmerism

I

All I believed is true!
   I am able yet
   All I want, to get
By a method as strange as new:
Dare I trust the same to you?

II

If at night, when doors are shut,
   And the wood-worm picks,
   And the death-watch ticks,
And the bar has a flag of smut,
And a cat's in the water-butt –   10

III

And the socket floats and flares,
   And the house-beams groan,
   And a foot unknown
Is surmised on the garret-stairs,
And the locks slip unawares –

IV

And the spider, to serve his ends,
   By a sudden thread,
   Arms and legs outspread,
On the table's midst descends,
Comes to find, God knows what friends! –   20

V

If since eve drew in, I say,
   I have sat and brought
   (So to speak) my thought
To bear on the woman away,
Till I felt my hair turn grey –

VI

Till I seemed to have and hold,
    In the vacancy
    'Twixt the wall and me,
From the hair-plait's chestnut gold
30 To the foot in its muslin fold –

VII

Have and hold, then and there,
    Her, from head to foot,
    Breathing and mute,
Passive and yet aware,
In the grasp of my steady stare –

VIII

Hold and have, there and then,
    All her body and soul
    That completes my whole,
All that women add to men,
40 In the clutch of my steady ken –

IX

Having and holding, till
    I imprint her fast
    On the void at last
As the sun does whom he will
By the calotypist's skill –

X

Then, – if my heart's strength serve,
    And through all and each
    Of the veils I reach
To her soul and never swerve,
50 Knitting an iron nerve –

XI

Command her soul to advance
    And inform the shape
    Which has made escape
And before my countenance
Answers me glance for glance –

XII

I, still with a gesture fit
   Of my hands that best
   Do my soul's behest,
Pointing the power from it,
While myself do steadfast sit –   60

XIII

Steadfast and still the same
   On my object bent,
   While the hands give vent
To my ardour and my aim
And break into very flame –

XIV

Then I reach, I must believe,
   Not her soul in vain,
   For to me again
It reaches, and past retrieve
Is wound in the toils I weave;   70

XV

And must follow as I require,
   As befits a thrall,
   Bringing flesh and all,
Essence and earth-attire,
To the source of the tractile fire:

XVI

Till the house called hers, not mine,
   With a growing weight
   Seems to suffocate
If she break not its leaden line
And escape from its close confine.   80

XVII

Out of doors into the night!
   On to the maze
   Of the wild wood-ways,
Not turning to left nor right
From the pathway, blind with sight –

XVIII

Making through rain and wind
　　O'er the broken shrubs,
　　'Twixt the stems and stubs,
With a still, composed, strong mind,
90 Nor a care for the world behind –

XIX

Swifter and still more swift,
　　As the crowding peace
　　Doth to joy increase
In the wide blind eyes uplift
Through the darkness and the drift!

XX

While I – to the shape, I too
　　Feel my soul dilate
　　Nor a whit abate,
And relax not a gesture due,
100 As I see my belief come true.

XXI

For, there! have I drawn or no
　　Life to that lip?
　　Do my fingers dip
In a flame which again they throw
On the cheek that breaks a-glow?

XXII

Ha! was the hair so first?
　　What, unfilleted,
　　Made alive, and spread
Through the void with a rich outburst,
110 Chestnut gold-interspersed?

XXIII

Like the doors of a casket-shrine,
　　See, on either side,
　　Her two arms divide
Till the heart betwixt makes sign,
Take me, for I am thine!

XXIV

'Now – now' – the door is heard!
   Hark, the stairs! and near –
   Nearer – and here –
'Now!' and at call the third
She enters without a word.   120

XXV

On doth she march and on
   To the fancied shape;
   It is, past escape,
Herself, now: the dream is done
And the shadow and she are one.

XXVI

First I will pray. Do Thou
   That ownest the soul,
   Yet wilt grant control
To another, nor disallow
For a time, restrain me now!   130

XXVII

I admonish me while I may,
   Not to squander guilt,
   Since require Thou wilt
At my hand its price one day!
What the price is, who can say?

A Serenade at the Villa

I

That was I, you heard last night,
    When there rose no moon at all,
Nor, to pierce the strained and tight
    Tent of heaven, a planet small:
Life was dead and so was light.

II

Not a twinkle from the fly,
    Not a glimmer from the worm;
When the crickets stopped their cry,
    When the owls forbore a term,
10 You heard music; that was I.

III

Earth turned in her sleep with pain,
    Sultrily suspired for proof:
In at heaven and out again,
    Lightning! – where it broke the roof,
Bloodlike, some few drops of rain.

IV

What they could my words expressed,
    O my love, my all, my one!
Singing helped the verses best,
    And when singing's best was done,
20 To my lute I left the rest.

V

So wore night; the East was grey,
    White the broad-faced hemlock-flowers:
There would be another day;
    Ere its first of heavy hours
Found me, I had passed away.

VI

What became of all the hopes,
    Words and song and lute as well?
Say, this struck you – 'When life gropes
    Feebly for the path where fell
Light last on the evening slopes,   30

VII

'One friend in that path shall be,
    To secure my step from wrong;
One to count night day for me,
    Patient through the watches long,
Serving most with none to see.'

VIII

Never say – as something bodes –
    'So, the worst has yet a worse!
When life halts 'neath double loads,
    Better the taskmaster's curse
Than such music on the roads!   40

IX

'When no moon succeeds the sun,
    Nor can pierce the midnight's tent
Any star, the smallest one,
    While some drops, where lightning rent,
Show the final storm begun –

X

'When the fire-fly hides its spot,
    When the garden-voices fail
In the darkness thick and hot, –
    Shall another voice avail,
That shape be where these are not?   50

XI

'Has some plague a longer lease,
    Proffering its help uncouth?
Can't one even die in peace?
    As one shuts one's eyes on youth,
Is that face the last one sees?'

XII

Oh how dark your villa was,
    Windows fast and obdurate!
How the garden grudged me grass
    Where I stood – the iron gate
60   Ground its teeth to let me pass!

'Childe Roland to the Dark Tower Came'

(See Edgar's song in *Lear*)

I

My first thought was, he lied in every word,
 That hoary cripple, with malicious eye
 Askance to watch the working of his lie
On mine, and mouth scarce able to afford
Suppression of the glee, that pursed and scored
 Its edge, at one more victim gained thereby.

II

What else should he be set for, with his staff?
 What, save to waylay with his lies, ensnare
 All travellers who might find him posted there,
And ask the road? I guessed what skull-like laugh   10
Would break, what crutch 'gin write my epitaph
 For pastime in the dusty thoroughfare,

III

If at his counsel I should turn aside
 Into that ominous tract which, all agree,
 Hides the Dark Tower. Yet acquiescingly
I did turn as he pointed: neither pride
Nor hope rekindling at the end descried,
 So much as gladness that some end might be.

IV

For, what with my whole world-wide wandering,
 What with my search drawn out through years, my hope   20
 Dwindled into a ghost not fit to cope
With that obstreperous joy success would bring, –
I hardly tried now to rebuke the spring
 My heart made, finding failure in its scope.

V

As when a sick man very near to death
    Seems dead indeed, and feels begin and end
    The tears and takes the farewell of each friend,
And hears one bid the other go, draw breath
Freelier outside, ('since all is o'er,' he saith,
30   'And the blow fallen no grieving can amend';)

VI

While some discuss if near the other graves
    Be room enough for this, and when a day
    Suits best for carrying the corpse away,
With care about the banners, scarves and staves:
And still the man hears all, and only craves
    He may not shame such tender love and stay.

VII

Thus, I had so long suffered in this quest,
    Heard failure prophesied so oft, been writ
    So many times among 'The Band' – to wit,
40   The knights who to the Dark Tower's search addressed
Their steps – that just to fail as they, seemed best,
    And all the doubt was now – should I be fit?

VIII

So, quiet as despair, I turned from him,
    That hateful cripple, out of his highway
    Into the path he pointed. All the day
Had been a dreary one at best, and dim
Was settling to its close, yet shot one grim
    Red leer to see the plain catch its estray.

IX

For mark! no sooner was I fairly found
50   Pledged to the plain, after a pace or two,
    Than, pausing to throw backward a last view
O'er the safe road, 'twas gone; grey plain all round:
Nothing but plain to the horizon's bound.
    I might go on; naught else remained to do.

X

So, on I went. I think I never saw
  Such starved ignoble nature; nothing throve:
  For flowers – as well expect a cedar grove!
But cockle, spurge, according to their law
Might propagate their kind, with none to awe,
  You'd think; a burr had been a treasure-trove.   60

XI

No! penury, inertness and grimace,
  In some strange sort, were the land's portion. 'See
  Or shut your eyes,' said Nature peevishly,
'It nothing skills: I cannot help my case:
'Tis the Last Judgement's fire must cure this place,
  Calcine its clods and set my prisoners free.'

XII

If there pushed any ragged thistle-stalk
  Above its mates, the head was chopped; the bents
  Were jealous else. What made those holes and rents
In the dock's harsh swarth leaves, bruised as to balk   70
All hope of greenness? 'tis a brute must walk
  Pashing their life out, with a brute's intents.

XIII

As for the grass, it grew as scant as hair
  In leprosy; thin dry blades pricked the mud
  Which underneath looked kneaded up with blood.
One stiff blind horse, his every bone a-stare,
Stood stupefied, however he came there:
  Thrust out past service from the devil's stud!

XIV

Alive? he might be dead for aught I know,
  With that red gaunt and colloped neck a-strain,   80
  And shut eyes underneath the rusty mane;
Seldom went such grotesqueness with such woe;
I never saw a brute I hated so;
  He must be wicked to deserve such pain.

XV

I shut my eyes and turned them on my heart.
   As a man calls for wine before he fights,
   I asked one draught of earlier, happier sights,
Ere fitly I could hope to play my part.
Think first, fight afterwards – the soldier's art:
90   One taste of the old time sets all to rights.

XVI

Not it! I fancied Cuthbert's reddening face
   Beneath its garniture of curly gold,
   Dear fellow, till I almost felt him fold
An arm in mine to fix me to the place,
That way he used. Alas, one night's disgrace!
   Out went my heart's new fire and left it cold.

XVII

Giles then, the soul of honour – there he stands
   Frank as ten years ago when knighted first.
   What honest man should dare (he said) he durst.
100   Good – but the scene shifts – faugh! what hangman-hands
Pin to his breast a parchment? His own bands
   Read it. Poor traitor, spit upon and curst!

XVIII

Better this present than a past like that;
   Back therefore to my darkening path again!
   No sound, no sight as far as eye could strain.
Will the night send a howlet or a bat?
I asked: when something on the dismal flat
   Came to arrest my thoughts and change their train.

XIX

A sudden little river crossed my path
110   As unexpected as a serpent comes.
   No sluggish tide congenial to the glooms;
This, as it frothed by, might have been a bath
For the fiend's glowing hoof – to see the wrath
   Of its black eddy bespate with flakes and spumes.

XX

So petty yet so spiteful! All along,
   Low scrubby alders kneeled down over it;
   Drenched willows flung them headlong in a fit
Of mute despair, a suicidal throng:
The river which had done them all the wrong,
   Whate'er that was, rolled by, deterred no whit.   120

XXI

Which, while I forded, – good saints, how I feared
   To set my foot upon a dead man's cheek,
   Each step, or feel the spear I thrust to seek
For hollows, tangled in his hair or beard!
– It may have been a water-rat I speared,
   But, ugh! it sounded like a baby's shriek.

XXII

Glad was I when I reached the other bank.
   Now for a better country. Vain presage!
   Who were the strugglers, what war did they wage,
Whose savage trample thus could pad the dank   130
Soil to a plash? Toads in a poisoned tank,
   Or wild cats in a red-hot iron cage –

XXIII

The fight must so have seemed in that fell cirque.
   What penned them there, with all the plain to choose?
   No foot-print leading to that horrid mews,
None out of it. Mad brewage set to work
Their brains, no doubt, like galley-slaves the Turk
   Pits for his pastime, Christians against Jews.

XXIV

And more than that – a furlong on – why, there!
   What bad use was that engine for, that wheel,   140
   Or brake, not wheel – that harrow fit to reel
Men's bodies out like silk? with all the air
Of Tophet's tool, on earth left unaware,
   Or brought to sharpen its rusty teeth of steel.

XXV

Then came a bit of stubbed ground, once a wood,
 Next a marsh, it would seem, and now mere earth
 Desperate and done with; (so a fool finds mirth,
Makes a thing and then mars it, till his mood
Changes and off he goes!) within a rood –
150 Bog, clay and rubble, sand and stark black dearth.

XXVI

Now blotches rankling, coloured gay and grim,
 Now patches where some leanness of the soil's
 Broke into moss or substances like boils;
Then came some palsied oak, a cleft in him
Like a distorted mouth that splits its rim
 Gaping at death, and dies while it recoils.

XXVII

And just as far as ever from the end!
 Naught in the distance but the evening, naught
 To point my footstep further! At the thought,
160 A great black bird, Apollyon's bosom-friend,
Sailed past, nor beat his wide wing dragon-penned
 That brushed my cap – perchance the guide I sought.

XXVIII

For, looking up, aware I somehow grew,
 'Spite of the dusk, the plain had given place
 All round to mountains – with such name to grace
Mere ugly heights and heaps now stolen in view.
How thus they had surprised me, – solve it, you!
 How to get from them was no clearer case.

XXIX

Yet half I seemed to recognize some trick
170 Of mischief happened to me, God knows when –
 In a bad dream perhaps. Here ended, then,
Progress this way. When, in the very nick
Of giving up, one time more, came a click
 As when a trap shuts – you're inside the den!

XXX

Burningly it came on me all at once,
   This was the place! those two hills on the right,
   Crouched like two bulls locked horn in horn in fight;
While to the left, a tall scalped mountain . . . Dunce,
Dotard, a-dozing at the very nonce,
   After a life spent training for the sight!   180

XXXI

What in the midst lay but the Tower itself?
   The round squat turret, blind as the fool's heart,
   Built of brown stone, without a counterpart
In the whole world. The tempest's mocking elf
Points to the shipman thus the unseen shelf
   He strikes on, only when the timbers start.

XXXII

Not see? because of night perhaps? – why, day
   Came back again for that! before it left,
   The dying sunset kindled through a cleft:
The hills, like giants at a hunting, lay,   190
Chin upon hand, to see the game at bay, –
   'Now stab and end the creature – to the heft!'

XXXIII

Not hear? when noise was everywhere! it tolled
   Increasing like a bell. Names in my ears
   Of all the lost adventurers my peers, –
How such a one was strong, and such was bold,
And such was fortunate, yet each of old
   Lost, lost! one moment knelled the woe of years.

XXXIV

There they stood, ranged along the hill-sides, met
   To view the last of me, a living frame   200
   For one more picture! in a sheet of flame
I saw them and I knew them all. And yet
Dauntless the slug-horn to my lips I set,
   And blew. *'Childe Roland to the Dark Tower came.'*

The Statue and the Bust

There's a palace in Florence, the world knows well,
And a statue watches it from the square,
And this story of both do our townsmen tell.

Ages ago, a lady there,
At the farthest window facing the East
Asked, 'Who rides by with the royal air?'

The bridesmaids' prattle around her ceased;
She leaned forth, one on either hand;
They saw how the blush of the bride increased –

10 They felt by its beats her heart expand –
As one at each ear and both in a breath
Whispered, 'The Great-Duke Ferdinand.'

That self-same instant, underneath,
The Duke rode past in his idle way,
Empty and fine like a swordless sheath.

Gay he rode, with a friend as gay,
Till he threw his head back – 'Who is she?'
– 'A bride the Riccardi brings home today.'

Hair in heaps lay heavily
20 Over a pale brow spirit-pure –
Carved like the heart of the coal-black tree,

Crisped like a war-steed's encolure –
And vainly sought to dissemble her eyes
Of the blackest black our eyes endure.

And lo, a blade for a knight's emprise
Filled the fine empty sheath of a man, –
The Duke grew straightway brave and wise.

He looked at her, as a lover can;
She looked at him, as one who awakes:
The past was a sleep, and her life began.　　　30

Now, love so ordered for both their sakes,
A feast was held that selfsame night
In the pile which the mighty shadow makes.

(For Via Larga is three-parts light,
But the palace overshadows one,
Because of a crime which may God requite!

To Florence and God the wrong was done,
Through the first republic's murder there
By Cosimo and his cursèd son.)

The Duke (with the statue's face in the square)　　40
Turned in the midst of his multitude
At the bright approach of the bridal pair.

Face to face the lovers stood
A single minute and no more,
While the bridegroom bent as a man subdued –

Bowed till his bonnet brushed the floor –
For the Duke on the lady a kiss conferred,
As the courtly custom was of yore.

In a minute can lovers exchange a word?
If a word did pass, which I do not think,　　50
Only one out of the thousand heard.

That was the bridegroom. At day's brink
He and his bride were alone at last
In a bedchamber by a taper's blink.

Calmly he said that her lot was cast,
That the door she had passed was shut on her
Till the final catafalque repassed.

The world meanwhile, its noise and stir,
Through a certain window facing the East,
She could watch like a convent's chronicler.　　60

Since passing the door might lead to a feast,
And a feast might lead to so much beside,
He, of many evils, chose the least.

'Freely I choose too,' said the bride –
'Your window and its world suffice,'
Replied the tongue, while the heart replied –

'If I spend the night with that devil twice,
May his window serve as my loop of hell
Whence a damned soul looks on paradise!

70 'I fly to the Duke who loves me well,
Sit by his side and laugh at sorrow
Ere I count another ave-bell.

''Tis only the coat of a page to borrow,
And tie my hair in a horse-boy's trim,
And I save my soul – but not tomorrow' –

(She checked herself and her eye grew dim)
'My father tarries to bless my state:
I must keep it one day more for him.

'Is one day more so long to wait?
80 Moreover the Duke rides past, I know;
We shall see each other, sure as fate.'

She turned on her side and slept. Just so!
So we resolve on a thing and sleep:
So did the lady, ages ago.

That night the Duke said, 'Dear or cheap
As the cost of this cup of bliss may prove
To body or soul, I will drain it deep.'

And on the morrow, bold with love,
He beckoned the bridegroom (close on call,
90 As his duty bade, by the Duke's alcove)

And smiled ''Twas a very funeral,
Your lady will think, this feast of ours, –
A shame to efface, whate'er befall!

'What if we break from the Arno bowers,
And try if Petraja, cool and green,
Cure last night's fault with this morning's flowers?'

The bridegroom, not a thought to be seen
On his steady brow and quiet mouth,
Said, 'Too much favour for me so mean!

'But, alas! my lady leaves the South;   100
Each wind that comes from the Apennine
Is a menace to her tender youth:

'Nor a way exists, the wise opine,
If she quits her palace twice this year,
To avert the flower of life's decline.'

Quoth the Duke, 'A sage and a kindly fear.
Moreover Petraja is cold this spring:
Be our feast tonight as usual here!'

And then to himself – 'Which night shall bring
Thy bride to her lover's embraces, fool –   110
Or I am the fool, and thou art the king!

'Yet my passion must wait a night, nor cool –
For tonight the Envoy arrives from France
Whose heart I unlock with thyself, my tool.

'I need thee still and might miss perchance.
Today is not wholly lost, beside,
With its hope of my lady's countenance:

'For I ride – what should I do but ride?
And passing her palace, if I list,
May glance at its window – well betide!'   120

So said, so done: nor the lady missed
One ray that broke from the ardent brow,
Nor a curl of the lips where the spirit kissed.

Be sure that each renewed the vow,
No morrow's sun should arise and set
And leave them then as it left them now.

But next day passed, and next day yet,
With still fresh cause to wait one day more
Ere each leaped over the parapet.

130 And still, as love's brief morning wore,
With a gentle start, half smile, half sigh,
They found love not as it seemed before.

They thought it would work infallibly,
But not in despite of heaven and earth:
The rose would blow when the storm passed by.

Meantime they could profit in winter's dearth
By store of fruits that supplant the rose:
The world and its ways have a certain worth:

And to press a point while these oppose
140 Were simple policy; better wait:
We lose no friends and we gain no foes.

Meantime, worse fates than a lover's fate,
Who daily may ride and pass and look
Where his lady watches behind the grate!

And she – she watched the square like a book
Holding one picture and only one,
Which daily to find she undertook:

When the picture was reached the book was done,
And she turned from the picture at night to scheme
150 Of tearing it out for herself next sun.

So weeks grew months, years; gleam by gleam
The glory dropped from their youth and love,
And both perceived they had dreamed a dream;

Which hovered as dreams do, still above:
But who can take a dream for a truth?
Oh, hide our eyes from the next remove!

One day as the lady saw her youth
Depart, and the silver thread that streaked
Her hair, and, worn by the serpent's tooth,

The brow so puckered, the chin so peaked, –   160
And wondered who the woman was,
Hollow-eyed and haggard-cheeked,

Fronting her silent in the glass –
'Summon here,' she suddenly said,
'Before the rest of my old self pass,

'Him, the Carver, a hand to aid,
Who fashions the clay no love will change,
And fixes a beauty never to fade.

'Let Robbia's craft so apt and strange
Arrest the remains of young and fair,   170
And rivet them while the seasons range.

'Make me a face on the window there,
Waiting as ever, mute the while,
My love to pass below in the square!

'And let me think that it may beguile
Dreary days which the dead must spend
Down in their darkness under the aisle,

'To say, "What matters it at the end?
I did no more while my heart was warm
Than does that image, my pale-faced friend."   180

'Where is the use of the lip's red charm,
The heaven of hair, the pride of the brow,
And the blood that blues the inside arm –

'Unless we turn, as the soul knows how,
The earthly gift to an end divine?
A lady of clay is as good, I trow.'

But long ere Robbia's cornice, fine,
With flowers and fruits which leaves enlace,
Was set where now is the empty shrine –

(And, leaning out of a bright blue space,   190
As a ghost might lean from a chink of sky,
The passionate pale lady's face –

Eyeing ever, with earnest eye
And quick-turned neck at its breathless stretch,
Some one who ever is passing by –)

The Duke had sighed like the simplest wretch
In Florence, 'Youth – my dream escapes!
Will its record stay?' And he bade them fetch

Some subtle moulder of brazen shapes –
200 'Can the soul, the will, die out of a man
Ere his body find the grave that gapes?

'John of Douay shall effect my plan,
Set me on horseback here aloft,
Alive, as the crafty sculptor can,

'In the very square I have crossed so oft:
That men may admire, when future suns
Shall touch the eyes to a purpose soft,

'While the mouth and the brow stay brave in bronze –
Admire and say, "When he was alive
210 How he would take his pleasure once!"

'And it shall go hard but I contrive
To listen the while, and laugh in my tomb
At idleness which aspires to strive.'

———————

So! While these wait the trump of doom,
How do their spirits pass, I wonder,
Nights and days in the narrow room?

Still, I suppose, they sit and ponder
What a gift life was, ages ago,
Six steps out of the chapel yonder.

220 Only they see not God, I know,
Nor all that chivalry of his,
The soldier-saints who, row on row,

Burn upward each to his point of bliss –
Since, the end of life being manifest,
He had burned his way through the world to this.

I hear you reproach, 'But delay was best,
For their end was a crime.' – Oh, a crime will do
As well, I reply, to serve for a test,

As a virtue golden through and through,
Sufficient to vindicate itself   230
And prove its worth at a moment's view!

Must a game be played for the sake of pelf?
Where a button goes, 'twere an epigram
To offer the stamp of the very Guelph.

The true has no value beyond the sham:
As well the counter as coin, I submit,
When your table's a hat, and your prize a dram.

Stake your counter as boldly every whit,
Venture as warily, use the same skill,
Do your best, whether winning or losing it,   240

If you choose to play! – is my principle.
Let a man contend to the uttermost
For his life's set prize, be it what it will!

The counter our lovers staked was lost
As surely as if it were lawful coin:
And the sin I impute to each frustrate ghost

Is – the unlit lamp and the ungirt loin,
Though the end in sight was a vice, I say.
You of the virtue (we issue join)
How strive you? *De te, fabula.*   250

How It Strikes a Contemporary

I only knew one poet in my life:
And this, or something like it, was his way.

    You saw go up and down Valladolid,
A man of mark, to know next time you saw.
His very serviceable suit of black
Was courtly once and conscientious still,
And many might have worn it, though none did:
The cloak, that somewhat shone and showed the threads,
Had purpose, and the ruff, significance.
10 He walked and tapped the pavement with his cane,
Scenting the world, looking it full in face,
An old dog, bald and blindish, at his heels.
They turned up, now, the alley by the church,
That leads nowhither; now, they breathed themselves
On the main promenade just at the wrong time:
You'd come upon his scrutinizing hat,
Making a peaked shade blacker than itself
Against the single window spared some house
Intact yet with its mouldered Moorish work, –
20 Or else surprise the ferrel of his stick
Trying the mortar's temper 'tween the chinks
Of some new shop a-building, French and fine.
He stood and watched the cobbler at his trade,
The man who slices lemons into drink,
The coffee-roaster's brazier, and the boys
That volunteer to help him turn its winch.
He glanced o'er books on stalls with half an eye,
And fly-leaf ballads on the vendor's string,
And broad-edge bold-print posters by the wall.
30 He took such cognizance of men and things,

If any beat a horse, you felt he saw;
If any cursed a woman, he took note;
Yet stared at nobody, – you stared at him,
And found, less to your pleasure than surprise,
He seemed to know you and expect as much.
So, next time that a neighbour's tongue was loosed,
It marked the shameful and notorious fact,
We had among us, not so much a spy,
As a recording chief-inquisitor,
The town's true master if the town but knew!   40
We merely kept a governor for form,
While this man walked about and took account
Of all thought, said and acted, then went home,
And wrote it fully to our Lord the King
Who has an itch to know things, he knows why,
And reads them in his bedroom of a night.
Oh, you might smile! there wanted not a touch,
A tang of . . . well, it was not wholly ease
As back into your mind the man's look came.
Stricken in years a little, – such a brow   50
His eyes had to live under! – clear as flint
On either side the formidable nose
Curved, cut and coloured like an eagle's claw.
Had he to do with A.'s surprising fate?
When altogether old B. disappeared
And young C. got his mistress, – was't our friend,
His letter to the King, that did it all?
What paid the bloodless man for so much pains?
Our Lord the King has favourites manifold,
And shifts his ministry some once a month;   60
Our city gets new governors at whiles, –
But never word or sign, that I could hear,
Notified to this man about the streets
The King's approval of those letters conned
The last thing duly at the dead of night.
Did the man love his office? Frowned our Lord,
Exhorting when none heard – 'Beseech me not!
Too far above my people, – beneath me!

I set the watch, – how should the people know?
70 Forget them, keep me all the more in mind!'
Was some such understanding 'twixt the two?

   I found no truth in one report at least –
That if you tracked him to his home, down lanes
Beyond the Jewry, and as clean to pace,
You found he ate his supper in a room
Blazing with lights, four Titians on the wall,
And twenty naked girls to change his plate!
Poor man, he lived another kind of life
In that new stuccoed third house by the bridge,
80 Fresh-painted, rather smart than otherwise!
The whole street might o'erlook him as he sat,
Leg crossing leg, one foot on the dog's back,
Playing a decent cribbage with his maid
(Jacynth, you're sure her name was) o'er the cheese
And fruit, three red halves of starved winter-pears,
Or treat of radishes in April. Nine,
Ten, struck the church clock, straight to bed went he.

   My father, like the man of sense he was,
Would point him out to me a dozen times;
90 ''St – 'St,' he'd whisper, 'the Corregidor!'
I had been used to think that personage
Was one with lacquered breeches, lustrous belt,
And feathers like a forest in his hat,
Who blew a trumpet and proclaimed the news,
Announced the bull-fights, gave each church its turn,
And memorized the miracle in vogue!
He had a great observance from us boys;
We were in error; that was not the man.

   I'd like now, yet had haply been afraid,
100 To have just looked, when this man came to die,
And seen who lined the clean gay garret-sides
And stood about the neat low truckle-bed,
With the heavenly manner of relieving guard.
Here had been, mark, the general-in-chief,

Through a whole campaign of the world's life and death,
Doing the King's work all the dim day long,
In his old coat and up to knees in mud,
Smoked like a herring, dining on a crust, –
And, now the day was won, relieved at once!
No further show or need for that old coat,   110
You are sure, for one thing! Bless us, all the while
How sprucely we are dressed out, you and I!
A second, and the angels alter that.
Well, I could never write a verse, – could you?
Let's to the Prado and make the most of time.

The Patriot
An Old Story

I

It was roses, roses, all the way,
   With myrtle mixed in my path like mad:
The house-roofs seemed to heave and sway,
   The church-spires flamed, such flags they had,
A year ago on this very day.

II

The air broke into a mist with bells,
   The old walls rocked with the crowd and cries.
Had I said, 'Good folk, mere noise repels –
   But give me your sun from yonder skies!'
10 They had answered, 'And afterward, what else?'

III

Alack, it was I who leaped at the sun
   To give it my loving friends to keep!
Naught man could do, have I left undone:
   And you see my harvest, what I reap
This very day, now a year is run.

IV

There's nobody on the house-tops now –
   Just a palsied few at the windows set;
For the best of the sight is, all allow,
   At the Shambles' Gate – or, better yet,
20 By the very scaffold's foot, I trow.

V

I go in the rain, and, more than needs,
   A rope cuts both my wrists behind;
And I think, by the feel, my forehead bleeds,
   For they fling, whoever has a mind,
Stones at me for my year's misdeeds.

VI

Thus I entered, and thus I go!
   In triumphs, people have dropped down dead.
'Paid by the world, what dost thou owe
   Me?' – God might question; now instead,
'Tis God shall repay: I am safer so.   30

Memorabilia

I

Ah, did you once see Shelley plain,
    And did he stop and speak to you
And did you speak to him again?
    How strange it seems and new!

II

But you were living before that,
    And also you are living after;
And the memory I started at –
    My starting moves your laughter.

III

I crossed a moor, with a name of its own
10   And a certain use in the world no doubt,
Yet a hand's-breadth of it shines alone
    'Mid the blank miles round about:

IV

For there I picked up on the heather
    And there I put inside my breast
A moulted feather, an eagle-feather!
    Well, I forget the rest.

Andrea del Sarto

(Called 'The Faultless Painter')

But do not let us quarrel any more,
No, my Lucrezia; bear with me for once:
Sit down and all shall happen as you wish.
You turn your face, but does it bring your heart?
I'll work then for your friend's friend, never fear,
Treat his own subject after his own way,
Fix his own time, accept too his own price,
And shut the money into this small hand
When next it takes mine. Will it? tenderly?
Oh, I'll content him, – but tomorrow, Love!   10
I often am much wearier than you think,
This evening more than usual, and it seems
As if – forgive now – should you let me sit
Here by the window with your hand in mine
And look a half-hour forth on Fiesole,
Both of one mind, as married people use,
Quietly, quietly the evening through,
I might get up tomorrow to my work
Cheerful and fresh as ever. Let us try.
Tomorrow, how you shall be glad for this!   20
Your soft hand is a woman of itself,
And mine the man's bared breast she curls inside.
Don't count the time lost, neither; you must serve
For each of the five pictures we require:
It saves a model. So! keep looking so –
My serpentining beauty, rounds on rounds!
– How could you ever prick those perfect ears,
Even to put the pearl there! oh, so sweet –
My face, my moon, my everybody's moon,

30 Which everybody looks on and calls his,
And, I suppose, is looked on by in turn,
While she looks – no one's: very dear, no less.
You smile? why, there's my picture ready made,
There's what we painters call our harmony!
A common greyness silvers everything, –
All in a twilight, you and I alike
– You, at the point of your first pride in me
(That's gone you know), – but I, at every point;
My youth, my hope, my art, being all toned down
40 To yonder sober pleasant Fiesole.
There's the bell clinking from the chapel-top;
That length of convent-wall across the way
Holds the trees safer, huddled more inside;
The last monk leaves the garden; days decrease,
And autumn grows, autumn in everything.
Eh? the whole seems to fall into a shape
As if I saw alike my work and self
And all that I was born to be and do,
A twilight-piece. Love, we are in God's hand.
50 How strange now, looks the life he makes us lead;
So free we seem, so fettered fast we are!
I feel he laid the fetter: let it lie!
This chamber for example – turn your head –
All that's behind us! You don't understand
Nor care to understand about my art,
But you can hear at least when people speak:
And that cartoon, the second from the door
– It is the thing, Love! so such things should be –
Behold Madonna! – I am bold to say.
60 I can do with my pencil what I know,
What I see, what at bottom of my heart
I wish for, if I ever wish so deep –
Do easily, too – when I say, perfectly,
I do not boast, perhaps: yourself are judge,
Who listened to the Legate's talk last week,
And just as much they used to say in France.
At any rate 'tis easy, all of it!

No sketches first, no studies, that's long past:
I do what many dream of, all their lives,
– Dream? strive to do, and agonize to do,   70
And fail in doing. I could count twenty such
On twice your fingers, and not leave this town,
Who strive – you don't know how the others strive
To paint a little thing like that you smeared
Carelessly passing with your robes afloat, –
Yet do much less, so much less, Someone says,
(I know his name, no matter) – so much less!
Well, less is more, Lucrezia: I am judged.
There burns a truer light of God in them,
In their vexed beating stuffed and stopped-up brain,   80
Heart, or whate'er else, than goes on to prompt
This low-pulsed forthright craftsman's hand of mine.
Their works drop groundward, but themselves, I know,
Reach many a time a heaven that's shut to me,
Enter and take their place there sure enough,
Though they come back and cannot tell the world.
My works are nearer heaven, but I sit here.
The sudden blood of these men! at a word –
Praise them, it boils, or blame them, it boils too.
I, painting from myself and to myself,   90
Know what I do, am unmoved by men's blame
Or their praise either. Somebody remarks
Morello's outline there is wrongly traced,
His hue mistaken; what of that? or else,
Rightly traced and well ordered; what of that?
Speak as they please, what does the mountain care?
Ah, but a man's reach should exceed his grasp,
Or what's a heaven for? All is silver-grey
Placid and perfect with my art: the worse!
I know both what I want and what might gain,   100
And yet how profitless to know, to sigh
'Had I been two, another and myself,
Our head would have o'erlooked the world!' No doubt.
Yonder's a work now, of that famous youth
The Urbinate who died five years ago.

('Tis copied, George Vasari sent it me.)
Well, I can fancy how he did it all,
Pouring his soul, with kings and popes to see,
Reaching, that heaven might so replenish him,
110   Above and through his art – for it gives way;
That arm is wrongly put – and there again –
A fault to pardon in the drawing's lines,
Its body, so to speak: its soul is right,
He means right – that, a child may understand.
Still, what an arm! and I could alter it:
But all the play, the insight and the stretch –
Out of me, out of me! And wherefore out?
Had you enjoined them on me, given me soul,
We might have risen to Rafael, I and you!
120   Nay, Love, you did give all I asked, I think –
More than I merit, yes, by many times.
But had you – oh, with the same perfect brow,
And perfect eyes, and more than perfect mouth,
And the low voice my soul hears, as a bird
The fowler's pipe, and follows to the snare –
Had you, with these the same, but brought a mind!
Some women do so. Had the mouth there urged
'God and the glory! never care for gain.
The present by the future, what is that?
130   Live for fame, side by side with Agnolo!
Rafael is waiting: up to God, all three!'
I might have done it for you. So it seems:
Perhaps not. All is as God over-rules.
Beside, incentives come from the soul's self;
The rest avail not. Why do I need you?
What wife had Rafael, or has Agnolo?
In this world, who can do a thing, will not;
And who would do it, cannot, I perceive:
Yet the will's somewhat – somewhat, too, the power –
140   And thus we half-men struggle. At the end,
God, I conclude, compensates, punishes.
'Tis safer for me, if the award be strict,
That I am something underrated here,

Poor this long while, despised, to speak the truth.
I dared not, do you know, leave home all day,
For fear of chancing on the Paris lords.
The best is when they pass and look aside;
But they speak sometimes; I must bear it all.
Well may they speak! That Francis, that first time,
And that long festal year at Fontainebleau!   150
I surely then could sometimes leave the ground,
Put on the glory, Rafael's daily wear,
In that humane great monarch's golden look, –
One finger in his beard or twisted curl
Over his mouth's good mark that made the smile,
One arm about my shoulder, round my neck,
The jingle of his gold chain in my ear,
I painting proudly with his breath on me,
All his court round him, seeing with his eyes,
Such frank French eyes, and such a fire of souls   160
Profuse, my hand kept plying by those hearts, –
And, best of all, this, this, this face beyond,
This in the background, waiting on my work,
To crown the issue with a last reward!
A good time, was it not, my kingly days?
And had you not grown restless . . . but I know –
'Tis done and past; 'twas right, my instinct said;
Too live the life grew, golden and not grey,
And I'm the weak-eyed bat no sun should tempt
Out of the grange whose four walls make his world.   170
How could it end in any other way?
You called me, and I came home to your heart.
The triumph was – to reach and stay there; since
I reached it ere the triumph, what is lost?
Let my hands frame your face in your hair's gold,
You beautiful Lucrezia that are mine!
'Rafael did this, Andrea painted that;
The Roman's is the better when you pray,
But still the other's Virgin was his wife –'
Men will excuse me. I am glad to judge   180
Both pictures in your presence; clearer grows

My better fortune, I resolve to think.
For, do you know, Lucrezia, as God lives,
Said one day Agnolo, his very self,
To Rafael . . . I have known it all these years . . .
(When the young man was flaming out his thoughts
Upon a palace-wall for Rome to see,
Too lifted up in heart because of it)
'Friend, there's a certain sorry little scrub
190   Goes up and down our Florence, none cares how,
Who, were he set to plan and execute
As you are, pricked on by your popes and kings,
Would bring the sweat into that brow of yours!'
To Rafael's! – And indeed the arm is wrong.
I hardly dare . . . yet, only you to see,
Give the chalk here – quick, thus the line should go!
Ay, but the soul! he's Rafael! rub it out!
Still, all I care for, if he spoke the truth,
(What he? why, who but Michel Agnolo?
200   Do you forget already words like those?)
If really there was such a chance, so lost, –
Is, whether you're – not grateful – but more pleased.
Well, let me think so. And you smile indeed!
This hour has been an hour! Another smile?
If you would sit thus by me every night
I should work better, do you comprehend?
I mean that I should earn more, give you more.
See, it is settled dusk now; there's a star;
Morello's gone, the watch-lights show the wall,
210   The cue-owls speak the name we call them by.
Come from the window, love, – come in, at last,
Inside the melancholy little house
We built to be so gay with. God is just.
King Francis may forgive me: oft at nights
When I look up from painting, eyes tired out,
The walls become illumined, brick from brick
Distinct, instead of mortar, fierce bright gold,
That gold of his I did cement them with!
Let us but love each other. Must you go?

That Cousin here again? he waits outside?   220
Must see you – you, and not with me? Those loans?
More gaming debts to pay? you smiled for that?
Well, let smiles buy me! have you more to spend?
While hand and eye and something of a heart
Are left me, work's my ware, and what's it worth?
I'll pay my fancy. Only let me sit
The grey remainder of the evening out,
Idle, you call it, and muse perfectly
How I could paint, were I but back in France,
One picture, just one more – the Virgin's face,   230
Not yours this time! I want you at my side
To hear them – that is, Michel Agnolo –
Judge all I do and tell you of its worth.
Will you? Tomorrow, satisfy your friend.
I take the subjects for his corridor,
Finish the portrait out of hand – there, there,
And throw him in another thing or two
If he demurs; the whole should prove enough
To pay for this same Cousin's freak. Beside,
What's better and what's all I care about,   240
Get you the thirteen scudi for the ruff!
Love, does that please you? Ah, but what does he,
The Cousin! what does he to please you more?

I am grown peaceful as old age tonight.
I regret little, I would change still less.
Since there my past life lies, why alter it?
The very wrong to Francis! – it is true
I took his coin, was tempted and complied,
And built this house and sinned, and all is said.
My father and my mother died of want.   250
Well, had I riches of my own? you see
How one gets rich! Let each one bear his lot.
They were born poor, lived poor, and poor they died:
And I have laboured somewhat in my time
And not been paid profusely. Some good son
Paint my two hundred pictures – let him try!

No doubt, there's something strikes a balance. Yes,
You loved me quite enough, it seems tonight.
This must suffice me here. What would one have?
260 In heaven, perhaps, new chances, one more chance –
Four great walls in the New Jerusalem,
Meted on each side by the angel's reed,
For Leonard, Rafael, Agnolo and me
To cover – the three first without a wife,
While I have mine! So – still they overcome
Because there's still Lucrezia, – as I choose.

Again the Cousin's whistle! Go, my Love.

In a Year

I

Never any more,
  While I live,
Need I hope to see his face
  As before.
Once his love grown chill,
  Mine may strive:
Bitterly we re-embrace,
  Single still.

II

Was it something said,
  Something done,   10
Vexed him? was it touch of hand,
  Turn of head?
Strange! that very way
  Love begun:
I as little understand
  Love's decay.

III

When I sewed or drew,
  I recall
How he looked as if I sung,
  – Sweetly too.   20
If I spoke a word,
  First of all
Up his cheek the colour sprung,
  Then he heard.

IV

Sitting by my side,
　　At my feet,
So he breathed but air I breathed,
　　Satisfied!
I, too, at love's brim
30　　Touched the sweet:
I would die if death bequeathed
　　Sweet to him.

V

'Speak, I love thee best!'
　　He exclaimed:
'Let thy love my own foretell!'
　　I confessed:
'Clasp my heart on thine
　　Now unblamed,
Since upon thy soul as well
40　　Hangeth mine!'

VI

Was it wrong to own,
　　Being truth?
Why should all the giving prove
　　His alone?
I had wealth and ease,
　　Beauty, youth:
Since my lover gave me love,
　　I gave these.

VII

That was all I meant,
50　　– To be just,
And the passion I had raised,
　　To content.
Since he chose to change
　　Gold for dust,
If I gave him what he praised
　　Was it strange?

VIII

Would he loved me yet,
　　On and on,
While I found some way undreamed
　　– Paid my debt!　　　　　　　60
Gave more life and more,
　　Till, all gone,
He should smile 'She never seemed
　　Mine before.

IX

'What, she felt the while,
　　Must I think?
Love's so different with us men!'
　　He should smile:
'Dying for my sake –
　　White and pink!　　　　　　70
Can't we touch these bubbles then
　　But they break?'

X

Dear, the pang is brief,
　　Do thy part,
Have thy pleasure! How perplexed
　　Grows belief!
Well, this cold clay clod
　　Was man's heart:
Crumble it, and what comes next?
　　Is it God?　　　　　　　　80

Cleon

'As certain also of your own poets have said' –

Cleon the poet (from the sprinkled isles,
Lily on lily, that o'erlace the sea,
And laugh their pride when the light wave lisps 'Greece') –
To Protus in his Tyranny: much health!

They give thy letter to me, even now:
I read and seem as if I heard thee speak.
The master of thy galley still unlades
Gift after gift; they block my court at last
And pile themselves along its portico
10 Royal with sunset, like a thought of thee:
And one white she-slave from the group dispersed
Of black and white slaves (like the chequer-work
Pavement, at once my nation's work and gift,
Now covered with this settle-down of doves),
One lyric woman, in her crocus vest
Woven of sea-wools, with her two white hands
Commends to me the strainer and the cup
Thy lip hath bettered ere it blesses mine.

Well-counselled, king, in thy munificence!
20 For so shall men remark, in such an act
Of love for him whose song gives life its joy,
Thy recognition of the use of life;
Nor call thy spirit barely adequate
To help on life in straight ways, broad enough
For vulgar souls, by ruling and the rest.
Thou, in the daily building of thy tower, –
Whether in fierce and sudden spasms of toil,
Or through dim lulls of unapparent growth,

Or when the general work 'mid good acclaim
Climbed with the eye to cheer the architect, –   30
Didst ne'er engage in work for mere work's sake –
Had'st ever in thy heart the luring hope
Of some eventual rest a-top of it,
Whence, all the tumult of the building hushed,
Thou first of men mightst look out to the East:
The vulgar saw thy tower, thou sawest the sun.
For this, I promise on thy festival
To pour libation, looking o'er the sea,
Making this slave narrate thy fortunes, speak
Thy great words, and describe thy royal face –   40
Wishing thee wholly where Zeus lives the most,
Within the eventual element of calm.

    Thy letter's first requirement meets me here.
It is as thou hast heard: in one short life
I, Cleon, have effected all those things
Thou wonderingly dost enumerate.
That epos on thy hundred plates of gold
Is mine, – and also mine the little chant,
So sure to rise from every fishing-bark
When, lights at prow, the seamen haul their net.   50
The image of the sun-god on the phare,
Men turn from the sun's self to see, is mine;
The Poecile, o'er-storied its whole length,
As thou didst hear, with painting, is mine too.
I know the true proportions of a man
And woman also, not observed before;
And I have written three books on the soul,
Proving absurd all written hitherto,
And putting us to ignorance again.
For music, – why, I have combined the moods,   60
Inventing one. In brief, all arts are mine;
Thus much the people know and recognize,
Throughout our seventeen islands. Marvel not.
We of these latter days, with greater mind
Than our forerunners, since more composite,

Look not so great, beside their simple way,
To a judge who only sees one way at once,
One mind-point and no other at a time, –
Compares the small part of a man of us
70 With some whole man of the heroic age,
Great in his way – not ours, nor meant for ours.
And ours is greater, had we skill to know:
For, what we call this life of men on earth,
This sequence of the soul's achievements here
Being, as I find much reason to conceive,
Intended to be viewed eventually
As a great whole, not analysed to parts,
But each part having reference to all, –
How shall a certain part, pronounced complete,
80 Endure effacement by another part?
Was the thing done? – then, what's to do again?
See, in the chequered pavement opposite,
Suppose the artist made a perfect rhomb,
And next a lozenge, then a trapezoid –
He did not overlay them, superimpose
The new upon the old and blot it out,
But laid them on a level in his work,
Making at last a picture; there it lies.
So, first the perfect separate forms were made,
90 The portions of mankind; and after, so,
Occurred the combination of the same.
For where had been a progress, otherwise?
Mankind, made up of all the single men, –
In such a synthesis the labour ends.
Now mark me! those divine men of old time
Have reached, thou sayest well, each at one point
The outside verge that rounds our faculty;
And where they reached, who can do more than reach?
It takes but little water just to touch
100 At some one point the inside of a sphere,
And, as we turn the sphere, touch all the rest
In due succession: but the finer air
Which not so palpably nor obviously,

Though no less universally, can touch
The whole circumference of that emptied sphere,
Fills it more fully than the water did;
Holds thrice the weight of water in itself
Resolved into a subtler element.
And yet the vulgar call the sphere first full
Up to the visible height – and after, void; 110
Not knowing air's more hidden properties.
And thus our soul, misknown, cries out to Zeus
To vindicate his purpose in our life:
Why stay we on the earth unless to grow?
Long since, I imaged, wrote the fiction out,
That he or other god descended here
And, once for all, showed simultaneously
What, in its nature, never can be shown,
Piecemeal or in succession; – showed, I say,
The worth both absolute and relative 120
Of all his children from the birth of time,
His instruments for all appointed work.
I now go on to image, – might we hear
The judgement which should give the due to each,
Show where the labour lay and where the ease,
And prove Zeus' self, the latent everywhere!
This is a dream: – but no dream, let us hope,
That years and days, the summers and the springs,
Follow each other with unwaning powers.
The grapes which dye thy wine are richer far, 130
Through culture, than the wild wealth of the rock;
The suave plum than the savage-tasted drupe;
The pastured honey-bee drops choicer sweet;
The flowers turn double, and the leaves turn flowers;
That young and tender crescent-moon, thy slave,
Sleeping above her robe as buoyed by clouds,
Refines upon the women of my youth.
What, and the soul alone deteriorates?
I have not chanted verse like Homer, no –
Nor swept string like Terpander, no – nor carved 140
And painted men like Phidias and his friend:

I am not great as they are, point by point.
But I have entered into sympathy
With these four, running these into one soul,
Who, separate, ignored each other's art.
Say, is it nothing that I know them all?
The wild flower was the larger; I have dashed
Rose-blood upon its petals, pricked its cup's
Honey with wine, and driven its seed to fruit,
150 And show a better flower if not so large:
I stand myself. Refer this to the gods
Whose gift alone it is! which, shall I dare
(All pride apart) upon the absurd pretext
That such a gift by chance lay in my hand,
Discourse of lightly or depreciate?
It might have fallen to another's hand: what then?
I pass too surely: let at least truth stay!

    And next, of what thou followest on to ask.
This being with me as I declare, O king,
160 My works, in all these varicoloured kinds,
So done by me, accepted so by men –
Thou askest, if (my soul thus in men's hearts)
I must not be accounted to attain
The very crown and proper end of life?
Inquiring thence how, now life closeth up,
I face death with success in my right hand:
Whether I fear death less than dost thyself
The fortunate of men? 'For' (writest thou)
'Thou leavest much behind, while I leave naught.
170 Thy life stays in the poems men shall sing,
The pictures men shall study; while my life,
Complete and whole now in its power and joy,
Dies altogether with my brain and arm,
Is lost indeed; since, what survives myself?
The brazen statue to o'erlook my grave,
Set on the promontory which I named.
And that – some supple courtier of my heir
Shall use its robed and sceptred arm, perhaps,

To fix the rope to, which best drags it down.
I go then: triumph thou, who dost not go!'　　　　　180

　　Nay, thou art worthy of hearing my whole mind.
Is this apparent, when thou turn'st to muse
Upon the scheme of earth and man in chief,
That admiration grows as knowledge grows?
That imperfection means perfection hid,
Reserved in part, to grace the after-time?
If, in the morning of philosophy,
Ere aught had been recorded, nay perceived,
Thou, with the light now in thee, couldst have looked
On all earth's tenantry, from worm to bird,　　　　　190
Ere man, her last, appeared upon the stage –
Thou wouldst have seen them perfect, and deduced
The perfectness of others yet unseen.
Conceding which, – had Zeus then questioned thee
'Shall I go on a step, improve on this,
Do more for visible creatures than is done?'
Thou wouldst have answered, 'Ay, by making each
Grow conscious in himself – by that alone.
All's perfect else: the shell sucks fast the rock,
The fish strikes through the sea, the snake both swims　200
And slides, forth range the beasts, the birds take flight,
Till life's mechanics can no further go –
And all this joy in natural life is put
Like fire from off thy finger into each,
So exquisitely perfect is the same.
But 'tis pure fire, and they mere matter are;
It has them, not they it: and so I choose
For man, thy last premeditated work
(If I might add a glory to the scheme)
That a third thing should stand apart from both,　　　210
A quality arise within his soul,
Which, intro-active, made to supervise
And feel the force it has, may view itself,
And so be happy.' Man might live at first
The animal life: but is there nothing more?

In due time, let him critically learn
How he lives; and, the more he gets to know
Of his own life's adaptabilities,
The more joy-giving will his life become.
220 Thus man, who hath this quality, is best.

But thou, king, hadst more reasonably said:
'Let progress end at once, – man make no step
Beyond the natural man, the better beast,
Using his senses, not the sense of sense.'
In man there's failure, only since he left
The lower and inconscious forms of life.
We called it an advance, the rendering plain
Man's spirit might grow conscious of man's life,
And, by new lore so added to the old,
230 Take each step higher over the brute's head.
This grew the only life, the pleasure-house,
Watch-tower and treasure-fortress of the soul,
Which whole surrounding flats of natural life
Seemed only fit to yield subsistence to;
A tower that crowns a country. But alas,
The soul now climbs it just to perish there!
For thence we have discovered ('tis no dream –
We know this, which we had not else perceived)
That there's a world of capability
240 For joy, spread round about us, meant for us,
Inviting us; and still the soul craves all,
And still the flesh replies, 'Take no jot more
Than ere thou clombst the tower to look abroad!
Nay, so much less as that fatigue has brought
Deduction to it.' We struggle, fain to enlarge
Our bounded physical recipiency,
Increase our power, supply fresh oil to life,
Repair the waste of age and sickness: no,
It skills not! life's inadequate to joy,
250 As the soul sees joy, tempting life to take.
They praise a fountain in my garden here
Wherein a Naiad sends the water-bow

Thin from her tube; she smiles to see it rise.
What if I told her, it is just a thread
From that great river which the hills shut up,
And mock her with my leave to take the same?
The artificer has given her one small tube
Past power to widen or exchange – what boots
To know she might spout oceans if she could?
She cannot lift beyond her first thin thread: 260
And so a man can use but a man's joy
While he sees God's. Is it for Zeus to boast,
'See, man, how happy I live, and despair –
That I may be still happier – for thy use!'
If this were so, we could not thank our lord,
As hearts beat on to doing; 'tis not so –
Malice it is not. Is it carelessness?
Still, no. If care – where is the sign? I ask,
And get no answer, and agree in sum,
O king, with thy profound discouragement,   270
Who seest the wider but to sigh the more.
Most progress is most failure: thou sayest well.

    The last point now: – thou dost except a case –
Holding joy not impossible to one
With artist-gifts – to such a man as I
Who leave behind me living works indeed;
For, such a poem, such a painting lives.
What? dost thou verily trip upon a word,
Confound the accurate view of what joy is
(Caught somewhat clearer by my eyes than thine)   280
With feeling joy? confound the knowing how
And showing how to live (my faculty)
With actually living? – Otherwise
Where is the artist's vantage o'er the king?
Because in my great epos I display
How divers men young, strong, fair, wise, can act –
Is this as though I acted? if I paint,
Carve the young Phoebus, am I therefore young?
Methinks I'm older that I bowed myself

290 The many years of pain that taught me art!
Indeed, to know is something, and to prove
How all this beauty might be enjoyed, is more:
But, knowing naught, to enjoy is something too.
Yon rower, with the moulded muscles there,
Lowering the sail, is nearer it than I.
I can write love-odes: thy fair slave's an ode.
I get to sing of love, when grown too grey
For being beloved: she turns to that young man,
The muscles all a-ripple on his back.

300 I know the joy of kingship: well, thou art king!

    'But,' sayest thou – (and I marvel, I repeat
To find thee trip on such a mere word) 'what
Thou writest, paintest, stays; that does not die:
Sappho survives, because we sing her songs,
And Aeschylus, because we read his plays!'
Why, if they live still, let them come and take
Thy slave in my despite, drink from thy cup,
Speak in my place. Thou diest while I survive?
Say rather that my fate is deadlier still,

310 In this, that every day my sense of joy
Grows more acute, my soul (intensified
By power and insight) more enlarged, more keen;
While every day my hairs fall more and more,
My hand shakes, and the heavy years increase –
The horror quickening still from year to year,
The consummation coming past escape
When I shall know most, and yet least enjoy –
When all my works wherein I prove my worth,
Being present still to mock me in men's mouths,

320 Alive still, in the praise of such as thou,
I, I the feeling, thinking, acting man,
The man who loved his life so over-much,
Sleep in my urn. It is so horrible,
I dare at times imagine to my need
Some future state revealed to us by Zeus,
Unlimited in capability

For joy, as this is in desire for joy,
– To seek which, the joy-hunger forces us:
That, stung by straitness of our life, made strait
On purpose to make prized the life at large –   330
Freed by the throbbing impulse we call death,
We burst there as the worm into the fly,
Who, while a worm still, wants his wings. But no!
Zeus has not yet revealed it; and alas,
He must have done so, were it possible!

   Live long and happy, and in that thought die:
Glad for what was! Farewell. And for the rest,
I cannot tell thy messenger aright
Where to deliver what he bears of thine
To one called Paulus; we have heard his fame   340
Indeed, if Christus be not one with him –
I know not, nor am troubled much to know.
Thou canst not think a mere barbarian Jew,
As Paulus proves to be, one circumcised,
Hath access to a secret shut from us?
Thou wrongest our philosophy, O king,
In stooping to inquire of such an one,
As if his answer could impose at all!
He writeth, doth he? well, and he may write.
Oh, the Jew findeth scholars! certain slaves   350
Who touched on this same isle, preached him and Christ;
And (as I gathered from a bystander)
Their doctrine could be held by no sane man.

Two in the Campagna

I

I wonder do you feel today
    As I have felt since, hand in hand,
We sat down on the grass, to stray
    In spirit better through the land,
This morn of Rome and May?

II

For me, I touched a thought, I know,
    Has tantalized me many times,
(Like turns of thread the spiders throw
    Mocking across our path) for rhymes
10 To catch at and let go.

III

Help me to hold it! First it left
    The yellowing fennel, run to seed
There, branching from the brickwork's cleft,
    Some old tomb's ruin: yonder weed
Took up the floating weft,

IV

Where one small orange cup amassed
    Five beetles, – blind and green they grope
Among the honey-meal: and last,
    Everywhere on the grassy slope
20 I traced it. Hold it fast!

V

The champaign with its endless fleece
    Of feathery grasses everywhere!
Silence and passion, joy and peace,
    An everlasting wash of air –
Rome's ghost since her decease.

VI

Such life here, through such lengths of hours,
    Such miracles performed in play,
Such primal naked forms of flowers,
    Such letting nature have her way
While heaven looks from its towers!   30

VII

How say you? Let us, O my dove,
    Let us be unashamed of soul,
As earth lies bare to heaven above!
    How is it under our control
To love or not to love?

VIII

I would that you were all to me,
    You that are just so much, no more.
Nor yours nor mine, nor slave nor free!
    Where does the fault lie? What the core
O' the wound, since wound must be?   40

IX

I would I could adopt your will,
    See with your eyes, and set my heart
Beating by yours, and drink my fill
    At your soul's springs, – your part my part
In life, for good and ill.

X

No. I yearn upward, touch you close,
    Then stand away. I kiss your cheek,
Catch your soul's warmth, – I pluck the rose
    And love it more than tongue can speak –
Then the good minute goes.   50

XI

Already how am I so far
    Out of that minute? Must I go
Still like the thistle-ball, no bar,
    Onward, whenever light winds blow,
Fixed by no friendly star?

XII

Just when I seemed about to learn!
    Where is the thread now? Off again!
The old trick! Only I discern –
    Infinite passion, and the pain
60 Of finite hearts that yearn.

A Grammarian's Funeral
Shortly after the Revival of Learning in Europe

Let us begin and carry up this corpse,
    Singing together.
Leave we the common crofts, the vulgar thorpes
    Each in its tether
Sleeping safe on the bosom of the plain,
    Cared-for till cock-crow:
Look out if yonder be not day again
    Rimming the rock-row!
That's the appropriate country; there, man's thought,
    Rarer, intenser,   10
Self-gathered for an outbreak, as it ought,
    Chafes in the censer.
Leave we the unlettered plain its herd and crop;
    Seek we sepulture
On a tall mountain, citied to the top,
    Crowded with culture!
All the peaks soar, but one the rest excels;
    Clouds overcome it;
No! yonder sparkle is the citadel's
    Circling its summit.   20
Thither our path lies; wind we up the heights:
    Wait ye the warning?
Our low life was the level's and the night's;
    He's for the morning.
Step to a tune, square chests, erect each head,
    'Ware the beholders!
This is our master, famous calm and dead,
    Borne on our shoulders.

Sleep, crop and herd! sleep, darkling thorpe and croft,

30   Safe from the weather!
He, whom we convoy to his grave aloft,
    Singing together,
He was a man born with thy face and throat,
    Lyric Apollo!
Long he lived nameless: how should spring take note
    Winter would follow?
Till lo, the little touch, and youth was gone!
    Cramped and diminished,
Moaned he, 'New measures, other feet anon!
40   My dance is finished?'
No, that's the world's way: (keep the mountain-side,
    Make for the city!)
He knew the signal, and stepped on with pride
    Over men's pity;
Left play for work, and grappled with the world
    Bent on escaping:
'What's in the scroll,' quoth he, 'thou keepest furled?
    Show me their shaping,
Theirs who most studied man, the bard and sage, –
50   Give!' – So, he gowned him,
Straight got by heart that book to its last page:
    Learned, we found him.
Yea, but we found him bald too, eyes like lead,
    Accents uncertain:
'Time to taste life,' another would have said,
    'Up with the curtain!'
This man said rather, 'Actual life comes next?
    Patience a moment!
Grant I have mastered learning's crabbed text,
60   Still there's the comment.
Let me know all! Prate not of most or least,
    Painful or easy!
Even to the crumbs I'd fain eat up the feast,
    Ay, nor feel queasy.'
Oh, such a life as he resolved to live,
    When he had learned it,
When he had gathered all books had to give!

Sooner, he spurned it.
Image the whole, then execute the parts –
  Fancy the fabric   70
Quite, ere you build, ere steel strike fire from quartz,
  Ere mortar dab brick!

(Here's the town-gate reached: there's the market-place
  Gaping before us.)
Yea, this in him was the peculiar grace
  (Hearten our chorus!)
That before living he'd learn how to live –
  No end to learning:
Earn the means first – God surely will contrive
  Use for our earning.   80
Others mistrust and say, 'But time escapes:
  Live now or never!'
He said, 'What's time? Leave Now for dogs and apes!
  Man has Forever.'
Back to his book then: deeper drooped his head:
  Calculus racked him:
Leaden before, his eyes grew dross of lead:
  Tussis attacked him.
'Now, master, take a little rest!' – not he!
  (Caution redoubled,   90
Step two abreast, the way winds narrowly!)
  Not a whit troubled
Back to his studies, fresher than at first,
  Fierce as a dragon
He (soul-hydroptic with a sacred thirst)
  Sucked at the flagon.
Oh, if we draw a circle premature,
  Heedless of far gain,
Greedy for quick returns of profit, sure
  Bad is our bargain!   100
Was it not great? did not he throw on God,
  (He loves the burthen) –
God's task to make the heavenly period
  Perfect the earthen?

Did not he magnify the mind, show clear
    Just what it all meant?
He would not discount life, as fools do here,
    Paid by instalment.
He ventured neck or nothing – heaven's success
110   Found, or earth's failure:
'Wilt thou trust death or not?' He answered 'Yes:
    Hence with life's pale lure!'
That low man seeks a little thing to do,
    Sees it and does it:
This high man, with a great thing to pursue,
    Dies ere he knows it.
That low man goes on adding one to one,
    His hundred's soon hit:
This high man, aiming at a million,
120   Misses an unit.
That, has the world here – should he need the next,
    Let the world mind him!
This, throws himself on God, and unperplexed
    Seeking shall find him.
So, with the throttling hands of death at strife,
    Ground he at grammar;
Still, through the rattle, parts of speech were rife:
    While he could stammer
He settled *Hoti's* business – let it be! –
130   Properly based *Oun* –
Gave us the doctrine of the enclitic *De*,
    Dead from the waist down.
Well, here's the platform, here's the proper place:
    Hail to your purlieus,
All ye highfliers of the feathered race,
    Swallows and curlews!
Here's the top-peak; the multitude below
    Live, for they can, there:
This man decided not to Live but Know –
140   Bury this man there?
Here – here's his place, where meteors shoot, clouds form,
    Lightnings are loosened,

Stars come and go! Let joy break with the storm,
    Peace let the dew send!
Lofty designs must close in like effects:
    Loftily lying,
Leave him – still loftier than the world suspects,
    Living and dying.

James Lee's Wife

I James Lee's Wife Speaks at the Window

I

Ah, Love, but a day
    And the world has changed!
The sun's away,
    And the bird estranged;
The wind has dropped,
    And the sky's deranged:
Summer has stopped.

II

Look in my eyes!
    Wilt thou change too?
Should I fear surprise?
    Shall I find aught new
In the old and dear,
    In the good and true,
With the changing year?

III

Thou art a man,
    But I am thy love.
For the lake, its swan;
    For the dell, its dove;
And for thee – (oh, haste!)
    Me, to bend above,
Me, to hold embraced.

II By the Fireside

I

Is all our fire of shipwreck wood,
   Oak and pine?
Oh, for the ills half-understood,
   The dim dead woe
   Long ago
Befallen this bitter coast of France!
Well, poor sailors took their chance;
   I take mine.

II

A ruddy shaft our fire must shoot   30
   O'er the sea:
Do sailors eye the casement – mute,
   Drenched and stark,
   From their bark –
And envy, gnash their teeth for hate
O' the warm safe house and happy freight
   – Thee and me?

III

God help you, sailors, at your need!
   Spare the curse!
For some ships, safe in port indeed,   40
   Rot and rust,
   Run to dust,
All through worms i' the wood, which crept,
Gnawed our hearts out while we slept:
   That is worse.

IV

Who lived here before us two?
   Old-world pairs.
Did a woman ever – would I knew! –
   Watch the man
   With whom began   50
Love's voyage full-sail, – (now, gnash your teeth!)
When planks start, open hell beneath
   Unawares?

145

III In the Doorway

I

The swallow has set her six young on the rail,
  And looks sea-ward:
The water's in stripes like a snake, olive-pale
  To the leeward, –
On the weather-side, black, spotted white with the wind.
'Good fortune departs, and disaster's behind,' –
60 Hark, the wind with its wants and its infinite wail!

II

Our fig-tree, that leaned for the saltness, has furled
  Her five fingers,
Each leaf like a hand opened wide to the world
  Where there lingers
No glint of the gold, Summer sent for her sake:
How the vines writhe in rows, each impaled on its stake!
My heart shrivels up and my spirit shrinks curled.

III

Yet here are we two; we have love, house enough,
  With the field there,
70 This house of four rooms, that field red and rough,
  Though it yield there,
For the rabbit that robs, scarce a blade or a bent;
If a magpie alight now, it seems an event;
And they both will be gone at November's rebuff.

IV

But why must cold spread? but wherefore bring change
  To the spirit,
God meant should mate his with an infinite range,
  And inherit
His power to put life in the darkness and cold?
80 Oh, live and love worthily, bear and be bold!
Whom Summer made friends of, let Winter estrange!

IV Along the Beach

I

I will be quiet and talk with you,
  And reason why you are wrong.
You wanted my love – is that much true?
And so I did love, so I do:
  What has come of it all along?

II

I took you – how could I otherwise?
  For a world to me, and more;
For all, love greatens and glorifies
Till God's a-glow, to the loving eyes,   90
  In what was mere earth before.

III

Yes, earth – yes, mere ignoble earth!
  Now do I mis-state, mistake?
Do I wrong your weakness and call it worth?
Expect all harvest, dread no dearth,
  Seal my sense up for your sake?

IV

Oh, Love, Love, no, Love! not so, indeed!
  You were just weak earth, I knew:
With much in you waste, with many a weed,
And plenty of passions run to seed,   100
  But a little good grain too.

V

And such as you were, I took you for mine:
  Did not you find me yours,
To watch the olive and wait the vine,
And wonder when rivers of oil and wine
  Would flow, as the Book assures?

VI

Well, and if none of these good things came,
  What did the failure prove?
The man was my whole world, all the same,

147

110 With his flowers to praise or his weeds to blame,
    And, either or both, to love.

VII

Yet this turns now to a fault – there! there!
    That I do love, watch too long,
And wait too well, and weary and wear;
And 'tis all an old story, and my despair
    Fit subject for some new song:

VIII

'How the light, light love, he has wings to fly
    At suspicion of a bond:
My wisdom has bidden your pleasure good-bye,
120 Which will turn up next in a laughing eye,
    And why should you look beyond?'

V *On the Cliff*

I

I leaned on the turf,
I looked at a rock
Left dry by the surf;
For the turf, to call it grass were to mock:
Dead to the roots, so deep was done
The work of the summer sun.

II

And the rock lay flat
As an anvil's face:
130 No iron like that!
Baked dry; of a weed, of a shell, no trace:
Sunshine outside, but ice at the core,
Death's altar by the lone shore.

III

On the turf, sprang gay
With his films of blue,
No cricket, I'll say,
But a warhorse, barded and chanfroned too,

The gift of a quixote-mage to his knight,
Real fairy, with wings all right.

IV

On the rock, they scorch   140
Like a drop of fire
From a brandished torch,
Fall two red fans of a butterfly:
No turf, no rock: in their ugly stead,
See, wonderful blue and red!

V

Is it not so
With the minds of men?
The level and low,
The burnt and bare, in themselves; but then
With such a blue and red grace, not theirs, –   150
Love settling unawares!

VI Reading a Book, Under the Cliff

I

'Still ailing, Wind? Wilt be appeased or no?
    Which needs the other's office, thou or I?
Dost want to be disburthened of a woe,
    And can, in truth, my voice untie
Its links, and let it go?

II

'Art thou a dumb wronged thing that would be righted,
    Entrusting thus thy cause to me? Forbear!
No tongue can mend such pleadings; faith, requited
    With falsehood, – love, at last aware   160
Of scorn, – hopes, early blighted, –

III

'We have them; but I know not any tone
    So fit as thine to falter forth a sorrow:
Does think men would go mad without a moan,
    If they knew any way to borrow
A pathos like thy own?

IV

'Which sigh wouldst mock, of all the sighs? The one
    So long escaping from lips starved and blue,
That lasts while on her pallet-bed the nun
170   Stretches her length; her foot comes through
The straw she shivers on;

V

'You had not thought she was so tall: and spent,
    Her shrunk lids open, her lean fingers shut
Close, close, their sharp and livid nails indent
    The clammy palm; then all is mute:
That way, the spirit went.

VI

'Or wouldst thou rather that I understand
    Thy will to help me? – like the dog I found
Once, pacing sad this solitary strand,
180   Who would not take my food, poor hound,
But whined and licked my hand.'

VII

All this, and more, comes from some young man's pride
    Of power to see, – in failure and mistake,
Relinquishment, disgrace, on every side, –
    Merely examples for his sake,
Helps to his path untried:

VIII

Instances he must – simply recognize?
    Oh, more than so! – must, with a learner's zeal,
Make doubly prominent, twice emphasize,
190   By added touches that reveal
The god in babe's disguise.

IX

Oh, he knows what defeat means, and the rest!
    Himself the undefeated that shall be:
Failure, disgrace, he flings them you to test, –
    His triumph, in eternity
Too plainly manifest!

X

Whence, judge if he learn forthwith what the wind
   Means in its moaning – by the happy prompt
Instinctive way of youth, I mean; for kind
   Calm years, exacting their accompt   200
Of pain, mature the mind:

XI

And some midsummer morning, at the lull
   Just about daybreak, as he looks across
A sparkling foreign country, wonderful
   To the sea's edge for gloom and gloss,
Next minute must annul, –

XII

Then, when the wind begins among the vines,
   So low, so low, what shall it say but this?
'Here is the change beginning, here the lines
   Circumscribe beauty, set to bliss   210
The limit time assigns.'

XIII

Nothing can be as it has been before;
   Better, so call it, only not the same.
To draw one beauty into our hearts' core,
   And keep it changeless! such our claim;
So answered, – Never more!

XIV

Simple? Why this is the old woe o' the world;
   Tune, to whose rise and fall we live and die.
Rise with it, then! Rejoice that man is hurled
   From change to change unceasingly,   220
His soul's wings never furled!

XV

That's a new question; still replies the fact,
   Nothing endures: the wind moans, saying so;
We moan in acquiescence: there's life's pact,
   Perhaps probation – do *I* know?
God does: endure his act!

XVI

Only, for man, how bitter not to grave
   On his soul's hands' palms one fair good wise thing
Just as he grasped it! For himself, death's wave;
230   While time first washes – ah, the sting! –
O'er all he'd sink to save.

VII Among the Rocks

I

Oh, good gigantic smile o' the brown old earth,
   This autumn morning! How he sets his bones
To bask i' the sun, and thrusts out knees and feet
For the ripple to run over in its mirth;
   Listening the while, where on the heap of stones
The white breast of the sea-lark twitters sweet.

II

That is the doctrine, simple, ancient, true;
   Such is life's trial, as old earth smiles and knows.
240 If you loved only what were worth your love,
Love were clear gain, and wholly well for you:
   Make the low nature better by your throes!
Give earth yourself, go up for gain above!

VIII Beside the Drawing-Board

I

'As like as a Hand to another Hand!'
   Whoever said that foolish thing,
Could not have studied to understand
   The counsels of God in fashioning,
Out of the infinite love of his heart,
This Hand, whose beauty I praise, apart
250 From the world of wonder left to praise,
If I tried to learn the other ways
Of love in its skill, or love in its power.
   'As like as a Hand to another Hand':
   Who said that, never took his stand,
Found and followed, like me, an hour,

The beauty in this, – how free, how fine
To fear, almost, – of the limit-line!
As I looked at this, and learned and drew,
   Drew and learned, and looked again,
While fast the happy minutes flew,   260
   Its beauty mounted into my brain,
   And a fancy seized me; I was fain
To efface my work, begin anew,
Kiss what before I only drew;
Ay, laying the red chalk 'twixt my lips,
   With soul to help if the mere lips failed,
   I kissed all right where the drawing ailed,
Kissed fast the grace that somehow slips
Still from one's soul-less finger-tips.

II

'Tis a clay cast, the perfect thing,   270
   From Hand live once, dead long ago:
Princess-like it wears the ring
   To fancy's eye, by which we know
That here at length a master found
   His match, a proud lone soul its mate,
As soaring genius sank to ground,
   And pencil could not emulate
The beauty in this, – how free, how fine
To fear almost! – of the limit-line.
Long ago the god, like me   280
The worm, learned, each in our degree:
Looked and loved, learned and drew,
   Drew and learned and loved again,
While fast the happy minutes flew,
   Till beauty mounted into his brain
And on the finger which outvied
   His art he placed the ring that's there,
Still by fancy's eye descried,
   In token of a marriage rare:
   For him on earth, his art's despair,   290
For him in heaven, his soul's fit bride.

III

Little girl with the poor coarse hand
   I turned from to a cold clay cast –
I have my lesson, understand
   The worth of flesh and blood at last.
Nothing but beauty in a Hand?
   Because he could not change the hue,
   Mend the lines and make them true
To this which met his soul's demand, –
300   Would Da Vinci turn from you?
I hear him laugh my woes to scorn –
   'The fool forsooth is all forlorn
Because the beauty, she thinks best,
Lived long ago or was never born, –
Because no beauty bears the test
In this rough peasant Hand! Confessed!
"Art is null and study void!"
   So sayest thou? So said not I,
   Who threw the faulty pencil by,
310 And years instead of hours employed,
Learning the veritable use
   Of flesh and bone and nerve beneath
   Lines and hue of the outer sheath,
If haply I might reproduce
One motive of the powers profuse,
Flesh and bone and nerve that make
   The poorest coarsest human hand
   An object worthy to be scanned
A whole life long for their sole sake.
320 Shall earth and the cramped moment-space
Yield the heavenly crowning grace?
Now the parts and then the whole!
Who art thou, with stinted soul
   And stunted body, thus to cry
"I love, – shall that be life's strait dole?
   I must live beloved or die!"
This peasant hand that spins the wool
   And bakes the bread, why lives it on,

Poor and coarse with beauty gone, –
What use survives the beauty?' Fool! 330
Go, little girl with the poor coarse hand!
I have my lesson, shall understand.

IX *On Deck*

I

There is nothing to remember in me,
 Nothing I ever said with a grace,
Nothing I did that you care to see,
 Nothing I was that deserves a place
In your mind, now I leave you, set you free.

II

Conceded! In turn, concede to me,
 Such things have been as a mutual flame.
Your soul's locked fast; but, love for a key, 340
 You might let it loose, till I grew the same
In your eyes, as in mine you stand: strange plea!

III

For then, then, what would it matter to me
 That I was the harsh ill-favoured one?
We both should be like as pea and pea;
 It was ever so since the world begun:
So, let me proceed with my reverie.

IV

How strange it were if you had all me,
 As I have all you in my heart and brain,
You, whose least word brought gloom or glee, 350
 Who never lifted the hand in vain –
Will hold mine yet, from over the sea!

V

Strange, if a face, when you thought of me,
 Rose like your own face present now,
With eyes as dear in their due degree,
 Much such a mouth, and as bright a brow,
Till you saw yourself, while you cried ''Tis She!'

VI

Well, you may, you must, set down to me
   Love that was life, life that was love;
360 A tenure of breath at your lips' decree,
   A passion to stand as your thoughts approve,
A rapture to fall where your foot might be.

VII

But did one touch of such love for me
   Come in a word or a look of yours,
Whose words and looks will, circling, flee
   Round me and round while life endures, –
Could I fancy 'As I feel, thus feels he';

VIII

Why, fade you might to a thing like me,
   And your hair grow these coarse hanks of hair,
370 Your skin, this bark of a gnarled tree, –
   You might turn myself! – should I know or care
When I should be dead of joy, James Lee?

Gold Hair:
A Story of Pornic

I

Oh, the beautiful girl, too white,
   Who lived at Pornic, down by the sea,
Just where the sea and the Loire unite!
   And a boasted name in Brittany
She bore, which I will not write.

II

Too white, for the flower of life is red;
   Her flesh was the soft seraphic screen
Of a soul that is meant (her parents said)
   To just see earth, and hardly be seen,
And blossom in heaven instead.   10

III

Yet earth saw one thing, one how fair!
   One grace that grew to its full on earth:
Smiles might be sparse on her cheek so spare,
   And her waist want half a girdle's girth,
But she had her great gold hair.

IV

Hair, such a wonder of flix and floss,
   Freshness and fragrance – floods of it, too!
Gold, did I say? Nay, gold's mere dross:
   Here, Life smiled, 'Think what I meant to do!'
And Love sighed, 'Fancy my loss!'   20

V

So, when she died, it was scarce more strange
   Than that, when delicate evening dies,
And you follow its spent sun's pallid range,

There's a shoot of colour startles the skies
With sudden, violent change, –

VI

That, while the breath was nearly to seek,
   As they put the little cross to her lips,
She changed; a spot came out on her cheek,
   A spark from her eye in mid-eclipse,
30 And she broke forth, 'I must speak!'

VII

'Not my hair!' made the girl her moan –
   'All the rest is gone or to go;
But the last, last grace, my all, my own,
   Let it stay in the grave, that the ghosts may know!
Leave my poor gold hair alone!'

VIII

The passion thus vented, dead lay she;
   Her parents sobbed their worst on that;
All friends joined in, nor observed degree:
   For indeed the hair was to wonder at,
40 As it spread – not flowing free,

IX

But curled around her brow, like a crown,
   And coiled beside her cheeks, like a cap,
And calmed about her neck – ay, down
   To her breast, pressed flat, without a gap
I' the gold, it reached her gown.

X

All kissed that face, like a silver wedge
   'Mid the yellow wealth, nor disturbed its hair:
E'en the priest allowed death's privilege,
   As he planted the crucifix with care
50 On her breast, 'twixt edge and edge.

XI

And thus was she buried, inviolate
   Of body and soul, in the very space

By the altar; keeping saintly state
 In Pornic church, for her pride of race,
Pure life and piteous fate.

XII

And in after-time would your fresh tear fall,
 Though your mouth might twitch with a dubious smile,
As they told you of gold, both robe and pall,
 How she prayed them leave it alone awhile,
So it never was touched at all.   60

XIII

Years flew; this legend grew at last
 The life of the lady; all she had done,
All been, in the memories fading fast
 Of lover and friend, was summed in one
Sentence survivors passed:

XIV

To wit, she was meant for heaven, not earth;
 Had turned an angel before the time:
Yet, since she was mortal, in such dearth
 Of frailty, all you could count a crime
Was – she knew her gold hair's worth.   70

————————

XV

At little pleasant Pornic church,
 It chanced, the pavement wanted repair,
Was taken to pieces: left in the lurch,
 A certain sacred space lay bare,
And the boys began research.

XVI

'Twas the space where our sires would lay a saint,
 A benefactor, – a bishop, suppose,
A baron with armour-adornments quaint,
 Dame with chased ring and jewelled rose,
Things sanctity saves from taint;   80

XVII

So we come to find them in after-days
　　When the corpse is presumed to have done with gauds
Of use to the living, in many ways:
　　For the boys get pelf, and the town applauds,
And the church deserves the praise.

XVIII

They grubbed with a will: and at length – *O cor*
　　Humanum, *pectora caeca*, and the rest! –
They found – no gaud they were prying for,
　　No ring, no rose, but – who would have guessed? –
90　A double Louis-d'or!

XIX

Here was a case for the priest: he heard,
　　Marked, inwardly digested, laid
Finger on nose, smiled, 'There's a bird
　　Chirps in my ear': then, 'Bring a spade,
Dig deeper!' – he gave the word.

XX

And lo, when they came to the coffin-lid,
　　Or rotten planks which composed it once,
Why, there lay the girl's skull wedged amid
　　A mint of money, it served for the nonce
100　To hold in its hair-heaps hid!

XXI

Hid there? Why? Could the girl be wont
　　(She the stainless soul) to treasure up
Money, earth's trash and heaven's affront?
　　Had a spider found out the communion-cup,
Was a toad in the christening-font?

XXII

Truth is truth: too true it was.
　　Gold! She hoarded and hugged it first,
Longed for it, leaned o'er it, loved it – alas –
　　Till the humour grew to a head and burst,
110　And she cried, at the final pass, –

XXIII

'Talk not of God, my heart is stone!
  Nor lover nor friend – be gold for both!
Gold I lack; and, my all, my own,
  It shall hide in my hair. I scarce die loth
If they let my hair alone!'

XXIV

Louis-d'or, some six times five,
  And duly double, every piece.
Now do you see? With the priest to shrive,
  With parents preventing her soul's release
By kisses that kept alive, –   120

XXV

With heaven's gold gates about to ope,
  With friends' praise, gold-like, lingering still,
An instinct had bidden the girl's hand grope
  For gold, the true sort – 'Gold in heaven, if you will;
But I keep earth's too, I hope.'

XXVI

Enough! The priest took the grave's grim yield:
  The parents, they eyed that price of sin
As if *thirty pieces* lay revealed
  On the place *to bury strangers in*,
The hideous Potter's Field.   130

XXVII

But the priest bethought him: '"Milk that's spilt"
  – You know the adage! Watch and pray!
Saints tumble to earth with so slight a tilt!
  It would build a new altar; that, we may!'
And the altar therewith was built.

XXVIII

Why I deliver this horrible verse?
  As the text of a sermon, which now I preach:
Evil or good may be better or worse
  In the human heart, but the mixture of each
Is a marvel and a curse.   140

XXIX

The candid incline to surmise of late
   That the Christian faith proves false, I find;
For our Essays-and-Reviews' debate
   Begins to tell on the public mind,
And Colenso's words have weight:

XXX

I still, to suppose it true, for my part,
   See reasons and reasons; this, to begin:
'Tis the faith that launched point-blank her dart
   At the head of a lie – taught Original Sin,
150   The Corruption of Man's Heart.

Dîs Aliter Visum; or, Le Byron de Nos Jours

I

Stop, let me have the truth of that!
   Is that all true? I say, the day
Ten years ago when both of us
   Met on a morning, friends – as thus
We meet this evening, friends or what? –

II

Did you – because I took your arm
   And sillily smiled, 'A mass of brass
That sea looks, blazing underneath!'
   While up the cliff-road edged with heath,
We took the turns nor came to harm –   10

III

Did you consider 'Now makes twice
   That I have seen her, walked and talked
With this poor pretty thoughtful thing,
   Whose worth I weigh: she tries to sing;
Draws, hopes in time the eye grows nice;

IV

'Reads verse and thinks she understands;
   Loves all, at any rate, that's great,
Good, beautiful; but much as we
   Down at the bath-house love the sea,
Who breathe its salt and bruise its sands: 20

V

'While . . . do but follow the fishing-gull
   That flaps and floats from wave to cave!
There's the sea-lover, fair my friend!
   What then? Be patient, mark and mend!
Had you the making of your skull?'

VI

And did you, when we faced the church
   With spire and sad slate roof, aloof
From human fellowship so far,
   Where a few graveyard crosses are,
30 And garlands for the swallows' perch, –

VII

Did you determine, as we stepped
   O'er the lone stone fence, 'Let me get
Her for myself, and what's the earth
   With all its art, verse, music, worth –
Compared with love, found, gained, and kept?

VIII

'Schumann's our music-maker now;
   Has his march-movement youth and mouth?
Ingres's the modern man that paints;
   Which will lean on me, of his saints?
40 Heine for songs; for kisses, how?'

IX

And did you, when we entered, reached
   The votive frigate, soft aloft
Riding on air this hundred years,
   Safe-smiling at old hopes and fears, –
Did you draw profit while she preached?

X

Resolving, 'Fools we wise men grow!
   Yes, I could easily blurt out curt
Some question that might find reply
   As prompt in her stopped lips, dropped eye,
50 And rush of red to cheek and brow:

XI

'Thus were a match made, sure and fast,
   'Mid the blue weed-flowers round the mound
Where, issuing, we shall stand and stay
   For one more look at baths and bay,
Sands, sea-gulls, and the old church last –

XII

'A match 'twixt me, bent, wigged and lamed,
  Famous, however, for verse and worse,
Sure of the Fortieth spare Arm-chair
  When gout and glory seat me there,
So, one whose love-freaks pass unblamed, –   60

XIII

'And this young beauty, round and sound
  As a mountain-apple, youth and truth
With loves and doves, at all events
  With money in the Three per Cents;
Whose choice of me would seem profound:-

XIV

'She might take me as I take her.
  Perfect the hour would pass, alas!
Climb high, love high, what matter? Still,
  Feet, feelings, must descend the hill:
An hour's perfection can't recur.   70

XV

'Then follows Paris and full time
  For both to reason: "Thus with us!"
She'll sigh, "Thus girls give body and soul
  At first word, think they gain the goal,
When 'tis the starting-place they climb!

XVI

'"My friend makes verse and gets renown;
  Have they all fifty years, his peers?
He knows the world, firm, quiet and gay;
  Boys will become as much one day:
They're fools; he cheats, with beard less brown.   80

XVII

'"For boys say, *Love me or I die!*
  He did not say, *The truth is, youth
I want, who am old and know too much;
  I'd catch youth: lend me sight and touch!
Drop heart's blood where life's wheels grate dry!*"

XVIII

'While I should make rejoinder' – (then
  It was, no doubt, you ceased that least
Light pressure of my arm in yours)
  '"I can conceive of cheaper cures
90 For a yawning-fit o'er books and men.

XIX

'"What? All I am, was, and might be,
  All, books taught, art brought, life's whole strife,
Painful results since precious, just
  Were fitly exchanged, in wise disgust,
For two cheeks freshened by youth and sea?

XX

'"All for a nosegay! – what came first;
  With fields on flower, untried each side;
I rally, need my books and men,
  And find a nosegay": drop it, then,
100 No match yet made for best or worst!'

XXI

That ended me. You judged the porch
  We left by, Norman; took our look
At sea and sky, wondered so few
  Find out the place for air and view;
Remarked the sun began to scorch;

XXII

Descended, soon regained the baths,
  And then, good-bye! Years ten since then:
Ten years! We meet: you tell me, now,
  By a window-seat for that cliff-brow,
110 On carpet-stripes for those sand-paths.

XXIII

Now I may speak: you fool, for all
  Your lore! Who made things plain in vain?
What was the sea for? What, the grey
  Sad church, that solitary day,
Crosses and graves and swallows' call?

XXIV

Was there naught better than to enjoy?
  No feat which, done, would make time break,
And let us pent-up creatures through
  Into eternity, our due?
No forcing earth teach heaven's employ?   120

XXV

No wise beginning, here and now,
  What cannot grow complete (earth's feat)
And heaven must finish, there and then?
  No tasting earth's true food for men,
Its sweet in sad, its sad in sweet?

XXVI

No grasping at love, gaining a share
  O' the sole spark from God's life at strife
With death, so, sure of range above
  The limits here? For us and love,
Failure; but, when God fails, despair.   130

XXVII

This you call wisdom? Thus you add
  Good unto good again, in vain?
You loved, with body worn and weak;
  I loved, with faculties to seek:
Were both loves worthless since ill-clad?

XXVIII

Let the mere star-fish in his vault
  Crawl in a wash of weed, indeed,
Rose-jacinth to the finger-tips:
  He, whole in body and soul, outstrips
Man, found with either in default.   140

XXIX

But what's whole, can increase no more,
  Is dwarfed and dies, since here's its sphere.
The devil laughed at you in his sleeve!
  You knew not? That I well believe;
Or you had saved two souls: nay, four.

XXX

For Stephanie sprained last night her wrist,
    Ankle or something. 'Pooh,' cry you?
At any rate she danced, all say,
    Vilely; her vogue has had its day.
150 Here comes my husband from his whist.

A Death in the Desert

[Supposed of Pamphylax the Antiochene:
It is a parchment, of my rolls the fifth,
Hath three skins glued together, is all Greek
And goeth from *Epsilon* down to *Mu*:
Lies second in the surnamed Chosen Chest,
Stained and conserved with juice of terebinth,
Covered with cloth of hair, and lettered *Xi*,
From Xanthus, my wife's uncle, now at peace:
Mu and *Epsilon* stand for my own name.
I may not write it, but I make a cross   10
To show I wait His coming, with the rest,
And leave off here: beginneth Pamphylax.]

I said, 'If one should wet his lips with wine,
And slip the broadest plantain-leaf we find,
Or else the lappet of a linen robe,
Into the water-vessel, lay it right,
And cool his forehead just above the eyes,
The while a brother, kneeling either side,
Should chafe each hand and try to make it warm, –
He is not so far gone but he might speak.'   20

This did not happen in the outer cave,
Nor in the secret chamber of the rock
Where, sixty days since the decree was out,
We had him, bedded on a camel-skin,
And waited for his dying all the while;
But in the midmost grotto: since noon's light
Reached there a little, and we would not lose
The last of what might happen on his face.

I at the head, and Xanthus at the feet,
30   With Valens and the Boy, had lifted him,
And brought him from the chamber in the depths,
And laid him in the light where we might see:
For certain smiles began about his mouth,
And his lids moved, presageful of the end.

Beyond, and half way up the mouth o' the cave,
The Bactrian convert, having his desire,
Kept watch, and made pretence to graze a goat
That gave us milk, on rags of various herb,
Plantain and quitch, the rocks' shade keeps alive:
40   So that if any thief or soldier passed,
(Because the persecution was aware)
Yielding the goat up promptly with his life,
Such man might pass on, joyful at a prize,
Nor care to pry into the cool o' the cave.
Outside was all noon and the burning blue.

'Here is wine,' answered Xanthus, – dropped a drop;
I stooped and placed the lap of cloth aright,
Then chafed his right hand, and the Boy his left:
But Valens had bethought him, and produced
50   And broke a ball of nard, and made perfume.
Only, he did – not so much wake, as – turn
And smile a little, as a sleeper does
If any dear one call him, touch his face –
And smiles and loves, but will not be disturbed.

Then Xanthus said a prayer, but still he slept:
It is the Xanthus that escaped to Rome,
Was burned, and could not write the chronicle.

Then the Boy sprang up from his knees, and ran,
Stung by the splendour of a sudden thought,
60   And fetched the seventh plate of graven lead
Out of the secret chamber, found a place,
Pressing with finger on the deeper dints,
And spoke, as 'twere his mouth proclaiming first,
'I am the Resurrection and the Life.'

Whereat he opened his eyes wide at once,
And sat up of himself, and looked at us;
And thenceforth nobody pronounced a word:
Only, outside, the Bactrian cried his cry
Like the lone desert-bird that wears the ruff,
As signal we were safe, from time to time.　　　　70

First he said, 'If a friend declared to me,
This my son Valens, this my other son,
Were James and Peter, – nay, declared as well
This lad was very John, – I could believe!
– Could, for a moment, doubtlessly believe:
So is myself withdrawn into my depths,
The soul retreated from the perished brain
Whence it was wont to feel and use the world
Through these dull members, done with long ago.
Yet I myself remain; I feel myself:　　　　80
And there is nothing lost. Let be, awhile!'

[This is the doctrine he was wont to teach,
How divers persons witness in each man,
Three souls which make up one soul: first, to wit,
A soul of each and all the bodily parts,
Seated therein, which works, and is what Does,
And has the use of earth, and ends the man
Downward: but, tending upward for advice,
Grows into, and again is grown into
By the next soul, which, seated in the brain,　　　　90
Useth the first with its collected use,
And feeleth, thinketh, willeth, – is what Knows:
Which, duly tending upward in its turn,
Grows into, and again is grown into
By the last soul, that uses both the first,
Subsisting whether they assist or no,
And, constituting man's self, is what Is –
And leans upon the former, makes it play,
As that played off the first: and, tending up,
Holds, is upheld by, God, and ends the man　　　　100
Upward in that dread point of intercourse,

Nor needs a place, for it returns to Him.
What Does, what Knows, what Is; three souls, one man.
I give the glossa of Theotypas.]

And then, 'A stick, once fire from end to end;
Now, ashes save the tip that holds a spark!
Yet, blow the spark, it runs back, spreads itself
A little where the fire was: thus I urge
The soul that served me, till it task once more
110   What ashes of my brain have kept their shape,
And these make effort on the last o' the flesh,
Trying to taste again the truth of things –'
(He smiled) – 'their very superficial truth;
As that ye are my sons, that it is long
Since James and Peter had release by death,
And I am only he, your brother John,
Who saw and heard, and could remember all.
Remember all! It is not much to say.
What if the truth broke on me from above
120   As once and oft-times? Such might hap again:
Doubtlessly He might stand in presence here,
With head wool-white, eyes flame, and feet like brass,
The sword and the seven stars, as I have seen –
I who now shudder only and surmise
"How did your brother bear that sight and live?"
'If I live yet, it is for good, more love
Through me to men: be naught but ashes here
That keep awhile my semblance, who was John, –
Still, when they scatter, there is left on earth
130   No one alive who knew (consider this!)
– Saw with his eyes and handled with his hands
That which was from the first, the Word of Life.
How will it be when none more saith "I saw"?

'Such ever was love's way: to rise, it stoops.
Since I, whom Christ's mouth taught, was bidden teach,
I went, for many years, about the world,
Saying "It was so; so I heard and saw,"

Speaking as the case asked: and men believed.
Afterward came the message to myself
In Patmos isle; I was not bidden teach,   140
But simply listen, take a book and write,
Nor set down other than the given word,
With nothing left to my arbitrament
To choose or change: I wrote, and men believed.
Then, for my time grew brief, no message more,
No call to write again, I found a way,
And, reasoning from my knowledge, merely taught
Men should, for love's sake, in love's strength believe;
Or I would pen a letter to a friend
And urge the same as friend, nor less nor more: 150
Friends said I reasoned rightly, and believed.
But at the last, why, I seemed left alive
Like a sea-jelly weak on Patmos strand,
To tell dry sea-beach gazers how I fared
When there was mid-sea, and the mighty things;
Left to repeat, "I saw, I heard, I knew,"
And go all over the old ground again,
With Antichrist already in the world,
And many Antichrists, who answered prompt
"Am I not Jasper as thyself art John?   160
Nay, young, whereas through age thou mayst forget:
Wherefore, explain, or how shall we believe?"
I never thought to call down fire on such,
Or, as in wonderful and early days,
Pick up the scorpion, tread the serpent dumb;
But patient stated much of the Lord's life
Forgotten or misdelivered, and let it work:
Since much that at the first, in deed and word,
Lay simply and sufficiently exposed,
Had grown (or else my soul was grown to match,   170
Fed through such years, familiar with such light,
Guarded and guided still to see and speak)
Of new significance and fresh result;
What first were guessed as points, I now knew stars,
And named them in the Gospel I have writ.

For men said, "It is getting long ago:
Where is the promise of His coming?" – asked
These young ones in their strength, as loth to wait,
Of me who, when their sires were born, was old.
180   I, for I loved them, answered, joyfully,
Since I was there, and helpful in my age;
And, in the main, I think such men believed.
Finally, thus endeavouring, I fell sick,
Ye brought me here; and I supposed the end,
And went to sleep with one thought that, at least,
Though the whole earth should lie in wickedness,
We had the truth, might leave the rest to God.
Yet now I wake in such decrepitude
As I had slidden down and fallen afar,
190   Past even the presence of my former self,
Grasping the while for stay at facts which snap,
Till I am found away from my own world,
Feeling for foot-hold through a blank profound,
Along with unborn people in strange lands,
Who say – I hear said or conceive they say –
"Was John at all, and did he say he saw?
Assure us, ere we ask what he might see!"

'And how shall I assure them? Can they share
– They, who have flesh, a veil of youth and strength
200   About each spirit, that needs must bide its time,
Living and learning still as years assist
Which wear the thickness thin, and let man see –
With me who hardly am withheld at all,
But shudderingly, scarce a shred between,
Lie bare to the universal prick of light?
Is it for nothing we grow old and weak,
We whom God loves? When pain ends, gain ends too.
To me, that story – ay, that Life and Death
Of which I wrote "it was" – to me, it is;
210   – Is, here and now: I apprehend naught else.
Is not God now i' the world His power first made?
Is not His love at issue still with sin

Visibly when a wrong is done on earth?
Love, wrong, and pain, what see I else around?
Yea, and the Resurrection and Uprise
To the right hand of the throne – what is it beside,
When such truth, breaking bounds, o'erfloods my soul.
And, as I saw the sin and death, even so
See I the need yet transiency of both,
The good and glory consummated thence?   220
I saw the power; I see the Love, once weak,
Resume the Power: and in this word "I see,"
Lo, there is recognized the Spirit of both
That moving o'er the spirit of man, unblinds
His eye and bids him look. These are, I see;
But ye, the children, His beloved ones too,
Ye need, – as I should use an optic glass
I wondered at erewhile, somewhere i' the world,
It had been given a crafty smith to make;
A tube, he turned on objects brought too close,   230
Lying confusedly insubordinate
For the unassisted eye to master once:
Look through his tube, at distance now they lay,
Become succinct, distinct, so small, so clear!
Just thus, ye needs must apprehend what truth
I see, reduced to plain historic fact,
Diminished into clearness, proved a point
And far away: ye would withdraw your sense
From out eternity, strain it upon time,
Then stand before that fact, that Life and Death,   240
Stay there at gaze, till it dispart, dispread,
As though a star should open out, all sides,
Grow the world on you, as it is my world.

'For life, with all it yields of joy and woe,
And hope and fear, – believe the aged friend, –
Is just our chance o' the prize of learning love,
How love might be, hath been indeed, and is;
And that we hold thenceforth to the uttermost
Such prize despite the envy of the world,

250 And, having gained truth, keep truth: that is all.
But see the double way wherein we are led,
How the soul learns diversely from the flesh!
With flesh, that hath so little time to stay,
And yields mere basement for the soul's emprise,
Expect prompt teaching. Helpful was the light,
And warmth was cherishing and food was choice
To every man's flesh, thousand years ago,
As now to yours and mine; the body sprang
At once to the height, and stayed: but the soul, – no!

260 Since sages who, this noontide, meditate
In Rome or Athens, may descry some point
Of the eternal power, hid yestereve;
And, as thereby the power's whole mass extends,
So much extends the aether floating o'er,
The love that tops the might, the Christ in God.
Then, as new lessons shall be learned in these
Till earth's work stop and useless time run out,
So duly, daily, needs provision be
For keeping the soul's prowess possible,

270 Building new barriers as the old decay,
Saving us from evasion of life's proof,
Putting the question ever, "Does God love,
And will ye hold that truth against the world?"
Ye know there needs no second proof with good
Gained for our flesh from any earthly source:
We might go freezing, ages, – give us fire,
Thereafter we judge fire at its full worth,
And guard it safe through every chance, ye know!
That fable of Prometheus and his theft,

280 How mortals gained Jove's fiery flower, grows old
(I have been used to hear the pagans own)
And out of mind; but fire, howe'er its birth,
Here is it, precious to the sophist now
Who laughs the myth of Aeschylus to scorn,
As precious to those satyrs of his play,
Who touched it in gay wonder at the thing.
While were it so with the soul, – this gift of truth

Once grasped, were this our soul's gain safe, and sure
To prosper as the body's gain is wont, –
Why, man's probation would conclude, his earth   290
Crumble; for he both reasons and decides,
Weighs first, then chooses: will he give up fire
For gold or purple once he knows its worth?
Could he give Christ up were His worth as plain?
Therefore, I say, to test man, the proofs shift,
Nor may he grasp that fact like other fact,
And straightway in his life acknowledge it,
As, say, the indubitable bliss of fire.
Sigh ye, "It had been easier once than now"?
To give you answer I am left alive;   300
Look at me who was present from the first!
Ye know what things I saw; then came a test,
My first, befitting me who so had seen:
"Forsake the Christ thou sawest transfigured, Him
Who trod the sea and brought the dead to life?
What should wring this from thee!" – ye laugh and ask.
What wrung it? Even a torchlight and a noise,
The sudden Roman faces, violent hands,
And fear of what the Jews might do! Just that,
And it is written, "I forsook and fled":   310
There was my trial, and it ended thus.
Ay, but my soul had gained its truth, could grow:
Another year or two, – what little child,
What tender woman that had seen no least
Of all my sights, but barely heard them told,
Who did not clasp the cross with a light laugh,
Or wrap the burning robe round, thanking God?
Well, was truth safe for ever, then? Not so.
Already had begun the silent work
Whereby truth, deadened of its absolute blaze,   320
Might need love's eye to pierce the o'erstretched doubt.
Teachers were busy, whispering "All is true
As the aged ones report; but youth can reach
Where age gropes dimly, weak with stir and strain,
And the full doctrine slumbers till today."

Thus, what the Roman's lowered spear was found,
A bar to me who touched and handled truth,
Now proved the glozing of some new shrewd tongue,
This Ebion, this Cerinthus or their mates,
330   Till imminent was the outcry "Save our Christ!"
Whereon I stated much of the Lord's life
Forgotten or misdelivered, and let it work.
Such work done, as it will be, what comes next?
What do I hear say, or conceive men say,
"Was John at all, and did he say he saw?
Assure us, ere we ask what he might see!"

'Is this indeed a burthen for late days,
And may I help to bear it with you all,
Using my weakness which becomes your strength?
340   For if a babe were born inside this grot,
Grew to a boy here, heard us praise the sun,
Yet had but yon sole glimmer in light's place, –
One loving him and wishful he should learn,
Would much rejoice himself was blinded first
Month by month here, so made to understand
How eyes, born darkling, apprehend amiss:
I think I could explain to such a child
There was more glow outside than gleams he caught,
Ay, nor need urge "I saw it, so believe!"
350   It is a heavy burthen you shall bear
In latter days, new lands, or old grown strange,
Left without me, which must be very soon.
What is the doubt, my brothers? Quick with it!
I see you stand conversing, each new face,
Either in fields, of yellow summer eves,
On islets yet unnamed amid the sea;
Or pace for shelter 'neath a portico
Out of the crowd in some enormous town
Where now the larks sing in a solitude;
360   Or muse upon blank heaps of stone and sand
Idly conjectured to be Ephesus:
And no one asks his fellow any more

"Where is the promise of His coming?" but
"Was he revealed in any of His lives,
As Power, as Love, as Influencing Soul?"

'Quick, for time presses, tell the whole mind out,
And let us ask and answer and be saved!
My book speaks on, because it cannot pass;
One listens quietly, nor scoffs but pleads
"Here is a tale of things done ages since;   370
What truth was ever told the second day?
Wonders, that would prove doctrine, go for naught.
Remains the doctrine, love; well, we must love,
And what we love most, power and love in one,
Let us acknowledge on the record here,
Accepting these in Christ: must Christ then be?
Has He been? Did not we ourselves make Him?
Our mind receives but what it holds, no more.
First of the love, then; we acknowledge Christ –
A proof we comprehend His love, a proof   380
We had such love already in ourselves,
Knew first what else we should not recognize.
'Tis mere projection from man's inmost mind,
And, what he loves, thus falls reflected back,
Becomes accounted somewhat out of him;
He throws it up in air, it drops down earth's,
With shape, name, story added, man's old way.
How prove you Christ came otherwise at least?
Next try the power: He made and rules the world:
Certes there is a world once made, now ruled,   390
Unless things have been ever as we see.
Our sires declared a charioteer's yoked steeds
Brought the sun up the east and down the west,
Which only of itself now rises, sets,
As if a hand impelled it and a will, –
Thus they long thought, they who had will and hands:
But the new question's whisper is distinct,
Wherefore must all force needs be like ourselves?
We have the hands, the will; what made and drives

400   The sun is force, is law, is named, not known,
       While will and love we do know; marks of these,
       Eye-witnesses attest, so books declare –
       As that, to punish or reward our race,
       The sun at undue times arose or set
       Or else stood still: what do not men affirm?
       But earth requires as urgently reward
       Or punishment today as years ago,
       And none expects the sun will interpose:
       Therefore it was mere passion and mistake,
410   Or erring zeal for right, which changed the truth.
       Go back, far, farther, to the birth of things;
       Ever the will, the intelligence, the love,
       Man's! – which he gives, supposing he but finds,
       As late he gave head, body, hands and feet,
       To help these in what forms he called his gods.
       First, Jove's brow, Juno's eyes were swept away,
       But Jove's wrath, Juno's pride continued long;
       As last, will, power, and love discarded these,
       So law in turn discards power, love, and will.
420   What proveth God is otherwise at least?
       All else, projection from the mind of man!"

       'Nay, do not give me wine, for I am strong,
       But place my gospel where I put my hands.

       'I say that man was made to grow, not stop;
       That help, he needed once, and needs no more,
       Having grown but an inch by, is withdrawn:
       For he hath new needs, and new helps to these.
       This imports solely, man should mount on each
       New height in view; the help whereby he mounts,
430   The ladder-rung his foot has left, may fall,
       Since all things suffer change save God the Truth.
       Man apprehends Him newly at each stage
       Whereat earth's ladder drops, its service done;
       And nothing shall prove twice what once was proved.
       You stick a garden-plot with ordered twigs
       To show inside lie germs of herbs unborn,

And check the careless step would spoil their birth;
But when herbs wave, the guardian twigs may go,
Since should ye doubt of virtues, question kinds,
It is no longer for old twigs ye look,   440
Which proved once underneath lay store of seed,
But to the herb's self, by what light ye boast,
For what fruit's signs are. This book's fruit is plain,
Nor miracles need prove it any more.
Doth the fruit show? Then miracles bade 'ware
At first of root and stem, saved both till now
From trampling ox, rough boar and wanton goat.
What? Was man made a wheelwork to wind up,
And be discharged, and straight wound up anew?
No! – grown, his growth lasts; taught, he ne'er forgets: 450
May learn a thousand things, not twice the same.

'This might be pagan teaching: now hear mine.

'I say, that as the babe, you feed awhile,
Becomes a boy and fit to feed himself,
So, minds at first must be spoon-fed with truth:
When they can eat, babe's-nurture is withdrawn.
I fed the babe whether it would or no:
I bid the boy or feed himself or starve.
I cried once, "That ye may believe in Christ,
Behold this blind man shall receive his sight!"   460
I cry now, "Urgest thou, *for I am shrewd
And smile at stories how John's word could cure –
Repeat that miracle and take my faith?*"
I say, that miracle was duly wrought
When, save for it, no faith was possible.
Whether a change were wrought i' the shows o' the world,
Whether the change came from our minds which see
Of shows o' the world so much as and no more
Than God wills for His purpose, – (what do I
See now, suppose you, there where you see rock   470
Round us?) – I know not; such was the effect,
So faith grew, making void more miracles
Because too much: they would compel, not help.

I say, the acknowledgement of God in Christ
Accepted by thy reason, solves for thee
All questions in the earth and out of it,
And has so far advanced thee to be wise.
Wouldst thou unprove this to re-prove the proved?
In life's mere minute, with power to use that proof,
480 Leave knowledge and revert to how it sprung?
Thou hast it; use it and forthwith, or die!

'For I say, this is death and the sole death,
When a man's loss comes to him from his gain,
Darkness from light, from knowledge ignorance,
And lack of love from love made manifest;
A lamp's death when, replete with oil, it chokes;
A stomach's when, surcharged with food, it starves.
With ignorance was surety of a cure.
When man, appalled at nature, questioned first
490 "What if there lurk a might behind this might?"
He needed satisfaction God could give,
And did give, as ye have the written word:
But when he finds might still redouble might,
Yet asks, "Since all is might, what use of will?"
– Will, the one source of might, – he being man
With a man's will and a man's might, to teach
In little how the two combine in large, –
That man has turned round on himself and stands,
Which in the course of nature is, to die.

500 'And when man questioned, "What if there be love
Behind the will and might, as real as they?" –
He needed satisfaction God could give,
And did give, as ye have the written word:
But when, beholding that love everywhere,
He reasons, "Since such love is everywhere,
And since ourselves can love and would be loved,
We ourselves make the love, and Christ was not," –
How shall ye help this man who knows himself,
That he must love and would be loved again,
510 Yet, owning his own love that proveth Christ,

Rejecteth Christ through very need of Him?
The lamp o'erswims with oil, the stomach flags
Loaded with nurture, and that man's soul dies.

'If he rejoin, "But this was all the while
A trick; the fault was, first of all, in thee,
Thy story of the places, names and dates,
Where, when and how the ultimate truth had rise,
– Thy prior truth, at last discovered none,
Whence now the second suffers detriment.
What good of giving knowledge if, because   520
O' the manner of the gift, its profit fail?
And why refuse what modicum of help
Had stopped the after-doubt, impossible
I' the face of truth – truth absolute, uniform?
Why must I hit of this and miss of that,
Distinguish just as I be weak or strong,
And not ask of thee and have answer prompt,
Was this once, was it not once? – then and now
And evermore, plain truth from man to man.
Is John's procedure just the heathen bard's?   530
Put question of his famous play again
How for the ephemerals' sake Jove's fire was filched,
And carried in a cane and brought to earth:
The fact is in the fable, cry the wise,
Mortals obtained the boon, so much is fact,
Though fire be spirit and produced on earth.
As with the Titan's, so now with thy tale:
Why breed in us perplexity, mistake,
Nor tell the whole truth in the proper words?"

'I answer, Have ye yet to argue out   540
The very primal thesis, plainest law,
– Man is not God but hath God's end to serve,
A master to obey, a course to take,
Somewhat to cast off, somewhat to become?
Grant this, then man must pass from old to new,
From vain to real, from mistake to fact,
From what once seemed good, to what now proves best.

How could man have progression otherwise?
Before the point was mooted "What is God?"
550 No savage man inquired "What am myself?"
Much less replied, "First, last, and best of things."
Man takes that title now if he believes
Might can exist with neither will nor love,
In God's case – what he names now Nature's Law –
While in himself he recognizes love
No less than might and will: and rightly takes.
Since if man prove the sole existent thing
Where these combine, whatever their degree,
However weak the might or will or love,
560 So they be found there, put in evidence, –
He is as surely higher in the scale
Than any might with neither love nor will,
As life, apparent in the poorest midge,
(When the faint dust-speck flits, ye guess its wing)
Is marvellous beyond dead Atlas' self –
Given to the nobler midge for resting-place!
Th·is, man proves best and highest – God, in fine,
And thus the victory leads but to defeat,
The gain to loss, best rise to the worst fall,
570 His life becomes impossible, which is death.

'But if, appealing thence, he cower, avouch
He is mere man, and in humility
Neither may know God nor mistake himself;
I point to the immediate consequence
And say, by such confession straight he falls
Into man's place, a thing nor God nor beast,
Made to know that he can know and not more:
Lower than God who knows all and can all,
Higher than beasts which know and can so far
580 As each beast's limit, perfect to an end,
Nor conscious that they know, nor craving more;
While man knows partly but conceives beside,
Creeps ever on from fancies to the fact,
And in this striving, this converting air

184

Into a solid he may grasp and use,
Finds progress, man's distinctive mark alone,
Not God's, and not the beasts': God is, they are,
Man partly is and wholly hopes to be.
Such progress could no more attend his soul
Were all it struggles after found at first   590
And guesses changed to knowledge absolute,
Than motion wait his body, were all else
Than it the solid earth on every side,
Where now through space he moves from rest to rest.
Man, therefore, thus conditioned, must expect
He could not, what he knows now, know at first;
What he considers that he knows today,
Come but tomorrow, he will find misknown;
Getting increase of knowledge, since he learns
Because he lives, which is to be a man,   600
Set to instruct himself by his past self:
First, like the brute, obliged by facts to learn,
Next, as man may, obliged by his own mind,
Bent, habit, nature, knowledge turned to law.
God's gift was that man should conceive of truth
And yearn to gain it, catching at mistake,
As midway help till he reach fact indeed.
The statuary ere he mould a shape
Boasts a like gift, the shape's idea, and next
The aspiration to produce the same;   610
So, taking clay, he calls his shape thereout,
Cries ever "Now I have the thing I see":
Yet all the while goes changing what was wrought,
From falsehood like the truth, to truth itself.
How were it had he cried "I see no face,
No breast, no feet i' the ineffectual clay"?
Rather commend him that he clapped his hands,
And laughed "It is my shape and lives again!"
Enjoyed the falsehood, touched it on to truth,
Until yourselves applaud the flesh indeed   620
In what is still flesh-imitating clay.
Right in you, right in him, such way be man's!

God only makes the live shape at a jet.
Will ye renounce this pact of creatureship?
The pattern on the Mount subsists no more,
Seemed awhile, then returned to nothingness;
But copies, Moses strove to make thereby,
Serve still and are replaced as time requires:
By these, make newest vessels, reach the type!
630   If ye demur, this judgement on your head,
Never to reach the ultimate, angels' law,
Indulging every instinct of the soul
There where law, life, joy, impulse are one thing!

'Such is the burthen of the latest time.
I have survived to hear it with my ears,
Answer it with my lips: does this suffice?
For if there be a further woe than such,
Wherein my brothers struggling need a hand,
So long as any pulse is left in mine,
640   May I be absent even longer yet,
Plucking the blind ones back from the abyss,
Though I should tarry a new hundred years!'

But he was dead; 'twas about noon, the day
Somewhat declining: we five buried him
That eve, and then, dividing, went five ways,
And I, disguised, returned to Ephesus.

By this, the cave's mouth must be filled with sand.
Valens is lost, I know not of his trace;
The Bactrian was but a wild childish man,
650   And could not write nor speak, but only loved:
So, lest the memory of this go quite,
Seeing that I tomorrow fight the beasts,
I tell the same to Phoebas, whom believe!
For many look again to find that face,
Beloved John's to whom I ministered,
Somewhere in life about the world; they err:
Either mistaking what was darkly spoke
At ending of his book, as he relates,

Or misconceiving somewhat of this speech
Scattered from mouth to mouth, as I suppose.   660
Believe ye will not see him any more
About the world with his divine regard!
For all was as I say, and now the man
Lies as he lay once, breast to breast with God.

———————————

[Cerinthus read and mused; one added this:

'If Christ, as thou affirmest, be of men
Mere man, the first and best but nothing more, –
Account Him, for reward of what He was,
Now and for ever, wretchedest of all.
For see; Himself conceived of life as love,   670
Conceived of love as what must enter in,
Fill up, make one with His each soul He loved:
Thus much for man's joy, all men's joy for Him.
Well, He is gone, thou sayest, to fit reward.
But by this time are many souls set free,
And very many still retained alive:
Nay, should His coming be delayed awhile,
Say, ten years longer (twelve years, some compute)
See if, for every finger of thy hands,
There be not found, that day the world shall end,   680
Hundreds of souls, each holding by Christ's word
That He will grow incorporate with all,
With me as Pamphylax, with him as John,
Groom for each bride! Can a mere man do this?
Yet Christ saith, this He lived and died to do.
Call Christ, then, the illimitable God,
Or lost!'

    But 'twas Cerinthus that is lost.]

Caliban upon Setebos; or, Natural Theology in the Island

'Thou thoughtest that I was altogether such a one as thyself.'

['Will sprawl, now that the heat of day is best,
Flat on his belly in the pit's much mire,
With elbows wide, fists clenched to prop his chin.
And, while he kicks both feet in the cool slush,
And feels about his spine small eft-things course,
Run in and out each arm, and make him laugh:
And while above his head a pompion-plant,
Coating the cave-top as a brow its eye,
Creeps down to touch and tickle hair and beard,
10 And now a flower drops with a bee inside,
And now a fruit to snap at, catch and crunch, –
He looks out o'er yon sea which sunbeams cross
And recross till they weave a spider-web
(Meshes of fire, some great fish breaks at times)
And talks to his own self, howe'er he please,
Touching that other, whom his dam called God.
Because to talk about Him, vexes – ha,
Could He but know! and time to vex is now,
When talk is safer than in winter-time.
20 Moreover Prosper and Miranda sleep
In confidence he drudges at their task,
And it is good to cheat the pair, and gibe,
Letting the rank tongue blossom into speech.]

Setebos, Setebos, and Setebos!
'Thinketh, He dwelleth i' the cold o' the moon.

'Thinketh He made it, with the sun to match,
But not the stars; the stars came otherwise;
Only made clouds, winds, meteors, such as that:

188

Also this isle, what lives and grows thereon,
And snaky sea which rounds and ends the same.   30

'Thinketh, it came of being ill at ease:
He hated that He cannot change His cold,
Nor cure its ache. 'Hath spied an icy fish
That longed to 'scape the rock-stream where she lived,
And thaw herself within the lukewarm brine
O' the lazy sea her stream thrusts far amid,
A crystal spike 'twixt two warm walls of wave;
Only, she ever sickened, found repulse
At the other kind of water, not her life
(Green-dense and dim-delicious, bred o' the sun)   40
Flounced back from bliss she was not born to breathe,
And in her old bounds buried her despair,
Hating and loving warmth alike: so He.

'Thinketh, He made thereat the sun, this isle,
Trees and the fowls here, beast and creeping thing.
Yon otter, sleek-wet, black, lithe as a leech;
Yon auk, one fire-eye in a ball of foam,
That floats and feeds; a certain badger brown
He hath watched hunt with that slant white-wedge eye
By moonlight; and the pie with the long tongue   50
That pricks deep into oakwarts for a worm,
And says a plain word when she finds her prize,
But will not eat the ants; the ants themselves
That build a wall of seeds and settled stalks
About their hole – He made all these and more,
Made all we see, and us, in spite: how else?
He could not, Himself, make a second self
To be His mate; as well have made Himself:
He would not make what he mislikes or slights,
An eyesore to Him, or not worth His pains: 60
But did, in envy, listlessness or sport,
Make what Himself would fain, in a manner, be –
Weaker in most points, stronger in a few,
Worthy, and yet mere playthings all the while,
Things He admires and mocks too, – that is it.

Because, so brave, so better though they be,
It nothing skills if He begin to plague.
Look now, I melt a gourd-fruit into mash,
Add honeycomb and pods, I have perceived,
70   Which bite like finches when they bill and kiss, –
Then, when froth rises bladdery, drink up all,
Quick, quick, till maggots scamper through my brain;
Last, throw me on my back i' the seeded thyme,
And wanton, wishing I were born a bird.
Put case, unable to be what I wish,
I yet could make a live bird out of clay:
Would not I take clay, pinch my Caliban
Able to fly? – for, there, see, he hath wings,
And great comb like the hoopoe's to admire,
80   And there, a sting to do his foes offence,
There, and I will that he begin to live,
Fly to yon rock-top, nip me off the horns
Of grigs high up that make the merry din,
Saucy through their veined wings, and mind me not.
In which feat, if his leg snapped, brittle clay,
And he lay stupid-like, – why, I should laugh;
And if he, spying me, should fall to weep,
Beseech me to be good, repair his wrong,
Bid his poor leg smart less or grow again, –
90   Well, as the chance were, this might take or else
Not take my fancy: I might hear his cry,
And give the mankin three sound legs for one,
Or pluck the other off, leave him like an egg,
And lessoned he was mine and merely clay.
Were this no pleasure, lying in the thyme,
Drinking the mash, with brain become alive,
Making and marring clay at will? So He.

'Thinketh, such shows nor right nor wrong in Him,
Nor kind, nor cruel: He is strong and Lord.
100   'Am strong myself compared to yonder crabs
That march now from the mountain to the sea,
'Let twenty pass, and stone the twenty-first,

Loving not, hating not, just choosing so.
'Say, the first straggler that boasts purple spots
Shall join the file, one pincer twisted off;
'Say, this bruised fellow shall receive a worm,
And two worms he whose nippers end in red;
As it likes me each time, I do: so He.

Well then, 'supposeth He is good i' the main,
Placable if His mind and ways were guessed,   110
But rougher than His handiwork, be sure!
Oh, He hath made things worthier than Himself,
And envieth that, so helped, such things do more
Than He who made them! What consoles but this?
That they, unless through Him, do naught at all,
And must submit: what other use in things?
'Hath cut a pipe of pithless elder-joint
That, blown through, gives exact the scream o' the jay
When from her wing you twitch the feathers blue:
Sound this, and little birds that hate the jay   120
Flock within stone's throw, glad their foe is hurt:
Put case such pipe could prattle and boast forsooth
'I catch the birds, I am the crafty thing,
I make the cry my maker cannot make
With his great round mouth; he must blow through mine!'
Would not I smash it with my foot? So He.

But wherefore rough, why cold and ill at ease?
Aha, that is a question! Ask, for that,
What knows, – the something over Setebos
That made Him, or He, may be, found and fought,   130
Worsted, drove off and did to nothing, perchance.
There may be something quiet o'er His head,
Out of His reach, that feels nor joy nor grief,
Since both derive from weakness in some way.
I joy because the quails come; would not joy
Could I bring quails here when I have a mind:
This Quiet, all it hath a mind to, doth.
'Esteemeth stars the outposts of its couch,
But never spends much thought nor care that way.

140   It may look up, work up, – the worse for those
It works on! 'Careth but for Setebos
The many-handed as a cuttle-fish,
Who, making Himself feared through what He does,
Looks up, first, and perceives he cannot soar
To what is quiet and hath happy life;
Next looks down here, and out of very spite
Makes this a bauble-world to ape yon real,
These good things to match those as hips do grapes.
'Tis solace making baubles, ay, and sport.

150   Himself peeped late, eyed Prosper at his books
Careless and lofty, lord now of the isle:
Vexed, 'stitched a book of broad leaves, arrow-shaped,
Wrote thereon, he knows what, prodigious words;
Has peeled a wand and called it by a name;
Weareth at whiles for an enchanter's robe
The eyed skin of a supple oncelot;
And hath an ounce sleeker than youngling mole,
A four-legged serpent he makes cower and couch,
Now snarl, now hold its breath and mind his eye,

160   And saith she is Miranda and my wife:
'Keeps for his Ariel a tall pouch-bill crane
He bids go wade for fish and straight disgorge;
Also a sea-beast, lumpish, which he snared,
Blinded the eyes of, and brought somewhat tame,
And split its toe-webs, and now pens the drudge
In a hole o' the rock and calls him Caliban;
A bitter heart that bides its time and bites.
'Plays thus at being Prosper in a way,
Taketh his mirth with make-believes: so He.

170   His dam held that the Quiet made all things
Which Setebos vexed only: 'holds not so.
Who made them weak, meant weakness He might vex.
Had He meant other, while His hand was in,
Why not make horny eyes no thorn could prick,
Or plate my scalp with bone against the snow,
Or overscale my flesh 'neath joint and joint,

Like an orc's armour? Ay, – so spoil His sport!
He is the One now: only He doth all.

'Saith, He may like, perchance, what profits Him.
Ay, himself loves what does him good; but why?　　　180
'Gets good no otherwise. This blinded beast
Loves whoso places flesh-meat on his nose,
But, had he eyes, would want no help, but hate
Or love, just as it liked him: He hath eyes.
Also it pleaseth Setebos to work,
Use all His hands, and exercise much craft,
By no means for the love of what is worked.
'Tasteth, himself, no finer good i' the world
When all goes right, in this safe summer-time,
And he wants little, hungers, aches not much,　　　190
Than trying what to do with wit and strength.
'Falls to make something: 'piled yon pile of turfs,
And squared and stuck there squares of soft white chalk,
And, with a fish-tooth, scratched a moon on each,
And set up endwise certain spikes of tree,
And crowned the whole with a sloth's skull a-top,
Found dead i' the woods, too hard for one to kill.
No use at all i' the work, for work's sole sake;
'Shall some day knock it down again: so He.

'Saith He is terrible: watch His feats in proof!　　　200
One hurricane will spoil six good months' hope.
He hath a spite against me, that I know,
Just as He favours Prosper, who knows why?
So it is, all the same, as well I find.
'Wove wattles half the winter, fenced them firm
With stone and stake to stop she-tortoises
Crawling to lay their eggs here: well, one wave,
Feeling the foot of Him upon its neck,
Gaped as a snake does, lolled out its large tongue,
And licked the whole labour flat: so much for spite.　　　210
'Saw a ball flame down late (yonder it lies)
Where, half an hour before, I slept i' the shade:

Often they scatter sparkles: there is force!
'Dug up a newt He may have envied once
And turned to stone, shut up inside a stone.
Please Him and hinder this? – What Prosper does?
Aha, if He would tell me how! Not He!
There is the sport: discover how or die!
All need not die, for of the things o' the isle
220   Some flee afar, some dive, some run up trees;
Those at His mercy, – why, they please Him most
When . . . when . . . well, never try the same way twice!
Repeat what act has pleased, He may grow wroth.
You must not know His ways, and play Him off,
Sure of the issue. 'Doth the like himself:
'Spareth a squirrel that it nothing fears
But steals the nut from underneath my thumb,
And when I threat, bites stoutly in defence:
'Spareth an urchin that contrariwise,
230   Curls up into a ball, pretending death
For fright at my approach: the two ways please.
But what would move my choler more than this,
That either creature counted on its life
Tomorrow and next day and all days to come,
Saying, forsooth, in the inmost of its heart,
'Because he did so yesterday with me,
And otherwise with such another brute,
So must he do henceforth and always.' – Ay?
Would teach the reasoning couple what 'must' means!
240   'Doth as he likes, or wherefore Lord? So He.

'Conceiveth all things will continue thus,
And we shall have to live in fear of Him
So long as He lives, keeps His strength: no change,
If He have done His best, make no new world
To please Him more, so leave off watching this, –
If He surprise not even the Quiet's self
Some strange day, – or, suppose, grow into it
As grubs grow butterflies: else, here are we,
And there is He, and nowhere help at all.

'Believeth with the life, the pain shall stop.   250
His dam held different, that after death
He both plagued enemies and feasted friends:
Idly! He doth His worst in this our life,
Giving just respite lest we die through pain,
Saving last pain for worst, – with which, an end.
Meanwhile, the best way to escape His ire
Is, not to seem too happy. 'Sees, himself,
Yonder two flies, with purple films and pink,
Bask on the pompion-bell above: kills both.
'Sees two black painful beetles roll their ball   260
On head and tail as if to save their lives:
Moves them the stick away they strive to clear.

Even so, 'would have Him misconceive, suppose
This Caliban strives hard and ails no less,
And always, above all else, envies Him;
Wherefore he mainly dances on dark nights,
Moans in the sun, gets under holes to laugh,
And never speaks his mind save housed as now:
Outside, 'groans, curses. If He caught me here,
O'erheard this speech, and asked 'What chuckles at?'   270
'Would, to appease Him, cut a finger off,
Or of my three kid yearlings burn the best,
Or let the toothsome apples rot on tree,
Or push my tame beast for the orc to taste:
While myself lit a fire, and made a song
And sung it, '*What I hate, be consecrate*
To celebrate Thee and Thy state, no mate
For Thee; what see for envy in poor me?'
Hoping the while, since evils sometimes mend,
Warts rub away and sores are cured with slime,   280
That some strange day, will either the Quiet catch
And conquer Setebos, or likelier He
Decrepit may doze, doze, as good as die.

[What, what? A curtain o'er the world at once!
Crickets stop hissing; not a bird – or, yes,
There scuds His raven that has told Him all!
It was fool's play, this prattling! Ha! The wind
Shoulders the pillared dust, death's house o' the move,
And fast invading fires begin! White blaze –
290   A tree's head snaps – and there, there, there, there, there,
His thunder follows! Fool to gibe at Him!
Lo! 'Lieth flat and loveth Setebos!
'Maketh his teeth meet through his upper lip,
Will let those quails fly, will not eat this month
One little mess of whelks, so he may 'scape!]

Confessions

I

What is he buzzing in my ears?
　'Now that I come to die,
Do I view the world as a vale of tears?'
　Ah, reverend sir, not I!

II

What I viewed there once, what I view again
　Where the physic bottles stand
On the table's edge, – is a suburb lane,
　With a wall to my bedside hand.

III

That lane sloped, much as the bottles do,
　From a house you could descry　　　10
O'er the garden-wall: is the curtain blue
　Or green to a healthy eye?

IV

To mine, it serves for the old June weather
　Blue above lane and wall;
And that farthest bottle labelled 'Ether'
　Is the house o'ertopping all.

V

At a terrace, somewhere near the stopper,
　There watched for me, one June,
A girl: I know, sir, it's improper,
　My poor mind's out of tune.　　　20

VI

Only, there was a way . . . you crept
  Close by the side, to dodge
Eyes in the house, two eyes except:
  They styled their house 'The Lodge.'

VII

What right had a lounger up their lane?
  But, by creeping very close,
With the good wall's help, – their eyes might strain
  And stretch themselves to Oes,

VIII

Yet never catch her and me together,
30   As she left the attic, there,
By the rim of the bottle labelled 'Ether,'
  And stole from stair to stair,

IX

And stood by the rose-wreathed gate. Alas,
  We loved, sir – used to meet:
How sad and bad and mad it was –
  But then, how it was sweet!

Youth and Art

I

It once might have been, once only:
   We lodged in a street together,
You, a sparrow on the housetop lonely,
   I, a lone she-bird of his feather.

II

Your trade was with sticks and clay,
   You thumbed, thrust, patted and polished,
Then laughed 'They will see some day
   Smith made, and Gibson demolished.'

III

My business was song, song, song;
   I chirped, cheeped, trilled and twittered,   10
'Kate Brown's on the boards ere long,
   And Grisi's existence embittered!'

IV

I earned no more by a warble
   Than you by a sketch in plaster;
You wanted a piece of marble,
   I needed a music-master.

V

We studied hard in our styles,
   Chipped each at a crust like Hindoos,
For air looked out on the tiles,
   For fun watched each other's windows.   20

VI

You lounged, like a boy of the South,
    Cap and blouse – nay, a bit of beard too;
Or you got it, rubbing your mouth
    With fingers the clay adhered to.

VII

And I – soon managed to find
    Weak points in the flower-fence facing,
Was forced to put up a blind
    And be safe in my corset-lacing.

VIII

No harm! It was not my fault
30   If you never turned your eye's tail up
As I shook upon E *in alt*,
    Or ran the chromatic scale up:

IX

For spring bade the sparrows pair,
    And the boys and girls gave guesses,
And stalls in our street looked rare
    With bulrush and watercresses.

X

Why did not you pinch a flower
    In a pellet of clay and fling it?
Why did not I put a power
40   Of thanks in a look, or sing it?

XI

I did look, sharp as a lynx,
    (And yet the memory rankles)
When models arrived, some minx
    Tripped up-stairs, she and her ankles.

XII

But I think I gave you as good!
    'That foreign fellow, – who can know
How she pays, in a playful mood,
    For his tuning her that piano?'

XIII

Could you say so, and never say
    'Suppose we join hands and fortunes,   50
And I fetch her from over the way,
    Her, piano, and long tunes and short tunes?'

XIV

No, no: you would not be rash,
    Nor I rasher and something over:
You've to settle yet Gibson's hash,
    And Grisi yet lives in clover.

XV

But you meet the Prince at the Board,
    I'm queen myself at *bals-paré*,
I've married a rich old lord,
    And you're dubbed knight and an R.A.   60

XVI

Each life unfulfilled, you see;
    It hangs still, patchy and scrappy:
We have not sighed deep, laughed free,
    Starved, feasted, despaired, – been happy.

XVII

And nobody calls you a dunce,
    And people suppose me clever:
This could but have happened once,
    And we missed it, lost it for ever.

A Likeness

Some people hang portraits up
In a room where they dine or sup:
    And the wife clinks tea-things under,
And her cousin, he stirs his cup,
    Asks, 'Who was the lady, I wonder?'
'' Tis a daub John bought at a sale,'
    Quoth the wife, – looks black as thunder:
'What a shade beneath her nose!
Snuff-taking, I suppose, –'
10 Adds the cousin, while John's corns ail.

Or else, there's no wife in the case,
But the portrait's queen of the place,
    Alone 'mid the other spoils
Of youth, – masks, gloves and foils,
And pipe-sticks, rose, cherry-tree, jasmine,
    And the long whip, the tandem-lasher,
And the cast from a fist ('not, alas! mine,
    But my master's, the Tipton Slasher'),
And the cards where pistol-balls mark ace,
20 And a satin shoe used for cigar-case,
And the chamois-horns ('shot in the Chablais')
    And prints – Rarey drumming on Cruiser,
    And Sayers, our champion, the bruiser,
And the little edition of Rabelais:
Where a friend, with both hands in his pockets,
    May saunter up close to examine it,
    And remark a good deal of Jane Lamb in it,
'But the eyes are half out of their sockets;
That hair's not so bad, where the gloss is,
30 But they've made the girl's nose a proboscis:
Jane Lamb, that we danced with at Vichy!
What, is not she Jane? Then, who is she?'

All that I own is a print,
An etching, a mezzotint;
'Tis a study, a fancy, a fiction,
Yet a fact (take my conviction)
Because it has more than a hint
    Of a certain face, I never
Saw elsewhere touch or trace of
In women I've seen the face of: 40
    Just an etching, and, so far, clever.

I keep my prints, an imbroglio,
Fifty in one portfolio.
When somebody tries my claret,
We turn round chairs to the fire,
Chirp over days in a garret,
    Chuckle o'er increase of salary,
Taste the good fruits of our leisure,
Talk about pencil and lyre,
    And the National Portrait Gallery: 50
Then I exhibit my treasure.
After we've turned over twenty,
    And the debt of wonder my crony owes
    Is paid to my Marc Antonios,
He stops me – '*Festina lentè!*
What's that sweet thing there, the etching?'
How my waistcoat-strings want stretching,
    How my cheeks grow red as tomatoes,
How my heart leaps! But hearts, after leaps, ache.

'By the by, you must take, for a keepsake,   60
    That other, you praised, of Volpato's.'
The fool! would he try a flight further and say –
He never saw, never before today,
What was able to take his breath away,
A face to lose youth for, to occupy age
With the dream of, meet death with, – why, I'll not engage
But that, half in a rapture and half in a rage,
I should toss him the thing's self – ''Tis only a duplicate,
A thing of no value! Take it, I supplicate!'

Mr Sludge, 'The Medium'

Now, don't, sir! Don't expose me! Just this once!
This was the first and only time, I'll swear, –
Look at me, – see, I kneel, – the only time,
I swear, I ever cheated, – yes, by the soul
Of Her who hears – (your sainted mother, sir!)
All, except this last accident, was truth –
This little kind of slip! – and even this,
It was your own wine, sir, the good champagne,
(I took it for Catawba, you're so kind)
Which put the folly in my head!

                              'Get up?'
You still inflict on me that terrible face?
You show no mercy? – Not for Her dear sake,
The sainted spirit's, whose soft breath even now
Blows on my cheek – (don't you feel something, sir?)
You'll tell?

           Go tell, then! Who the devil cares
What such a rowdy chooses to . . .
                           Aie – aie – aie!
Please, sir! your thumbs are through my windpipe, sir!
Ch – ch!

           Well, sir, I hope you've done it now!
Oh Lord! I little thought, sir, yesterday,
When your departed mother spoke those words
Of peace through me, and moved you, sir, so much,
You gave me – (very kind it was of you)
These shirt-studs – (better take them back again,
Please, sir) – yes, little did I think so soon
A trifle of trick, all through a glass too much

204

Of his own champagne, would change my best of friends
Into an angry gentleman!

                Though, 'twas wrong.
I don't contest the point; your anger's just:
Whatever put such folly in my head,
I know 'twas wicked of me. There's a thick   30
Dusk undeveloped spirit (I've observed)
Owes me a grudge – a negro's, I should say,
Or else an Irish emigrant's; yourself
Explained the case so well last Sunday, sir,
When we had summoned Franklin to clear up
A point about those shares i' the telegraph:
Ay, and he swore . . . or might it be Tom Paine? . . .
Thumping the table close by where I crouched,
He'd do me soon a mischief: that's come true!

Why, now your face clears! I was sure it would!   40
Then, this one time . . . don't take your hand away,
Through yours I surely kiss your mother's hand . . .
You'll promise to forgive me? – or, at least,
Tell nobody of this? Consider, sir!
What harm can mercy do? Would but the shade
Of the venerable dead-one just vouchsafe
A rap or tip! What bit of paper's here?
Suppose we take a pencil, let her write,
Make the least sign, she urges on her child
Forgiveness? There now! Eh? Oh! 'Twas your foot,   50
And not a natural creak, sir?

                Answer, then!
Once, twice, thrice . . . see, I'm waiting to say 'thrice!'
All to no use? No sort of hope for me?
It's all to post to Greeley's newspaper?

What? If I told you all about the tricks?
Upon my soul! – the whole truth, and naught else,
And how there's been some falsehood – for your part,
Will you engage to pay my passage out,
And hold your tongue until I'm safe on board?

60 England's the place, not Boston – no offence!
    I see what makes you hesitate: don't fear!
    I mean to change my trade and cheat no more,
    Yes, this time really it's upon my soul!
    Be my salvation! – under Heaven, of course.
    I'll tell some queer things. Sixty Vs must do.
    A trifle, though, to start with! We'll refer
    The question to this table?

                      How you're changed!
    Then split the difference; thirty more, we'll say.
    Ay, but you leave my presents! Else I'll swear
70 'Twas all through those: you wanted yours again,
    So, picked a quarrel with me, to get them back!
    Tread on a worm, it turns, sir! If I turn,
    Your fault! 'Tis you'll have forced me! Who's obliged
    To give up life yet try no self-defence?
    At all events, I'll run the risk. Eh?

                           Done!
    May I sit, sir? This dear old table, now!
    Please, sir, a parting egg-nog and cigar!
    I've been so happy with you! Nice stuffed chairs,
    And sympathetic sideboards; what an end
80 To all the instructive evenings! (It's alight.)
    Well, nothing lasts, as Bacon came and said.
    Here goes, – but keep your temper, or I'll scream!

    Fol-lol-the-rido-liddle-iddle-ol!
    You see, sir, it's your own fault more than mine;
    It's all your fault, you curious gentlefolk!
    You're prigs, – excuse me, – like to look so spry,
    So clever, while you cling by half a claw

    To the perch whereon you puff yourselves at roost,
    Such piece of self-conceit as serves for perch
90 Because you chose it, so it must be safe.
    Oh, otherwise you're sharp enough! You spy
    Who slips, who slides, who holds by help of wing,
    Wanting real foothold, – who can't keep upright

On the other perch, your neighbour chose, not you:
There's no outwitting you respecting him!
For instance, men love money – that, you know
And what men do to gain it: well, suppose
A poor lad, say a help's son in your house,
Listening at keyholes, hears the company
Talk grand of dollars, V-notes, and so forth,   100
How hard they are to get, how good to hold,
How much they buy, – if, suddenly, in pops he –
'*I*'ve got a V-note!' – what do you say to him?
What's your first word which follows your last kick?
'Where did you steal it, rascal?' That's because
He finds you, fain would fool you, off your perch,
Not on the special piece of nonsense, sir,
Elected your parade-ground: let him try
Lies to the end of the list, – 'He picked it up,
His cousin died and left it him by will,   110
The President flung it to him, riding by,
An actress trucked it for a curl of his hair,
He dreamed of luck and found his shoe enriched,
He dug up clay, and out of clay made gold' –
How would you treat such possibilities?
Would not you, prompt, investigate the case
With cow-hide? 'Lies, lies, lies,' you'd shout: and why?
Which of the stories might not prove mere truth?
This last, perhaps, that clay was turned to coin!
Let's see, now, give him me to speak for him!   120
How many of your rare philosophers,
In plaguy books I've had to dip into,
Believed gold could be made thus, saw it made
And made it? Oh, with such philosophers
You're on your best behaviour! While the lad –
With him, in a trice, you settle likelihoods,
Nor doubt a moment how he got his prize:
In his case, you hear, judge and execute,
All in a breath: so would most men of sense.

But let the same lad hear you talk as grand   130

At the same keyhole, you and company,
Of signs and wonders, the invisible world;
How wisdom scouts our vulgar unbelief
More than our vulgarest credulity;
How good men have desired to see a ghost,
What Johnson used to say, what Wesley did,
Mother Goose thought, and fiddle-diddle-dee: –
If he break in with, 'Sir, *I* saw a ghost!'
Ah, the ways change! He finds you perched and prim;
140 It's a conceit of yours that ghosts may be:
There's no talk now of cow-hide. 'Tell it out!
Don't fear us! Take your time and recollect!
Sit down first: try a glass of wine, my boy!
And, David, (is not that your Christian name?)
Of all things, should this happen twice – it may –
Be sure, while fresh in mind, you let us know!'
Does the boy blunder, blurt out this, blab that,
Break down in the other, as beginners will?
All's candour, all's considerateness – 'No haste!
150 Pause and collect yourself! We understand!
That's the bad memory, or the natural shock,
Or the unexplained *phenomena*!'

                                Egad,
The boy takes heart of grace; finds, never fear,
The readiest way to ope your own heart wide,
Show – what I call your peacock-perch, pet post
To strut, and spread the tail, and squawk upon!
'Just as you thought, much as you might expect!
There be more things in heaven and earth, Horatio,' . . .
And so on. Shall not David take the hint,
160 Grow bolder, stroke you down at quickened rate?
If he ruffle a feather, it's 'Gently, patiently!
Manifestations are so weak at first!
Doubting, moreover, kills them, cuts all short,
Cures with a vengeance!'

                                There, sir, that's your style!
You and your boy – such pains bestowed on him,

Or any headpiece of the average worth,
To teach, say, Greek, would perfect him apace,
Make him a Person ('Porson?' thank you, sir!)
Much more, proficient in the art of lies.
You never leave the lesson! Fire alight,   170
Catch you permitting it to die! You've friends;
There's no withholding knowledge, – least from those
Apt to look elsewhere for their souls' supply:
Why should not you parade your lawful prize?
Who finds a picture, digs a medal up,
Hits on a first edition, – he henceforth
Gives it his name, grows notable: how much more,
Who ferrets out a 'medium'? 'David's yours,
You highly-favoured man? Then, pity souls
Less privileged! Allow us share your luck!'   180
So, David holds the circle, rules the roast,
Narrates the vision, peeps in the glass ball,
Sets-to the spirit-writing, hears the raps,
As the case may be.

          Now mark! To be precise –
Though I say, 'lies' all these, at this first stage,
'Tis just for science' sake: I call such grubs
By the name of what they'll turn to, dragonflies.
Strictly, it's what good people style untruth;
But yet, so far, not quite the full-grown thing:
It's fancying, fable-making, nonsense-work –   190
What never meant to be so very bad –
The knack of story-telling, brightening up
Each dull old bit of fact that drops its shine.
One does see somewhat when one shuts one's eyes,
If only spots and streaks; tables do tip
In the oddest way of themselves: and pens, good Lord,
Who knows if you drive them or they drive you?
'Tis but a foot in the water and out again;
Not that duck-under which decides your dive.
Note this, for it's important: listen why.   200

I'll prove, you push on David till he dives

And ends the shivering. Here's your circle, now:
Two-thirds of them, with heads like you their host,
Turn up their eyes, and cry, as you expect,
'Lord, who'd have thought it!' But there's always one
Looks wise, compassionately smiles, submits
'Of your veracity no kind of doubt,
But – do you feel so certain of that boy's?
Really, I wonder! I confess myself
210 More chary of my faith!' That's galling, sir!
What, he the investigator, he the sage,
When all's done? Then, you just have shut your eyes,
Opened your mouth, and gulped down David whole,
You! Terrible were such catastrophe!
So, evidence is redoubled, doubled again,
And doubled besides; once more, 'He heard, we heard,
You and they heard, your mother and your wife,
Your children and the stranger in your gates:
Did they or did they not?' So much for him,
220 The black sheep, guest without the wedding-garb,
The doubting Thomas! Now's your turn to crow:
'He's kind to think you such a fool: Sludge cheats?
Leave you alone to take precautions!'
                                        Straight
The rest join chorus. Thomas stands abashed,
Sips silent some such beverage as this,
Considers if it be harder, shutting eyes
And gulping David in good fellowship,
Than going elsewhere, getting, in exchange,
With no egg-nog to lubricate the food,
230 Some just as tough a morsel. Over the way,
Holds Captain Sparks his court: is it better there?
Have not you hunting-stories, scalping-scenes,
And Mexican War exploits to swallow plump
If you'd be free o' the stove-side, rocking-chair,
And trio of affable daughters?
                                    Doubt succumbs!
Victory! All your circle's yours again!
Out of the clubbing of submissive wits,

David's performance rounds, each chink gets patched,
Every protrusion of a point's filed fine,
All's fit to set a-rolling round the world,   240
And then return to David finally,
Lies seven-feet thick about his first half-inch.
Here's a choice birth o' the supernatural,
Poor David's pledged to! You've employed no tool
That laws exclaim at, save the devil's own,
Yet screwed him into henceforth gulling you
To the top o' your bent, – all out of one half-lie!

You hold, if there's one half or a hundredth part
Of a lie, that's his fault, – his be the penalty!
I dare say! You'd prove firmer in his place?   250
You'd find the courage, – that first flurry over,
That mild bit of romancing-work at end, –
To interpose with 'It gets serious, this;
Must stop here. Sir, I saw no ghost at all.
Inform your friends I made . . . well, fools of them,
And found you ready-made. I've lived in clover
These three weeks: take it out in kicks of me!'
I doubt it. Ask your conscience! Let me know,
Twelve months hence, with how few embellishments
You've told almighty Boston of this passage   260
Of arms between us, your first taste o' the foil
From Sludge who could not fence, sir! Sludge, your boy!
I lied, sir, – there! I got up from my gorge
On offal in the gutter, and preferred
Your canvas-backs: I took their carver's size,
Measured his modicum of intelligence,
Tickled him on the cockles of his heart
With a raven feather, and next week found myself
Sweet and clean, dining daintily, dizened smart,
Set on a stool buttressed by ladies' knees,   270
Every soft smiler calling me her pet,
Encouraging my story to uncoil
And creep out from its hole, inch after inch,
'How last night, I no sooner snug in bed,

Tucked up, just as they left me, – than came raps!
While a light whisked' . . . 'Shaped somewhat like a star?'
'Well, like some sort of stars, ma'am.' – 'So we thought!
And any voice? Not yet? Try hard, next time,
If you can't hear a voice; we think you may:
280   At least, the Pennsylvanian "mediums" did.'
Oh, next time comes the voice! 'Just as we hoped!'
Are not the hopers proud now, pleased, profuse
O' the natural acknowledgement?

                    Of course!
So, off we push, illy-oh-yo, trim the boat,
On we sweep with a cataract ahead,
We're midway to the Horseshoe: stop, who can,
The dance of bubbles gay about our prow!
Experiences become worth waiting for,
Spirits now speak up, tell their inmost mind,
290   And compliment the 'medium' properly,
Concern themselves about his Sunday coat,
See rings on his hand with pleasure. Ask yourself
How you'd receive a course of treats like these!
Why, take the quietest hack and stall him up,
Cram him with corn a month, then out with him
Among his mates on a bright April morn,
With the turf to tread; see if you find or no
A caper in him, if he bucks or bolts!
Much more a youth whose fancies sprout as rank
300   As toadstool-clump from melon-bed. 'Tis soon,
'Sirrah, you spirit, come, go, fetch and carry,
Read, write, rap, rub-a-dub, and hang yourself!'
I'm spared all further trouble; all's arranged;
Your circle does my business; I may rave
Like an epileptic dervish in the books,
Foam, fling myself flat, rend my clothes to shreds;
No matter: lovers, friends and countrymen
Will lay down spiritual laws, read wrong things right
By the rule o' reverse. If Francis Verulam
310   Styles himself Bacon, spells the name beside

With a *y* and a *k*, says he drew breath in York,
Gave up the ghost in Wales when Cromwell reigned,
(As, sir, we somewhat fear he was apt to say,
Before I found the useful book that knows)
Why, what harm's done? The circle smiles apace,
'It was not Bacon, after all, you see!
We understand; the trick's but natural:
Such spirits' individuality
Is hard to put in evidence: they incline
To gibe and jeer, these undeveloped sorts.   320
You see, their world's much like a gaol broke loose,
While this of ours remains shut, bolted, barred,
With a single window to it. Sludge, our friend,
Serves as this window, whether thin or thick,
Or stained or stainless; he's the medium-pane
Through which, to see us and be seen, they peep:
They crowd each other, hustle for a chance,
Tread on their neighbour's kibes, play tricks enough!
Does Bacon, tired of waiting, swerve aside?
Up in his place jumps Barnum – "I'm your man,   330
I'll answer you for Bacon!" Try once more!'

Or else it's – 'What's a "medium"? He's a means,
Good, bad, indifferent, still the only means
Spirits can speak by; he may misconceive,
Stutter and stammer, – he's their Sludge and drudge,
Take him or leave him; they must hold their peace,
Or else, put up with having knowledge strained
To half-expression through his ignorance.
Suppose, the spirit Beethoven wants to shed
New music he's brimful of; why, he turns   340
The handle of this organ, grinds with Sludge,
And what he poured in at the mouth o' the mill
As a Thirty-third Sonata, (fancy now!)
Comes from the hopper as bran-new Sludge, naught else,
The Shakers' Hymn in G, with a natural F,
Or the "Stars and Stripes" set to consecutive fourths.'

Sir, where's the scrape you did not help me through,
You that are wise? And for the fools, the folk
Who came to see, – the guests, (observe that word!)
350 Pray do you find guests criticize your wine,
Your furniture, your grammar, or your nose?
Then, why your 'medium'? What's the difference?
Prove your madeira red-ink and gamboge, –
Your Sludge, a cheat – then, somebody's a goose
For vaunting both as genuine. 'Guests!' Don't fear!
They'll make a wry face, nor too much of that,
And leave you in your glory.

                    'No, sometimes
They doubt and say as much!' Ay, doubt they do!
And what's the consequence? 'Of course they doubt' –
360 (You triumph) 'that explains the hitch at once!
Doubt posed our "medium," puddled his pure mind;
He gave them back their rubbish: pitch chaff in,
Could flour come out o' the honest mill?' So, prompt
Applaud the faithful: cases flock in point,
'How, when a mocker willed a "medium" once
Should name a spirit James whose name was George,
"James" cried the "medium," – 'twas the test of truth!'
In short, a hit proves much, a miss proves more.

Does this convince? The better: does it fail?
370 Time for the double-shotted broadside, then –
The grand means, last resource. Look black and big!
'You style us idiots, therefore – why stop short?
Accomplices in rascality: this we hear
In our own house, from our invited guest
Found brave enough to outrage a poor boy
Exposed by our good faith! Have you been heard?
Now, then, hear us; one man's not quite worth twelve.
You see a cheat? Here's some twelve see an ass:
Excuse me if I calculate: good day!'
380 Out slinks the sceptic, all the laughs explode,
Sludge waves his hat in triumph!

Or – he don't.
There's something in real truth (explain who can!)
One casts a wistful eye at, like the horse
Who mopes beneath stuffed hay-racks and won't munch
Because he spies a corn-bag: hang that truth,
It spoils all dainties proffered in its place!
I've felt at times when, cockered, cosseted
And coddled by the aforesaid company,
Bidden enjoy their bullying, – never fear,
But o'er their shoulders spit at the flying man, –   390
I've felt a child; only, a fractious child
That, dandled soft by nurse, aunt, grandmother,
Who keep him from the kennel, sun and wind,
Good fun and wholesome mud, – enjoined be sweet,
And comely and superior, – eyes askance
The ragged sons o' the gutter at their game,
Fain would be down with them i' the thick o' the filth,
Making dirt-pies, laughing free, speaking plain,
And calling granny the grey old cat she is.
I've felt a spite, I say, at you, at them,   400
Huggings and humbug – gnashed my teeth to mark
A decent dog pass! It's too bad, I say,
Ruining a soul so!

But what's 'so,' what's fixed,
Where may one stop? Nowhere! The cheating's nursed
Out of the lying, softly and surely spun
To just your length, sir! I'd stop soon enough:
But you're for progress. 'All old, nothing new?
Only the usual talking through the mouth,
Or writing by the hand? I own, I thought
This would develop, grow demonstrable,   410
Make doubt absurd, give figures we might see,
Flowers we might touch. There's no one doubts you, Sludge!
You dream the dreams, you see the spiritual sights,
The speeches come in your head, beyond dispute.
Still, for the sceptics' sake, to stop all mouths,
We want some outward manifestation! – well,

The Pennsylvanians gained such; why not Sludge?
He may improve with time!'

                      Ay, that he may!
He sees his lot: there's no avoiding fate.

420 'Tis a trifle at first. 'Eh, David? Did you hear?
You jogged the table, your foot caused the squeak,
This time you're . . . joking, are you not, my boy?'
'N-n-no!' – and I'm done for, bought and sold henceforth.
The old good easy jog-trot way, the . . . eh?
The . . . not so very false, as falsehood goes,
The spinning out and drawing fine, you know, –
Really mere novel-writing of a sort,
Acting, or improvising, make-believe,
Surely not downright cheatery, – any how,

430 'Tis done with and my lot cast; Cheat's my name:
The fatal dash of brandy in your tea
Has settled what you'll have the souchong's smack:
The caddy gives way to the dram-bottle.

Then, it's so cruel easy! Oh, those tricks
That can't be tricks, those feats by sleight of hand,
Clearly no common conjurer's! – no indeed!
A conjurer? Choose me any craft i' the world
A man puts hand to; and with six months' pains,
I'll play you twenty tricks miraculous

440 To people untaught the trade: have you seen glass blown,
Pipes pierced? Why, just this biscuit that I chip,
Did you ever watch a baker toss one flat
To the oven? Try and do it! Take my word,
Practise but half as much, while limbs are lithe,
To turn, shove, tilt a table, crack your joints,
Manage your feet, dispose your hands aright,
Work wires that twitch the curtains, play the glove
At end o' your slipper, – then put out the lights
And . . . there, there, all you want you'll get, I hope!

450 I found it slip, easy as an old shoe.

Now, lights on table again! I've done my part,
You take my place while I give thanks and rest.

'Well, Judge Humgruffin, what's your verdict, sir?
You, hardest head in the United States, –
Did you detect a cheat here? Wait! Let's see!
Just an experiment first, for candour's sake!
I'll try and cheat you, Judge! The table tilts:
Is it I that move it? Write! I'll press your hand:
Cry when I push, or guide your pencil, Judge!'
Sludge still triumphant! 'That a rap, indeed?   460
That, the real writing? Very like a whale!
Then, if, sir you – a most distinguished man,
And, were the Judge not here, I'd say, . . . no matter!
Well, sir, if you fail, you can't take us in, –
There's little fear that Sludge will!'

                       Won't he, ma'am?
But what if our distinguished host, like Sludge,
Bade God bear witness that he played no trick,
While you believed that what produced the raps
Was just a certain child who died, you know,
And whose last breath you thought your lips had felt?   470
Eh? That's a capital point, ma'am: Sludge begins
At your entreaty with your dearest dead,
The little voice set lisping once again,
The tiny hand made feel for yours once more,
The poor lost image brought back, plain as dreams,
Which image, if a word had chanced recall,
The customary cloud would cross your eyes,
Your heart return the old tick, pay its pang!
A right mood for investigation, this!
One's at one's ease with Saul and Jonathan,   480
Pompey and Caesar: but one's own lost child . . .
I wonder, when you heard the first clod drop
From the spadeful at the grave-side, felt you free
To investigate who twitched your funeral scarf
Or brushed your flounces? Then, it came of course
You should be stunned and stupid; then, (how else?)
Your breath stopped with your blood, your brain struck work.
But now, such causes fail of such effects,

All's changed, – the little voice begins afresh,
490 Yet you, calm, consequent, can test and try
And touch the truth. 'Tests? Didn't the creature tell
Its nurse's name, and say it lived six years,
And rode a rocking-horse? Enough of tests!
Sludge never could learn that!'

                       He could not, eh?
You compliment him. 'Could not?' Speak for yourself!
I'd like to know the man I ever saw
Once, – never mind where, how, why, when, – once saw,
Of whom I do not keep some matter in mind
He'd swear I 'could not' know, sagacious soul!
500 What? Do you live in this world's blow of blacks,
Palaver, gossipry, a single hour
Nor find one smut has settled on your nose,
Of a smut's worth, no more, no less? – one fact
Out of the drift of facts, whereby you learn
What someone was, somewhere, somewhen, somewhy?
You don't tell folk – 'See what has stuck to me!
Judge Humgruffin, our most distinguished man,
Your uncle was a tailor, and your wife
Thought to have married Miggs, missed him, hit you!' –
510 Do you, sir, though, you see him twice a-week?
'No,' you reply, 'what use retailing it?
Why should I?' But, you see, one day you *should*,
Because one day there's much use, – when this fact
Brings you the Judge upon both gouty knees
Before the supernatural; proves that Sludge
Knows, as you say, a thing he 'could not' know:
Will not Sludge thenceforth keep an outstretched face
The way the wind drives?

                    'Could not!' Look you now,
I'll tell you a story! There's a whiskered chap,
520 A foreigner, that teaches music here
And gets his bread, – knowing no better way:
He says, the fellow who informed of him
And made him fly his country and fall West

Was a hunchback cobbler, sat, stitched soles and sang,
In some outlandish place, the city Rome,
In a cellar by their Broadway, all day long;
Never asked questions, stopped to listen or look,
Nor lifted nose from lapstone; let the world
Roll round his three-legged stool, and news run in
The ears he hardly seemed to keep pricked up.   530
Well, that man went on Sundays, touched his pay,
And took his praise from government, you see;
For something like two dollars every week,
He'd engage tell you some one little thing
Of some one man, which led to many more,
(Because one truth leads right to the world's end)
And make you that man's master – when he dined
And on what dish, where walked to keep his health
And to what street. His trade was, throwing thus
His sense out, like an ant-eater's long tongue,   540
Soft, innocent, warm, moist, impassible,
And when 'twas crusted o'er with creatures – slick,
Their juice enriched his palate. 'Could not Sludge!'

I'll go yet a step further, and maintain,
Once the imposture plunged its proper depth
I' the rotten of your natures, all of you, –
(If one's not mad nor drunk, and hardly then)
It's impossible to cheat – that's, be found out!
Go tell your brotherhood this first slip of mine,
All today's tale, how you detected Sludge,   550
Behaved unpleasantly, till he was fain confess,
And so has come to grief! You'll find, I think,
Why Sludge still snaps his fingers in your face.
There now, you've told them! What's their prompt reply?
'Sir, did that youth confess he had cheated me,
I'd disbelieve him. He may cheat at times;
That's in the "medium"-nature, thus they're made,
Vain and vindictive, cowards, prone to scratch.
And so all cats are; still, a cat's the beast
You coax the strange electric sparks from out,   560

By rubbing back its fur; not so a dog,
Nor lion, nor lamb: 'tis the cat's nature, sir!
Why not the dog's? Ask God, who made them beasts!
D'ye think the sound, the nicely-balanced man
('Like me' – aside) – 'like you yourself,' – (aloud)
'– He's stuff to make a "medium"? Bless your soul,
'Tis these hysteric, hybrid half-and-halfs,
Equivocal, worthless vermin yield the fire!
We take such as we find them, 'ware their tricks,
570   Wanting their service. Sir, Sludge took in you –
How, I can't say, not being there to watch:
He was tried, was tempted by your easiness, –
He did not take in me!'

               Thank you for Sludge!
I'm to be grateful to such patrons, eh,
When what you hear's my best word? 'Tis a challenge;
'Snap at all strangers, half-tamed prairie-dog,
So you cower duly at your keeper's beck!
Cat, show what claws were made for, muffling them
Only to me! Cheat others if you can,
580   Me, if you dare!' And, my wise sir, I dared –
Did cheat you first, made you cheat others next,
And had the help o' your vaunted manliness
To bully the incredulous. You used me?
Have not I used you, taken full revenge,
Persuaded folk they knew not their own name,
And straight they'd own the error! Who was the fool
When, to an awe-struck wide-eyed open-mouthed
Circle of sages, Sludge would introduce
Milton composing baby-rhymes, and Locke
590   Reasoning in gibberish, Homer writing Greek
In noughts and crosses, Asaph setting psalms
To crotchet and quaver? I've made a spirit squeak
In sham voice for a minute, then outbroke
Bold in my own, defying the imbeciles –
Have copied some ghost's pothooks, half a page,
Then ended with my own scrawl undisguised.

'All right! The ghost was merely using Sludge,
Suiting itself from his imperfect stock!'
Don't talk of gratitude to me! For what?
For being treated as a showman's ape,   600
Encouraged to be wicked and make sport,
Fret or sulk, grin or whimper, any mood
So long as the ape be in it and no man –
Because a nut pays every mood alike.
Curse your superior, superintending sort,
Who, since you hate smoke, send up boys that climb
To cure your chimney, bid a 'medium' lie
To sweep you truth down! Curse your women too,
Your insolent wives and daughters, that fire up
Or faint away if a male hand squeeze theirs,   610
Yet, to encourage Sludge, may play with Sludge
As only a 'medium,' only the kind of thing
They must humour, fondle . . . oh, to misconceive
Were too preposterous! But I've paid them out!
They've had their wish – called for the naked truth,
And in she tripped, sat down and bade them stare:
They had to blush a little and forgive!
'The fact is, children talk so; in next world
All our conventions are reversed, – perhaps
Made light of: something like old prints, my dear!   620
The Judge has one, he brought from Italy,
A metropolis in the background, – o'er a bridge,
A team of trotting roadsters, – cheerful groups
Of wayside travellers, peasants at their work,
And, full in front, quite unconcerned, why not?
Three nymphs conversing with a cavalier,
And never a rag among them: "fine," folk cry –
And heavenly manners seem not much unlike!
Let Sludge go on; we'll fancy it's in print!'

If such as came for wool, sir, went home shorn,   630
Where is the wrong I did them? 'Twas their choice;
They tried the adventure, ran the risk, tossed up
And lost, as some one's sure to do in games;

They fancied I was made to lose, – smoked glass
Useful to spy the sun through, spare their eyes:
And had I proved a red-hot iron plate
They thought to pierce, and, for their pains, grew blind,
Whose were the fault but theirs? While, as things go,
Their loss amounts to gain, the more's the shame!
640   They've had their peep into the spirit-world,
And all this world may know it! They've fed fat
Their self-conceit which else had starved: what chance
Save this, of cackling o'er a golden egg
And compassing distinction from the flock,
Friends of a feather? Well, they paid for it,
And not prodigiously; the price o' the play,
Not counting certain pleasant interludes,
Was scarce a vulgar play's worth. When you buy
The actor's talent, do you dare propose
650   For his soul beside? Whereas my soul you buy!
Sludge acts Macbeth, obliged to be Macbeth,
Or you'll not hear his first word! Just go through
That slight formality, swear himself's the Thane,
And thenceforth he may strut and fret his hour,
Spout, spawl, or spin his target, no one cares!
Why hadn't I leave to play tricks, Sludge as Sludge?

Enough of it all! I've wiped out scores with you –
Vented your fustian, let myself be streaked
Like tom-fool with your ochre and carmine,
660   Worn patchwork your respectable fingers sewed
To metamorphose somebody, – yes, I've earned
My wages, swallowed down my bread of shame,
And shake the crumbs off – where but in your face?

As for religion – why, I served it, sir!
I'll stick to that! With my *phenomena*
I laid the atheist sprawling on his back,
Propped up Saint Paul, or, at least, Swedenborg!
In fact, it's just the proper way to balk
These troublesome fellows – liars, one and all,

Are not these sceptics? Well, to baffle them,   670
No use in being squeamish: lie yourself!
Erect your buttress just as wide o' the line,
Your side, as they build up the wall on theirs;
Where both meet, midway in a point, is truth
High overhead: so, take your room, pile bricks,
Lie! Oh, there's titillation in all shame!
What snow may lose in white, snow gains in rose!
Miss Stokes turns – Rahab, – nor a bad exchange!
Glory be on her, for the good she wrought,
Breeding belief anew 'neath ribs of death,   680
Browbeating now the unabashed before,
Ridding us of their whole life's gathered straws
By a live coal from the altar! Why, of old,
Great men spent years and years in writing books
To prove we've souls, and hardly proved it then:
Miss Stokes with her live coal, for you and me!
Surely, to this good issue, all was fair –
Not only fondling Sludge, but, even suppose
He let escape some spice of knavery, – well,
In wisely being blind to it! Don't you praise   690
Nelson for setting spy-glass to blind eye
And saying . . . what was it – that he could not see
The signal he was bothered with? Ay, indeed!

I'll go beyond: there's a real love of a lie,
Liars find ready-made for lies they make,
As hand for glove, or tongue for sugar-plum.
At best, 'tis never pure and full belief;
Those furthest in the quagmire, – don't suppose
They strayed there with no warning, got no chance
Of a filth-speck in their face, which they clenched teeth,   700
Bent brow against! Be sure they had their doubts,
And fears, and fairest challenges to try
The floor o' the seeming solid sand! But no!
Their faith was pledged, acquaintance too apprised,
All but the last step ventured, kerchiefs waved,
And Sludge called 'pet': 'twas easier marching on

To the promised land, join those who, Thursday next,
Meant to meet Shakespeare; better follow Sludge –
Prudent, oh sure! – on the alert, how else? –
710 But making for the mid-bog, all the same!
To hear your outcries, one would think I caught
Miss Stokes by the scruff o' the neck, and pitched her flat,
Foolish-face-foremost! Hear these simpletons,
That's all I beg, before my work's begun,
Before I've touched them with my finger-tip!
Thus they await me (do but listen, now!
It's reasoning, this is, – I can't imitate
The baby voice, though) 'In so many tales
Must be some truth, truth though a pin-point big,
720 Yet, some: a single man's deceived, perhaps –
Hardly, a thousand: to suppose one cheat
Can gull all these, were more miraculous far
Than aught we should confess a miracle' –
And so on. Then the Judge sums up – (it's rare)
Bids you respect the authorities that leap
To the judgement-seat at once, – why don't you note
The limpid nature, the unblemished life,
The spotless honour, indisputable sense
Of the first upstart with his story? What –
730 Outrage a boy on whom you ne'er till now
Set eyes, because he finds raps trouble him?

Fools, these are: ay, and how of their opposites
Who never did, at bottom of their hearts,
Believe for a moment? – Men emasculate,
Blank of belief, who played, as eunuchs use,
With superstition safely, – cold of blood,
Who saw what made for them i' the mystery,
Took their occasion, and supported Sludge
– As proselytes? No, thank you, far too shrewd!
740 – But promisers of fair play, encouragers
O' the claimant; who in candour needs must hoist
Sludge up on Mars' Hill, get speech out of Sludge
To carry off, criticize, and cant about!

Didn't Athens treat Saint Paul so? – at any rate,
It's 'a new thing' philosophy fumbles at.

Then there's the other picker-out of pearl
From dung-heaps, – ay, your literary man,
Who draws on his kid gloves to deal with Sludge
Daintily and discreetly, – shakes a dust
O' the doctrine, flavours thence, he well knows how,   750
The narrative or the novel, – half-believes,
All for the book's sake, and the public's stare,
And the cash that's God's sole solid in this world!
Look at him! Try to be too bold, too gross
For the master! Not you! He's the man for muck;
Shovel it forth, full-splash, he'll smooth your brown
Into artistic richness, never fear!
Find him the crude stuff; when you recognize
Your lie again, you'll doff your hat to it,
Dressed out for company! 'For company,'   760
I say, since there's the relish of success:
Let all pay due respect, call the lie truth,
Save the soft silent smirking gentleman
Who ushered in the stranger: you must sigh
'How melancholy, he, the only one
Fails to perceive the bearing of the truth
Himself gave birth to!' – There's the triumph's smack!
That man would choose to see the whole world roll
I' the slime o' the slough, so he might touch the tip
Of his brush with what I call the best of browns –   770
Tint ghost-tales, spirit-stories, past the power
Of the outworn umber and bistre!

                              Yet I think
There's a more hateful form of foolery –
The social sage's, Solomon of saloons
And philosophic diner-out, the fribble
Who wants a doctrine for a chopping-block
To try the edge of his faculty upon,
Prove how much common sense he'll hack and hew
I' the critical minute 'twixt the soup and fish!

780 These were my patrons: these, and the like of them
Who, rising in my soul now, sicken it, –
These I have injured! Gratitude to these?
The gratitude, forsooth, of a prostitute
To the greenhorn and the bully – friends of hers,
From the wag that wants the queer jokes for his club,
To the snuff-box-decorator, honest man,
Who just was at his wits' end where to find
So genial a Pasiphae! All and each
Pay, compliment, protect from the police:
790 And how she hates them for their pains, like me!
So much for my remorse at thanklessness
Toward a deserving public!

                         But, for God?
Ay, that's a question! Well, sir, since you press –
(How you do tease the whole thing out of me!
I don't mean you, you know, when I say 'them':
Hate you, indeed! But that Miss Stokes, that Judge!
Enough, enough – with sugar: thank you, sir!)
Now, for it, then! Will you believe me, though?
You've heard what I confess; I don't unsay
800 A single word: I cheated when I could,
Rapped with my toe-joints, set sham hands at work,
Wrote down names weak in sympathetic ink,
Rubbed odic lights with ends of phosphor-match,
And all the rest; believe that: believe this,
By the same token, though it seem to set
The crooked straight again, unsay the said,
Stick up what I've knocked down; I can't help that.
It's truth! I somehow vomit truth today.
This trade of mine – I don't know, can't be sure
810 But there was something in it, tricks and all!
Really, I want to light up my own mind.
They were tricks, – true, but what I mean to add
Is also true. First, – don't it strike you, sir?
Go back to the beginning, – the first fact
We're taught is, there's a world beside this world,

With spirits, not mankind, for tenantry;
That much within that world once sojourned here,
That all upon this world will visit there,
And therefore that we, bodily here below,
Must have exactly such an interest   820
In learning what may be the ways o' the world
Above us, as the disembodied folk
Have (by all analogic likelihood)
In watching how things go in the old home
With us, their sons, successors, and what not.
Oh yes, with added powers probably,
Fit for the novel state, – old loves grown pure,
Old interests understood aright, – they watch!
Eyes to see, ears to hear, and hands to help,
Proportionate to advancement: they're ahead,   830
That's all – do what we do, but noblier done –
Use plate, whereas we eat our meals off delf,
(To use a figure).

                    Concede that, and I ask
Next what may be the mode of intercourse
Between us men here, and those once-men there?
First comes the Bible's speech; then, history
With the supernatural element, – you know –
All that we sucked in with our mothers' milk,
Grew up with, got inside of us at last,
Till it's found bone of bone and flesh of flesh.   840
See now, we start with the miraculous,
And know it used to be, at all events:
What's the first step we take, and can't but take,
In arguing from the known to the obscure?
Why this: 'What was before, may be today.
Since Samuel's ghost appeared to Saul, of course
My brother's spirit may appear to me.'
Go tell your teacher that! What's his reply?
What brings a shade of doubt for the first time
O'er his brow late so luminous with faith?   850
'Such things have been,' says he, 'and there's no doubt

Such things may be: but I advise mistrust
Of eyes, ears, stomach, and, more than all, your brain,
Unless it be of your great-grandmother,
Whenever they propose a ghost to you!'
The end is, there's a composition struck;
'Tis settled, we've some way of intercourse
Just as in Saul's time; only, different:
How, when and where, precisely, – find it out!
860   I want to know, then, what's so natural
As that a person born into this world
And seized on by such teaching, should begin
With firm expectancy and a frank look-out
For his own allotment, his especial share
I' the secret, – his particular ghost, in fine?
I mean, a person born to look that way,
Since natures differ: take the painter-sort,
One man lives fifty years in ignorance
Whether grass be green or red, – 'No kind of eye
870   For colour,' say you; while another picks
And puts away even pebbles, when a child,
Because of bluish spots and pinky veins –
'Give him forthwith a paint-box!' Just the same
Was I born . . . 'medium,' you won't let me say, –
Well, seer of the supernatural
Everywhen, everyhow and everywhere, –
Will that do?

          I and all such boys of course
Started with the same stock of Bible-truth;
Only, – what in the rest you style their sense,
880   Instinct, blind reasoning but imperative,
This, betimes, taught them the old world had one law
And ours another: 'New world, new laws,' cried they:
'None but old laws, seen everywhere at work,'
Cried I, and by their help explained my life
The Jews' way, still a working way to me.
Ghosts made the noises, fairies waved the lights,
Or Santa Claus slid down on New Year's Eve

And stuffed with cakes the stocking at my bed,
Changed the worn shoes, rubbed clean the fingered slate
O' the sum that came to grief the day before.   890

This could not last long: soon enough I found
Who had worked wonder thus, and to what end:
But did I find all easy, like my mates?
Henceforth no supernatural any more?
Not a whit: what projects the billiard-balls?
'A cue,' you answer: 'Yes, a cue,' said I;
'But what hand, off the cushion, moved the cue?
What unseen agency, outside the world,
Prompted its puppets to do this and that,
Put cakes and shoes and slates into their mind,   900
These mothers and aunts, nay even schoolmasters?'

Thus high I sprang, and there have settled since.
Just so I reason, in sober earnest still,
About the greater godsends, what you call
The serious gains and losses of my life.
What do I know or care about your world
Which either is or seems to be? This snap
O' my fingers, sir! My care is for myself;
Myself am whole and sole reality
Inside a raree-show and a market-mob   910
Gathered about it: that's the use of things.
'Tis easy saying they serve vast purposes,
Advantage their grand selves: be it true or false,
Each thing may have two uses. What's a star?
A world, or a world's sun: doesn't it serve
As taper also, time-piece, weather-glass,
And almanac? Are stars not set for signs
When we should shear our sheep, sow corn, prune trees?
The Bible says so.

                    Well, I add one use
To all the acknowledged uses, and declare   920
If I spy Charles's Wain at twelve tonight,
It warns me, 'Go, nor lose another day,

And have your hair cut, Sludge!' You laugh: and why?
Were such a sign too hard for God to give?
No: but Sludge seems too little for such grace:
Thank you, sir! So you think, so does not Sludge!
When you and good men gape at Providence,
Go into history and bid us mark
Not merely powder-plots prevented, crowns
930   Kept on kings' heads by miracle enough,
But private mercies – oh, you've told me, sir,
Of such interpositions! How yourself
Once, missing on a memorable day
Your handkerchief – just setting out, you know, –
You must return to fetch it, lost the train,
And saved your precious self from what befell
The thirty-three whom Providence forgot.
You tell, and ask me what I think of this?
Well, sir, I think then, since you needs must know,
940   What matter had you and Boston city to boot
Sailed skyward, like burnt onion-peelings? Much
To you, no doubt: for me – undoubtedly
The cutting of my hair concerns me more,
Because, however sad the truth may seem,
Sludge is of all-importance to himself.
You set apart that day in every year
For special thanksgiving, were a heathen else:
Well, I who cannot boast the like escape,
Suppose I said 'I don't thank Providence
950   For my part, owing it no gratitude'?
'Nay, but you owe as much' – you'd tutor me,
'You, every man alive, for blessings gained
In every hour o' the day, could you but know!
I saw my crowning mercy: all have such,
Could they but see!' Well, sir, why don't they see?
'Because they won't look, – or perhaps, they can't.'
Then, sir, suppose I can, and will, and do
Look, microscopically as is right,
Into each hour with its infinitude
960   Of influences at work to profit Sludge?

For that's the case: I've sharpened up my sight
To spy a providence in the fire's going out,
The kettle's boiling, the dime's sticking fast
Despite the hole i' the pocket. Call such facts
Fancies, too petty a work for Providence,
And those same thanks which you exact from me
Prove too prodigious payment: thanks for what,
If nothing guards and guides us little men?

No, no, sir! You must put away your pride,
Resolve to let Sludge into partnership!   970
I live by signs and omens: looked at the roof
Where the pigeons settle – 'If the further bird,
The white, takes wing first, I'll confess when thrashed;
Not, if the blue does' – so I said to myself
Last week, lest you should take me by surprise:
Off flapped the white, – and I'm confessing, sir!
Perhaps 'tis Providence's whim and way
With only me, i' the world: how can you tell?
'Because unlikely!' Was it likelier, now,
That this our one out of all worlds beside,   980
The what-d'you-call-'em millions, should be just
Precisely chosen to make Adam for,
And the rest o' the tale? Yet the tale's true, you know:
Such undeserving clod was graced so once;
Why not graced likewise undeserving Sludge?

Are we merit-mongers, flaunt we filthy rags?
All you can bring against my privilege
Is, that another way was taken with you, –
Which I don't question. It's pure grace, my luck:
I'm broken to the way of nods and winks,   990
And need no formal summoning. You've a help;
Holloa his name or whistle, clap your hands,
Stamp with your foot or pull the bell: all's one,
He understands you want him, here he comes.
Just so, I come at the knocking: you, sir, wait
The tongue o' the bell, nor stir before you catch
Reason's clear tingle, nature's clapper brisk,

Or that traditional peal was wont to cheer
Your mother's face turned heavenward: short of these
1000 There's no authentic intimation, eh?
Well, when you hear, you'll answer them, start up
And stride into the presence, top of toe,
And there find Sludge beforehand, Sludge that sprang
At noise o' the knuckle on the partition-wall

I think myself the more religious man.
Religion's all or nothing; it's no mere smile
O' contentment, sigh of aspiration, sir –
No quality o' the finelier-tempered clay
Like its whiteness or its lightness; rather, stuff
1010 O' the very stuff, life of life, and self of self.
I tell you, men won't notice; when they do,
They'll understand. I notice nothing else:
I'm eyes, ears, mouth of me, one gaze and gape,
Nothing eludes me, everything's a hint,
Handle and help. It's all absurd, and yet
There's something in it all, I know: how much?
No answer! What does that prove? Man's still man,
Still meant for a poor blundering piece of work
When all's done; but, if somewhat's done, like this,
1020 Or not done, is the case the same? Suppose
I blunder in my guess at the true sense
O' the knuckle-summons, nine times out of ten, –
What if the tenth guess happen to be right?
If the tenth shovel-load of powdered quartz
Yield me the nugget? I gather, crush, sift all,
Pass o'er the failure, pounce on the success.

To give you a notion, now – (let who wins, laugh!)
When first I see a man, what do I first?
Why, count the letters which make up his name,
1030 And as their number chances, even or odd,
Arrive at my conclusion, trim my course:
Hiram H. Horsefall is your honoured name,
And haven't I found a patron, sir, in you?
'Shall I cheat this stranger?' I take apple-pips,

Stick one in either canthus of my eye,
And if the left drops first – (your left, sir, stuck)
I'm warned, I let the trick alone this time.
You, sir, who smile, superior to such trash,
You judge of character by other rules:
Don't your rules sometimes fail you? Pray, what rule   1040
Have you judged Sludge by hitherto?

                       Oh, be sure,
You, everybody blunders, just as I,
In simpler things than these by far! For see:
I knew two farmers, – one, a wiseacre
Who studied seasons, rummaged almanacs,
Quoted the dew-point, registered the frost,
And then declared, for outcome of his pains,
Next summer must be dampish: 'twas a drought.
His neighbour prophesied such drought would fall,
Saved hay and corn, made cent. per cent. thereby,   1050
And proved a sage indeed: how came his lore?
Because one brindled heifer, late in March,
Stiffened her tail of evenings, and somehow
He got into his head that drought was meant!

I don't expect all men can do as much:
Such kissing goes by favour. You must take
A certain turn of mind for this, – a twist
I' the flesh, as well. Be lazily alive,
Open-mouthed, like my friend the ant-eater,
Letting all nature's loosely-guarded motes   1060
Settle and, slick, be swallowed! Think yourself
The one i' the world, the one for whom the world
Was made, expect it tickling at your mouth!
Then will the swarm of busy buzzing flies,
Clouds of coincidence, break egg-shell, thrive,
Breed, multiply, and bring you food enough.

I can't pretend to mind your smiling, sir!
Oh, what you mean is this! Such intimate way,
Close converse, frank exchange of offices,

1070   Strict sympathy of the immeasurably great
With the infinitely small, betokened here
By a course of signs and omens, raps and sparks, –
How does it suit the dread traditional text
O' the 'Great and Terrible Name'? Shall the Heaven of
    Heavens
Stoop to such child's play?

                   Please, sir, go with me
A moment, and I'll try to answer you.
The '*Magnum et terribile*' (is that right?)
Well, folk began with this in the early day;
And all the acts they recognized in proof
1080   Were thunders, lightnings, earthquakes, whirlwinds, dealt
Indisputably on men whose death they caused.
There, and there only, folk saw Providence
At work, – and seeing it, 'twas right enough
All heads should tremble, hands wring hands amain,
And knees knock hard together at the breath
O' the Name's first letter; why, the Jews, I'm told,
Won't write it down, no, to this very hour,
Nor speak aloud: you know best if't be so.
Each ague-fit of fear at end, they crept
1090   (Because somehow people once born must live)
Out of the sound, sight, swing and sway o' the Name,
Into a corner, the dark rest of the world,
And safe space where as yet no fear had reached;
'Twas there they looked about them, breathed again,
And felt indeed at home, as we might say.
The current o' common things, the daily life,
This had their due contempt; no Name pursued
Man from the mountain-top where fires abide,
To his particular mouse-hole at its foot
1100   Where he ate, drank, digested, lived in short:
Such was man's vulgar business, far too small
To be worth thunder: 'small,' folk kept on, 'small,'
With much complacency in those great days!
A mote of sand, you know, a blade of grass –

234

What was so despicable as mere grass,
Except perhaps the life o' the worm or fly
Which fed there? These were 'small' and men were great.
Well, sir, the old way's altered somewhat since,
And the world wears another aspect now:
Somebody turns our spyglass round, or else   1110
Puts a new lens in it: grass, worm, fly grow big:
We find great things are made of little things,
And little things go lessening till at last
Comes God behind them. Talk of mountains now?
We talk of mould that heaps the mountain, mites
That throng the mould, and God that makes the mites.
The Name comes close behind a stomach-cyst,
The simplest of creations, just a sac
That's mouth, heart, legs and belly at once, yet lives
And feels, and could do neither, we conclude,   1120
If simplified still further one degree:
The small becomes the dreadful and immense!
Lightning, forsooth? No word more upon that!
A tin-foil bottle, a strip of greasy silk,
With a bit of wire and knob of brass, and there's
Your dollar's-worth of lightning! But the cyst –
The life of the least of the little things?

                                   No, no!
Preachers and teachers try another tack,
Come near the truth this time: they put aside
Thunder and lightning: 'That's mistake,' they cry,   1130
'Thunderbolts fall for neither fright nor sport,
But do appreciable good, like tides,
Changes o' the wind, and other natural facts –
"Good" meaning good to man, his body or soul.
Mediate, immediate, all things minister
To man, – that's settled: be our future text
"We are His children!"' So, they now harangue
About the intention, the contrivance, all
That keeps up an incessant play of love, –
See the Bridgewater book.

1140   Amen to it!
Well, sir, I put this question: I'm a child?
I lose no time, but take you at your word:
How shall I act a child's part properly?
Your sainted mother, sir, – used you to live
With such a thought as this a-worrying you?
'She has it in her power to throttle me,
Or stab or poison: she may turn me out
Or lock me in, – nor stop at this today,
But cut me off tomorrow from the estate
1150 I look for' – (long may you enjoy it, sir!)
'In brief, she may unchild the child I am.'
You never had such crotchets? Nor have I!
Who, frank confessing childship from the first,
Cannot both fear and take my ease at once,
So, don't fear, – know what might be, well enough,
But know too, child-like, that it will not be,
At least in my case, mine, the son and heir
O' the kingdom, as yourself proclaim my style.

But do you fancy I stop short at this?
1160 Wonder if suit and service, son and heir
Needs must expect, I dare pretend to find?
If, looking for signs proper to such an one,
I straight perceive them irresistible?
Concede that homage is a son's plain right,
And, never mind the nods and raps and winks,
'Tis the pure obvious supernatural
Steps forward, does its duty: why, of course!
I have presentiments; my dreams come true:
I fancy a friend stands whistling all in white
1170 Blithe as a boblink, and he's dead I learn.
I take dislike to a dog my favourite long,
And sell him; he goes mad next week and snaps.
I guess that stranger will turn up today
I have not seen these three years; there's his knock.
I wager 'sixty peaches on that tree!' –
That I pick up a dollar in my walk,

That your wife's brother's cousin's name was George –
And win on all points. Oh, you wince at this?
You'd fain distinguish between gift and gift,
Washington's oracle and Sludge's itch   1180
O' the elbow when at whist he ought to trump?
With Sludge it's too absurd? *Fine, draw the line
Somewhere, but, sir, your somewhere is not mine!*

Bless us, I'm turning poet! It's time to end.
How you have drawn me out, sir! All I ask
Is – am I heir or not heir? If I'm he,
Then, sir, remember, that same personage
(To judge by what we read i' the newspaper)
Requires, beside one nobleman in gold
To carry up and down his coronet,   1190
Another servant, probably a duke,
To hold egg-nog in readiness: why want
Attendance, sir, when helps in his father's house
Abound, I'd like to know?

                              Enough of talk!
My fault is that I tell too plain a truth.
Why, which of those who say they disbelieve,
Your clever people, but has dreamed his dream,
Caught his coincidence, stumbled on his fact
He can't explain, (he'll tell you smilingly)
Which he's too much of a philosopher   1200
To count as supernatural, indeed,
So calls a puzzle and problem, proud of it, –
Bidding you still be on your guard, you know,
Because one fact don't make a system stand,
Nor prove this an occasional escape
Of spirit beneath the matter: that's the way!
Just so wild Indians picked up, piece by piece,
The fact in California, the fine gold
That underlay the gravel – hoarded these,
But never made a system stand, nor dug!   1210
So wise men hold out in each hollowed palm
A handful of experience, sparkling fact

They can't explain; and since their rest of life
Is all explainable, what proof in this?
Whereas I take the fact, the grain of gold,
And fling away the dirty rest of life,
And add this grain to the grain each fool has found
O' the million other such philosophers, –
Till I see gold, all gold and only gold,
1220   Truth questionless though unexplainable,
And the miraculous proved the commonplace!
The other fools believed in mud, no doubt –
Failed to know gold they saw: was that so strange?
Are all men born to play Bach's fiddle-fugues,
'Time' with the foil in carte, jump their own height,
Cut the mutton with the broadsword, skate a five,
Make the red hazard with the cue, clip nails
While swimming, in five minutes row a mile,
Pull themselves three feet up with the left arm,
1230   Do sums of fifty figures in their head,
And so on, by the scores of instances?
The Sludge with luck, who sees the spiritual facts
His fellows strive and fail to see, may rank
With these, and share the advantage.

                              Ay, but share
The drawback! Think it over by yourself;
I have not heart, sir, and the fire's gone grey.
Defect somewhere compénsates for success,
Everyone knows that. Oh, we're equals, sir!
The big-legged fellow has a little arm
1240   And a less brain, though big legs win the race:
Do you suppose I 'scape the common lot?
Say, I was born with flesh so sensitive,
Soul so alert, that, practice helping both,
I guess what's going on outside the veil,
Just as a prisoned crane feels pairing-time
In the islands where his kind are, so must fall
To capering by himself some shiny night,
As if your back-yard were a plot of spice –

Thus am I 'ware o' the spirit-world: while you,
Blind as a beetle that way, – for amends,   1250
Why, you can double fist and floor me, sir!
Ride that hot hardmouthed horrid horse of yours,
Laugh while it lightens, play with the great dog,
Speak your mind though it vex some friend to hear,
Never brag, never bluster, never blush, –
In short, you've pluck, when I'm a coward – there!
I know it, I can't help it, – folly or no,
I'm paralysed, my hand's no more a hand,
Nor my head a head, in danger: you can smile
And change the pipe in your cheek. Your gift's not mine.   1260
Would you swap for mine? No! but you'd add my gift
To yours: I dare say! I too sigh at times,
Wish I were stouter, could tell truth nor flinch,
Kept cool when threatened, did not mind so much
Being dressed gaily, making strangers stare,
Eating nice things; when I'd amuse myself,
I shut my eyes and fancy in my brain
I'm – now the President, now Jenny Lind,
Now Emerson, now the Benicia Boy –
With all the civilized world a-wondering   1270
And worshipping. I know it's folly and worse;
I feel such tricks sap, honeycomb the soul,
But I can't cure myself: despond, despair,
And then, hey, presto, there's a turn o' the wheel,
Under comes uppermost, fate makes full amends;
Sludge knows and sees and hears a hundred things
You all are blind to, – I've my taste of truth,
Likewise my touch of falsehood, – vice no doubt,
But you've your vices also: I'm content.

What, sir? You won't shake hands? 'Because I cheat!'   1280
'You've found me out in cheating!' That's enough
To make an apostle swear! Why, when I cheat,
Mean to cheat, do cheat, and am caught in the act,
Are you, or, rather, am I sure o' the fact?
(There's verse again, but I'm inspired somehow.)

239

Well then I'm not sure! I may be, perhaps,
Free as a babe from cheating: how it began,
My gift, – no matter; what 'tis got to be
In the end now, that's the question; answer that!
1290   Had I seen, perhaps, what hand was holding mine,
Leading me whither, I had died of fright:
So, I was made believe I led myself.
If I should lay a six-inch plank from roof
To roof, you would not cross the street, one step,
Even at your mother's summons: but, being shrewd,
If I paste paper on each side the plank
And swear 'tis solid pavement, why, you'll cross
Humming a tune the while, in ignorance
Beacon Street stretches a hundred feet below:
1300   I walked thus, took the paper-cheat for stone.
Some impulse made me set a thing o' the move
Which, started once, ran really by itself;
Beer flows thus, suck the siphon; toss the kite,
It takes the wind and floats of its own force.
Don't let truth's lump rot stagnant for the lack
Of a timely helpful lie to leaven it!
Put a chalk-egg beneath the clucking hen,
She'll lay a real one, laudably deceived,
Daily for weeks to come. I've told my lie,
1310   And seen truth follow, marvels none of mine;
All was not cheating, sir, I'm positive!
I don't know if I move your hand sometimes
When the spontaneous writing spreads so far,
If my knee lifts the table all that height,
Why the inkstand don't fall off the desk a-tilt,
Why the accordion plays a prettier waltz
Than I can pick out on the pianoforte,
Why I speak so much more than I intend,
Describe so many things I never saw.
1320   I tell you, sir, in one sense, I believe
Nothing at all, – that everybody can,
Will, and does cheat: but in another sense
I'm ready to believe my very self –

That every cheat's inspired, and every lie
Quick with a germ of truth.

     You ask perhaps
Why I should condescend to trick at all
If I know a way without it? This is why!
There's a strange secret sweet self-sacrifice
In any desecration of one's soul
To a worthy end, – isn't it Herodotus   1330
(I wish I could read Latin!) who describes
The single gift o' the land's virginity,
Demanded in those old Egyptian rites,
(I've but a hazy notion – help me, sir!)
For one purpose in the world, one day in a life,
One hour in a day – thereafter, purity,
And a veil thrown o'er the past for evermore!
Well, now, they understood a many things
Down by Nile city, or wherever it was!
I've always vowed, after the minute's lie,   1340
And the end's gain, – truth should be mine henceforth.
This goes to the root o' the matter, sir, – this plain
Plump fact: accept it and unlock with it
The wards of many a puzzle!

      Or, finally,
Why should I set so fine a gloss on things?
What need I care? I cheat in self-defence,
And there's my answer to a world of cheats!
Cheat? To be sure, sir! What's the world worth else?
Who takes it as he finds, and thanks his stars?
Don't it want trimming, turning, furbishing up   1350
And polishing over? Your so-styled great men,
Do they accept one truth as truth is found,
Or try their skill at tinkering? What's your world?
Here are you born, who are, I'll say at once,
Of the luckiest kind, whether in head and heart,
Body and soul, or all that helps them both.
Well, now, look back: what faculty of yours

Came to its full, had ample justice done
By growing when rain fell, biding its time,
1360   Solidifying growth when earth was dead,
Spiring up, broadening wide, in seasons due?
Never! You shot up and frost nipped you off,
Settled to sleep when sunshine bade you sprout;
One faculty thwarted its fellow: at the end,
All you boast is 'I had proved a topping tree
In other climes' – yet this was the right clime
Had you foreknown the seasons. Young, you've force
Wasted like well-streams: old, – oh, then indeed,
Behold a labyrinth of hydraulic pipes
1370   Through which you'd play off wondrous waterwork;
Only, no water's left to feed their play.
Young, – you've a hope, an aim, a love: it's tossed
And crossed and lost: you struggle on, some spark
Shut in your heart against the puffs around,
Through cold and pain; these in due time subside,
Now then for age's triumph, the hoarded light
You mean to loose on the altered face of things, –
Up with it on the tripod! It's extinct.
Spend your life's remnant asking, which was best,
1380   Light smothered up that never peeped forth once,
Or the cold cresset with full leave to shine?
Well, accept this too, – seek the fruit of it
Not in enjoyment, proved a dream on earth,
But knowledge, useful for a second chance,
Another life, – you've lost this world – you've gained
Its knowledge for the next. What knowledge, sir,
Except that you know nothing? Nay, you doubt
Whether 'twere better have made you man or brute,
If aught be true, if good and evil clash.
1390   No foul, no fair, no inside, no outside,
There's your world!

              Give it me! I slap it brisk
With harlequin's pasteboard sceptre: what's it now?
Changed like a rock-flat, rough with rusty weed,

At first wash-over o' the returning wave!
All the dry dead impracticable stuff
Starts into life and light again; this world
Pervaded by the influx from the next.
I cheat, and what's the happy consequence?
You find full justice straightway dealt you out,
Each want supplied, each ignorance set at ease,   1400
Each folly fooled. No life-long labour now
As the price of worse than nothing! No mere film
Holding you chained in iron, as it seems,
Against the outstretch of your very arms
And legs i' the sunshine moralists forbid!
What would you have? Just speak and, there, you see!
You're supplemented, made a whole at last,
Bacon advises, Shakespeare writes you songs,
And Mary Queen of Scots embraces you.
Thus it goes on, not quite like life perhaps,   1410
But so near, that the very difference piques,
Shows that e'en better than this best will be –
This passing entertainment in a hut
Whose bare walls take your taste since, one stage more,
And you arrive at the palace: all half real,
And you, to suit it, less than real beside,
In a dream, lethargic kind of death in life,
That helps the interchange of natures, flesh
Transfused by souls, and such souls! Oh, 'tis choice!
And if at whiles the bubble, blown too thin,   1420
Seem nigh on bursting, – if you nearly see
The real world through the false, – what *do* you see?
Is the old so ruined? You find you're in a flock
O' the youthful, earnest, passionate – genius, beauty,
Rank and wealth also, if you care for these:
And all depose their natural rights, hail you,
(That's me, sir) as their mate and yoke-fellow,
Participate in Sludgehood – nay, grow mine,
I veritably possess them – banish doubt,
And reticence and modesty alike!   1430
Why, here's the Golden Age, old Paradise

Or new Eutopia! Here's true life indeed,
And the world well won now, mine for the first time!

And all this might be, may be, and with good help
Of a little lying shall be: so, Sludge lies!
Why, he's at worst your poet who sings how Greeks
That never were, in Troy which never was,
Did this or the other impossible great thing!
He's Lowell – it's a world (you smile applause),
1440 Of his own invention – wondrous Longfellow,
Surprising Hawthorne! Sludge does more than they,
And acts the books they write: the more his praise!

But why do I mount to poets? Take plain prose –
Dealers in common sense, set these at work,
What can they do without their helpful lies?
Each states the law and fact and face o' the thing
Just as he'd have them, finds what he thinks fit,
Is blind to what missuits him, just records
What makes his case out, quite ignores the rest.
1450 It's a History of the world, the Lizard Age,
The Early Indians, the Old Country War,
Jerome Napoleon, whatsoever you please,
All as the author wants it. Such a scribe
You pay and praise for putting life in stones,
Fire into fog, making the past your world.
There's plenty of 'How did you contrive to grasp
The thread which led you through this labyrinth?
How build such solid fabric out of air?
How on so slight foundation found this tale,
1460 Biography, narrative?' or, in other words,
'How many lies did it require to make
The portly truth you here present us with?'
'Oh,' quoth the penman, purring at your praise,
' 'Tis fancy all; no particle of fact:
I was poor and threadbare when I wrote that book
"Bliss in the Golden City." I, at Thebes?
We writers paint out of our heads, you see!'
'– Ah, the more wonderful the gift in you,

The more creativeness and godlike craft!'
But I, do I present you with my piece,   1470
It's 'What, Sludge? When my sainted mother spoke
The verses Lady Jane Grey last composed
About the rosy bower in the seventh heaven
Where she and Queen Elizabeth keep house, –
You made the raps? 'Twas your invention that?
Cur, slave and devil!' – eight fingers and two thumbs
Stuck in my throat!

        Well, if the marks seem gone
'Tis because stiffish cocktail, taken in time,
Is better for a bruise than arnica.

There, sir! I bear no malice: 'tisn't in me.   1480
I know I acted wrongly: still, I've tried
What I could say in my excuse, – to show
The devil's not all devil . . . I don't pretend,
He's angel, much less such a gentleman
As you, sir! And I've lost you, lost myself,
Lost all-l-l-l- . . .

       No – are you in earnest, sir?
O yours, sir, is an angel's part! I know
What prejudice prompts, and what's the common course
Men take to soothe their ruffled self-conceit:
Only you rise superior to it all!   1490
No, sir, it don't hurt much; it's speaking long
That makes me choke a little: the marks will go!
What? Twenty V-notes more, and outfit, too,
And not a word to Greeley? One – one kiss
O' the hand that saves me! You'll not let me speak,
I well know, and I've lost the right, too true!
But I must say, sir, if She hears (she does)
Your sainted . . . Well, sir, – be it so! That's, I think,
My bed-room candle. Good night! Bl-l-less you, sir!

R-r-r, you brute-beast and blackguard! Cowardly scamp! 1500
I only wish I dared burn down the house

And spoil your sniggering! Oh what, you're the man?
You're satisfied at last? You've found out Sludge?
We'll see that presently: my turn, sir, next!
I too can tell my story: brute, – do you hear? –
You throttled your sainted mother, that old hag,
In just such a fit of passion: no, it was . . .
To get this house of hers, and many a note
Like these . . . I'll pocket them, however . . . five,
1510 Ten, fifteen . . . ay, you gave her throat the twist,
Or else you poisoned her! Confound the cuss!
Where was my head? I ought to have prophesied
He'll die in a year and join her: that's the way.

I don't know where my head is: what had I done?
How did it all go? I said he poisoned her,
And hoped he'd have grace given him to repent,
Whereon he picked this quarrel, bullied me
And called me cheat: I thrashed him, – who could help?
He howled for mercy, prayed me on his knees
1520 To cut and run and save him from disgrace:
I do so, and once off, he slanders me.
An end of him! Begin elsewhere anew!
Boston's a hole, the herring-pond is wide,
V-notes are something, liberty still more.
Beside, is he the only fool in the world?

Apparent Failure

'We shall soon lose a celebrated building.' *Paris Newspaper*

I

No, for I'll save it! Seven years since,
   I passed through Paris, stopped a day
To see the baptism of your Prince;
   Saw, made my bow, and went my way:
Walking the heat and headache off,
   I took the Seine-side, you surmise,
Thought of the Congress, Gortschakoff,
   Cavour's appeal and Buol's replies,
So sauntered till – what met my eyes?

II

Only the Doric little Morgue!   10
   The dead-house where you show your drowned:
Petrarch's Vaucluse makes proud the Sorgue,
   Your Morgue has made the Seine renowned.
One pays one's debt in such a case;
   I plucked up heart and entered, – stalked,
Keeping a tolerable face
   Compared with some whose cheeks were chalked:
Let them! No Briton's to be balked!

III

First came the silent gazers; next,
   A screen of glass, we're thankful for;   20
Last, the sight's self, the sermon's text;
   The three men who did most abhor
Their life in Paris yesterday,
   So killed themselves: and now, enthroned

Each on his copper couch, they lay
   Fronting me, waiting to be owned.
I thought, and think, their sin's atoned.

IV

Poor men, God made, and all for that!
   The reverence struck me; o'er each head
30 Religiously was hung its hat,
   Each coat dripped by the owner's bed,
Sacred from touch: each had his berth,
   His bounds, his proper place of rest,
Who last night tenanted on earth
   Some arch, where twelve such slept abreast, –
Unless the plain asphalt seemed best.

V

How did it happen, my poor boy?
   You wanted to be Buonaparte
And have the Tuileries for toy,
40   And could not, so it broke your heart?
You, old one by his side, I judge,
   Were, red as blood, a socialist,
A leveller! Does the Empire grudge
   You've gained what no Republic missed?
Be quiet, and unclench your fist!

VI

And this – why, he was red in vain,
   Or black, – poor fellow that is blue!
What fancy was it turned your brain?
   Oh, women were the prize for you!
50 Money gets women, cards and dice
   Get money, and ill-luck gets just
The copper couch and one clear nice
   Cool squirt of water o'er your bust,
The right thing to extinguish lust!

VII
It's wiser being good than bad;
 It's safer being meek than fierce:
It's fitter being sane than mad.
 My own hope is, a sun will pierce
The thickest cloud earth ever stretched;
 That, after Last, returns the First,   60
Though a wide compass round be fetched;
 That what began best, can't end worst,
Nor what God blessed once, prove accurst.

Epilogue [*to* Dramatis Personae]

First Speaker, as David

I

On the first of the Feast of Feasts,
 The Dedication Day,
When the Levites joined the Priests
 At the Altar in robed array,
Gave signal to sound and say, –

II

When the thousands, rear and van,
 Swarming with one accord
Became as a single man
 (Look, gesture, thought and word)
10 In praising and thanking the Lord, –

III

When the singers lift up their voice,
 And the trumpets made endeavour,
Sounding, 'In God rejoice!'
 Saying, 'In Him rejoice
Whose mercy endureth for ever!' –

IV

Then the Temple filled with a cloud,
 Even the House of the Lord;
Porch bent and pillar bowed:
 For the presence of the Lord,
20 In the glory of His cloud,
 Had filled the House of the Lord.

Second Speaker, as Renan

Gone now! All gone across the dark so far,
   Sharpening fast, shuddering ever, shutting still,
Dwindling into the distance, dies that star
   Which came, stood, opened once! We gazed our fill
With upturned faces on as real a Face
   That, stooping from grave music and mild fire,
Took in our homage, made a visible place
   Through many a depth of glory, gyre on gyre,
For the dim human tribute. Was this true?   30
   Could man indeed avail, mere praise of his,
To help by rapture God's own rapture too,
   Thrill with a heart's red tinge that pure pale bliss?
Why did it end? Who failed to beat the breast,
   And shriek, and throw the arms protesting wide,
When a first shadow showed the star addressed
   Itself to motion, and on either side
The rims contracted as the rays retired;
   The music, like a fountain's sickening pulse,
Subsided on itself; awhile transpired   40
   Some vestige of a Face no pangs convulse,
No prayers retard; then even this was gone,
   Lost in the night at last. We, lone and left
Silent through centuries, ever and anon
   Venture to probe again the vault bereft
Of all now save the lesser lights, a mist
   Of multitudinous points, yet suns, men say –
And this leaps ruby, this lurks amethyst,
   But where may hide what came and loved our clay?
How shall the sage detect in yon expanse   50
   The star which chose to stoop and stay for us?
Unroll the records! Hailed ye such advance
   Indeed, and did your hope evanish thus?
Watchers of twilight, is the worst averred?
   We shall not look up, know ourselves are seen,
Speak, and be sure that we again are heard,
   Acting or suffering, have the disk's serene

Reflect our life, absorb an earthly flame,
　　Nor doubt that, were mankind inert and numb,
60　Its core had never crimsoned all the same,
　　　Nor, missing ours, its music fallen dumb?
　　Oh, dread succession to a dizzy post,
　　　Sad sway of sceptre whose mere touch appals,
　　Ghastly dethronement, cursed by those the most
　　　On whose repugnant brow the crown next falls!

Third Speaker

I

Witless alike of will and way divine,
How heaven's high with earth's low should intertwine!
Friends, I have seen through your eyes: now use mine!

II

Take the least man of all mankind, as I;
70　Look at his head and heart, find how and why
He differs from his fellows utterly:

III

Then, like me, watch when nature by degrees
Grows alive round him, as in Arctic seas
(They said of old) the instinctive water flees

IV

Toward some elected point of central rock,
As though, for its sake only, roamed the flock
Of waves about the waste: awhile they mock

V

With radiance caught for the occasion, – hues
Of blackest hell now, now such reds and blues
80　As only heaven could fitly interfuse, –

VI

The mimic monarch of the whirlpool, king
O' the current for a minute: then they wring
Up by the roots and oversweep the thing,

VII

And hasten off, to play again elsewhere
The same part, choose another peak as bare,
They find and flatter, feast and finish there.

VIII

When you see what I tell you, – nature dance
About each man of us, retire, advance,
As though the pageant's end were to enhance

IX

His worth, and – once the life, his product, gained –   90
Roll away elsewhere, keep the strife sustained,
And show thus real, a thing the North but feigned –

X

When you acknowledge that one world could do
All the diverse work, old yet ever new,
Divide us, each from other, me from you, –

XI

Why, where's the need of Temple, when the walls
O' the world are that? What use of swells and falls
From Levites' choir, Priests' cries, and trumpet-calls?

XII

That one Face, far from vanish, rather grows,
Or decomposes but to recompose,   100
Become my universe that feels and knows.

House

I

Shall I sonnet-sing you about myself?
   Do I live in a house you would like to see?
Is it scant of gear, has it store of pelf?
   'Unlock my heart with a sonnet-key?'

II

Invite the world, as my betters have done?
   'Take notice: this building remains on view,
Its suites of reception every one,
   Its private apartment and bedroom too;

III

'For a ticket, apply to the Publisher.'
10   No: thanking the public, I must decline.
A peep through my window, if folk prefer;
   But, please you, no foot over threshold of mine!

IV

I have mixed with a crowd and heard free talk
   In a foreign land where an earthquake chanced:
And a house stood gaping, naught to balk
   Man's eye wherever he gazed or glanced.

V

The whole of the frontage shaven sheer,
   The inside gaped: exposed to day,
Right and wrong and common and queer,
20   Bare, as the palm of your hand, it lay.

VI

The owner? Oh, he had been crushed, no doubt!
  'Odd tables and chairs for a man of wealth!
What a parcel of musty old books about!
  He smoked, – no wonder he lost his health!

VII

'I doubt if he bathed before he dressed.
  A brasier? – the pagan, he burned perfumes!
You see it is proved, what the neighbours guessed:
  His wife and himself had separate rooms.'

VIII

Friends, the goodman of the house at least
  Kept house to himself till an earthquake came: 30
'Tis the fall of its frontage permits you feast
  On the inside arrangement you praise or blame.

IX

Outside should suffice for evidence:
  And whoso desires to penetrate
Deeper, must dive by the spirit-sense –
  No optics like yours, at any rate!

X

'Hoity toity! A street to explore,
  Your house the exception! *"With this same key
Shakespeare unlocked his heart,"* once more!'
  Did Shakespeare? If so, the less Shakespeare he!   40

Saint Martin's Summer

I

No protesting, dearest!
  Hardly kisses even!
    Don't we both know how it ends?
How the greenest leaf turns serest,
  Bluest outbreak – blankest heaven,
    Lovers – friends?

II

You would build a mansion,
  I would weave a bower
    – Want the heart for enterprise.
10 Walls admit of no expansion:
    Trellis-work may haply flower
      Twice the size.

III

What makes glad Life's Winter?
  New buds, old blooms after.
    Sad the sighing 'How suspect
Beams would ere mid-Autumn splinter,
  Rooftree scarce support a rafter,
    Walls lie wrecked?'

IV

You are young, my princess!
20 I am hardly older:
    Yet – I steal a glance behind.
Dare I tell you what convinces
  Timid me that you, if bolder,
    Bold – are blind?

V

Where we plan our dwelling
  Glooms a graveyard surely!
    Headstone, footstone moss may drape, –
Name, date, violets hide from spelling, –
  But, though corpses rot obscurely,
    Ghosts escape.   30

VI

Ghosts! O breathing Beauty,
  Give my frank word pardon!
    What if I – somehow, somewhere –
Pledged my soul to endless duty
  Many a time and oft? Be hard on
    Love – laid there?

VII

Nay, blame grief that's fickle,
  Time that proves a traitor,
    Chance, change, all that purpose warps, –
Death who spares to thrust the sickle   40
  Laid Love low, through flowers which later
    Shroud the corpse!

VIII

And you, my winsome lady,
  Whisper with like frankness!
    Lies nothing buried long ago?
Are yon – which shimmer 'mid the shady
  Where moss and violet run to rankness –
    Tombs or no?

IX

Who taxes you with murder?
  My hands are clean – or nearly!   50
    Love being mortal needs must pass.
Repentance? Nothing were absurder.
  Enough: we felt Love's loss severely;
    Though now – alas!

X

Love's corpse lies quiet therefore,
    Only Love's ghost plays truant,
    And warns us have in wholesome awe
Durable mansionry; that's wherefore
    I weave but trellis-work, pursuant
60   – Life, to law.

XI

The solid, not the fragile,
    Tempts rain and hail and thunder.
        If bower stand firm at Autumn's close,
Beyond my hope, – why, boughs were agile;
    If bower fall flat, we scarce need wonder
        Wreathing – rose!

XII

So, truce to the protesting,
    So, muffled be the kisses!
        For, would we but avow the truth,
70 Sober is genuine joy. No jesting!
    Ask else Penelope, Ulysses –
        Old in youth!

XIII

For why should ghosts feel angered?
    Let all their interference
        Be faint march-music in the air!
'Up! Join the rear of us the vanguard!
    Up, lovers, dead to all appearance,
        Laggard pair!'

XIV

The while you clasp me closer,
80   The while I press you deeper,
        As safe we chuckle, – under breath,
Yet all the slyer, the jocoser, –
    'So, life can boast its day, like leap-year,
        Stolen from death!'

XV

Ah me – the sudden terror!
    Hence quick – avaunt, avoid me,
        You cheat, the ghostly flesh-disguised!
Nay, all the ghosts in one! Strange error!
    So, 'twas Death's self that clipped and coyed me,
        Loved – and lied!   90

XVI

Ay, dead loves are the potent!
    Like any cloud they used you,
        Mere semblance you, but substance they!
Build we no mansion, weave we no tent!
    Mere flesh – their spirit interfused you!
        Hence, I say!

XVII

All theirs, none yours the glamour!
    Theirs each low word that won me,
        Soft look that found me Love's, and left
What else but you – the tears and clamour   100
    That's all your very own! Undone me –
        Ghost-bereft!

Ned Bratts

'Twas Bedford Special Assize, one daft Midsummer's Day:
A broiling blasting June, – was never its like, men say.
Corn stood sheaf-ripe already, and trees looked yellow as that;
Ponds drained dust-dry, the cattle lay foaming around each
    flat.
Inside town, dogs went mad, and folk kept bibbing beer
While the parsons prayed for rain. 'Twas horrible, yes – but
    queer:
Queer – for the sun laughed gay, yet nobody moved a hand
To work one stroke at his trade: as given to understand
That all was come to a stop, work and such worldly ways,
10 And the world's old self about to end in a merry blaze.
Midsummer's Day moreover was the first of Bedford Fair,
With Bedford Town's tag-rag and bobtail a-bowsing there.

But the Court House, Quality crammed: through doors ope,
    windows wide,
High on the Bench you saw sit Lordships side by side.
There frowned Chief Justice Jukes, fumed learned Brother
    Small,
And fretted their fellow Judge: like threshers, one and all,
Of a reek with laying down the law in a furnace. Why?
Because their lungs breathed flame – the regular crowd
    forbye –
From gentry pouring in – quite a nosegay, to be sure!
20 How else could they pass the time, six mortal hours endure
Till night should extinguish day, when matters might haply
    mend?
Meanwhile no bad resource was – watching begin and end
Some trial for life and death, in a brisk five minutes' space,
And betting which knave would 'scape, which hang, from his
    sort of face.

So, their Lordships toiled and moiled, and a deal of work was
 done
(I warrant) to justify the mirth of the crazy sun,
As this and 'tother lout, struck dumb at the sudden show
Of red robes and white wigs, boggled nor answered 'Boh!'
When asked why he, Tom Styles, should not – because Jack
 Nokes
Had stolen the horse – be hanged: for Judges must have their   30
 jokes,
And louts must make allowance – let's say, for some blue fly
Which punctured a dewy scalp where the frizzles stuck awry –
Else Tom had fleered scot-free, so nearly over and done
Was the main of the job. Full-measure, the gentles enjoyed
 their fun,
As a twenty-five were tried, rank puritans caught at prayer
In a cow-house and laid by the heels, – have at 'em, devil may
 care! –
And ten were prescribed the whip, and ten a brand on the
 cheek,
And five a slit of the nose – just leaving enough to tweak.

Well, things at jolly high-tide, amusement steeped in fire,
While noon smote fierce the roof's red tiles to heart's desire,   40
The Court a-simmer with smoke, one ferment of oozy flesh,
One spirituous humming musk mount-mounting until its
 mesh
Entoiled all heads in a fluster, and Serjeant Postlethwayte
– Dashing the wig oblique as he mopped his oily pate –
Cried 'Silence, or I grow grease! No loophole lets in air?
Jurymen, – Guilty, Death! Gainsay me if you dare!'
– Things at this pitch, I say, – what hubbub without the doors?
What laughs, shrieks, hoots and yells, what rudest of uproars?

Bounce through the barrier throng a bulk comes rolling vast!
Thumps, kicks, – no manner of use! – spite of them rolls at   50
 last
Into the midst a ball which, bursting, brings to view
Publican Black Ned Bratts and Tabby his big wife too:
Both in a muck-sweat, both . . . were never such eyes uplift

At the sight of yawning hell, such nostrils – snouts that sniffed
Sulphur, such mouths a-gape ready to swallow flame!
Horrified, hideous, frank fiend-faces! yet, all the same,
Mixed with a certain . . . eh? how shall I dare style – mirth,
The desperate grin of the guess that, could they break from
    earth,
Heaven was above, and hell might rage in impotence
60 Below the saved, the saved!

                  'Confound you! (no offence!)
Out of our way, – push, wife! Yonder their Worships be!'
Ned Bratts has reached the bar, and 'Hey, my Lords,' roars
    he,
'A Jury of life and death, Judges the prime of the land,
Constables, javelineers, – all met, if I understand,
To decide so knotty a point as whether 'twas Jack or Joan
Robbed the henroost, pinched the pig, hit the "King's Arms"
    with a stone,
Dropped the baby down the well, left the tithesman in the
    lurch,
Or, three whole Sundays running, not once attended church!
What a pother – do these deserve the parish-stocks or whip,
70 More or less brow to brand, much or little nose to snip, –
When, in our Public, plain stand we – that's we stand here,
I and my Tab, brass-bold, brick-built of beef and beer,
– Do not we, slut? Step forth and show your beauty, jade!
Wife of my bosom – that's the word now! What a trade
We drove! None said us nay: nobody loved his life
So little as wag a tongue against us, – did they, wife?
Yet they knew us all the while, in their hearts, for what we are
– Worst couple, rogue and quean, unhanged – search near and
    far!
Eh, Tab? The pedlar, now – o'er his noggin – who warned a
    mate
80 To cut and run, nor risk his pack where its loss of weight
Was the least to dread, – aha, how we two laughed a-good
As, stealing round the midden, he came on where I stood
With billet poised and raised, – you, ready with the rope, –

Ah, but that's past, that's sin repented of, we hope!
Men knew us for that same, yet safe and sound stood we!
The lily-livered knaves knew too (I've balked a d—)
Our keeping the "Pied Bull" was just a mere pretence:
Too slow the pounds make food, drink, lodging, from out the
    pence!
There's not a stoppage to travel has chanced, this ten long
    year,
No break into hall or grange, no lifting of nag or steer,   90
Not a single roguery, from the clipping of a purse
To the cutting of a throat, but paid us toll. Od's curse!
When Gypsy Smouch made bold to cheat us of our due,
– Eh, Tab? the Squire's strong-box we helped the rascal to –
I think he pulled a face, next Sessions' swinging-time!
He danced the jig that needs no floor, – and, here's the
    prime,
'Twas Scroggs that houghed the mare! Ay, those were busy
    days!

'Well, there we flourished brave, like scripture-trees called
    bays,
Faring high, drinking hard, in money up to head
– Not to say, boots and shoes, when . . . Zounds, I nearly   100
    said –
Lord, to unlearn one's language! How shall we labour, wife?
Have you, fast hold, the Book? Grasp, grip it, for your life!
See, sirs, here's life, salvation! Here's – hold but out my
    breath –
When did I speak so long without once swearing? 'Sdeath,
No, nor unhelped by ale since man and boy! And yet
All yesterday I had to keep my whistle wet
While reading Tab this Book: book? don't say "book" –
    they're plays,
Songs, ballads and the like: here's no such strawy blaze,
But sky wide ope, sun, moon, and seven stars out full-flare!
Tab, help and tell! I'm hoarse. A mug! or – no, a prayer!   110
Dip for one out of the Book! Who wrote it in the Jail
– He plied his pen unhelped by beer, sirs, I'll be bail!

'I've got my second wind. In trundles she – that's Tab.
"Why, Gammer, what's come now, that – bobbing like a crab
On Yule-tide bowl – your head's a-work and both your eyes
Break loose? Afeard, you fool? As if the dead can rise!
Say – Bagman Dick was found last May with fuddling-cap
Stuffed in his mouth: to choke's a natural mishap!"
"Gaffer, be – blessed," cries she, "and Bagman Dick as
    well!

120 I, you, and he are damned: this Public is our hell:
We live in fire: live coals don't feel! – once quenched, they
    learn –
Cinders do, to what dust they moulder while they burn!"

'"If you don't speak straight out," says I – belike I swore –
"A knobstick, well you know the taste of, shall, once more,
Teach you to talk, my maid!" She ups with such a face,
Heart sunk inside me. "Well, pad on, my prate-apace!"

'"I've been about those laces we need for . . . never mind!
If henceforth they tie hands, 'tis mine they'll have to bind.
You know who makes them best – the Tinker in our cage,

130 Pulled-up for gospelling, twelve years ago: no age
To try another trade, – yet, so he scorned to take
Money he did not earn, he taught himself the make
Of laces, tagged and tough – Dick Bagman found them so!
Good customers were we! Well, last week, you must know,
His girl, – the blind young chit, who hawks about his wares, –
She takes it in her head to come no more – such airs
These hussies have! Yet, since we need a stoutish lace, –
'I'll to the gaol-bird father, abuse her to his face!'
So, first I filled a jug to give me heart, and then,

140 Primed to the proper pitch, I posted to their den –
Patmore – they style their prison! I tip the turnkey, catch
My heart up, fix my face, and fearless lift the latch –
Both arms a-kimbo, in bounce with a good round oath
Ready for rapping out: no 'Lawks' nor 'By my troth!'

'"There sat my man, the father. He looked up: what one feels
When heart that leapt to mouth drops down again to heels!

He raised his hand . . . Hast seen, when drinking out the
   night,
And in, the day, earth grow another something quite
Under the sun's first stare? I stood a very stone.

'"'Woman!' (a fiery tear he put in every tone),   150
'How should my child frequent your house where lust is sport,
Violence – trade? Too true! I trust no vague report.
Her angel's hand, which stops the sight of sin, leaves clear
The other gate of sense, lets outrage through the ear.
What has she heard! – which, heard shall never be again.
Better lack food than feast, a Dives in the – wain
Or reign or train – of Charles!' (His language was not ours:
'Tis my belief, God spoke: no tinker has such powers).
'Bread, only bread they bring – my laces: if we broke
Your lump of leavened sin, the loaf's first crumb would   160
   choke!'

'"Down on my marrow-bones! Then all at once rose he:
His brown hair burst a-spread, his eyes were suns to see:
Up went his hands: 'Through flesh, I reach, I read thy soul!
So may some stricken tree look blasted, bough and bole,
Champed by the fire-tooth, charred without, and yet,
   thrice-bound
With dreriment about, within may life be found,
A prisoned power to branch and blossom as before,
Could but the gardener cleave the cloister, reach the core,
Loosen the vital sap: yet where shall help be found?
Who says "How save it?" – nor "Why cumbers it the ground?" 170
Woman, that tree art thou! All sloughed about with scurf,
Thy stag-horns fright the sky, thy snake-roots sting the turf!
Drunkenness, wantonness, theft, murder gnash and gnarl
Thine outward, case thy soul with coating like the marle
Satan stamps flat upon each head beneath his hoof!
And how deliver such? The strong men keep aloof,
Lover and friend stand far, the mocking ones pass by,
Tophet gapes wide for prey: lost soul, despair and die!
What then? "Look unto me and be ye saved!" saith God:
"I strike the rock, outstreats the life-stream at my rod!   180

Be your sins scarlet, wool shall they seem like, – although
As crimson red, yet turn white as the driven snow!"'

'"There, there, there! All I seem to somehow understand
Is – that, if I reached home, 'twas through the guiding hand
Of his blind girl which led and led me through the streets
And out of town and up to door again. What greets
First thing my eye, as limbs recover from their swoon?
A book – this Book she gave at parting. 'Father's boon –
The Book he wrote: it reads as if he spoke himself:
190 He cannot preach in bonds, so, – take it down from shelf
When you want counsel, – think you hear his very voice!'

'"Wicked dear Husband, first despair and then rejoice!
Dear wicked Husband, waste no tick of moment more,
Be saved like me, bald trunk! There's greenness yet at core,
Sap under slough! Read, read!"

                               'Let me take breath, my lords!
I'd like to know, are these – hers, mine, or Bunyan's words?
I'm 'wildered – scarce with drink, – nowise with drink alone!
You'll say, with heat: but heat's no stuff to split a stone
Like this black boulder – this flint heart of mine: the Book –
200 That dealt the crashing blow! Sirs, here's the fist that shook
His beard till Wrestler Jem howled like a just-lugged bear!
You had brained me with a feather: at once I grew aware
Christmas was meant for me. A burden at your back,
Good Master Christmas? Nay, – yours was that Joseph's sack,
– Or whose it was, – which held the cup, – compared with
    mine!
Robbery loads my loins, perjury cracks my chine,
Adultery . . . nay, Tab, you pitched me as I flung!
One word, I'll up with fist . . . No, sweet spouse, hold your
    tongue!

'I'm hasting to the end. The Book, sirs – take and read!
210 You have my history in a nutshell, – ay, indeed!
It must off, my burden! See, – slack straps and into pit,
Roll, reach the bottom, rest, rot there – a plague on it!
For a mountain's sure to fall and bury Bedford Town,

"Destruction" – that's the name, and fire shall burn it down!
O 'scape the wrath in time! Time's now, if not too late.
How can I pilgrimage up to the wicket-gate?
Next comes Despond the slough: not that I fear to pull
Through mud, and dry my clothes at brave House Beautiful –
But it's late in the day, I reckon: had I left years ago
Town, wife, and children dear . . . Well, Christmas did, you   220
    know! –
Soon I had met in the valley and tried my cudgel's strength
On the enemy horned and winged, a-straddle across its
    length!
Have at his horns, thwick – thwack: they snap, see! Hoof and
    hoof –
Bang, break the fetlock-bones! For love's sake, keep aloof
Angels! I'm man and match, – this cudgel for my flail, –
To thresh him, hoofs and horns, bat's wing and serpent's tail!
A chance gone by! But then, what else does Hopeful ding
Into the deafest ear except – hope, hope's the thing?
Too late i' the day for me to thrid the windings: but
There's still a way to win the race by death's short cut!   230
Did Master Faithful need climb the Delightful Mounts?
No, straight to Vanity Fair, – a fair, by all accounts,
Such as is held outside, – lords, ladies, grand and gay, –
Says he in the face of them, just what you hear me say.
And the Judges brought him in guilty, and brought him out
To die in the market-place – Saint Peter's Green's about
The same thing: there they flogged, flayed, buffeted, lanced
    with knives,
Pricked him with swords, – I'll swear, he'd full a cat's nine
    lives, –
So to his end at last came Faithful, – ha, ha, he!
Who holds the highest card? for there stands hid, you see,   240
Behind the rabble-rout, a chariot, pair and all:
He's in, he's off, he's up, through clouds, at trumpet-call,
Carried the nearest way to Heaven-gate! Odds my life –
Has nobody a sword to spare? not even a knife?
Then hang me, draw and quarter! Tab – do the same by her!
O Master Worldly-Wiseman . . . that's Master Interpreter,

Take the will, not the deed! Our gibbet's handy close:
Forestall Last Judgement-Day! Be kindly, not morose!
There wants no earthly judge-and-jurying: here we stand –
250 Sentence our guilty selves: so, hang us out of hand!
Make haste for pity's sake! A single moment's loss
Means – Satan's lord once more: his whisper shoots across
All singing in my heart, all praying in my brain,
"It comes of heat and beer!" – hark how he guffaws plain!
"Tomorrow you'll wake bright, and, in a safe skin, hug
Your sound selves, Tab and you, over a foaming jug!
You've had such qualms before, time out of mind!" He's right!
Did not we kick and cuff and curse away, that night
When home we blindly reeled and left poor humpback Joe
260 I' the lurch to pay for what . . . somebody did, you know!
Both of us maundered then "Lame humpback, – never more
Will he come limping, drain his tankard at our door!
He'll swing, while – somebody . . ." Says Tab, "No, for I'll
        peach!"
"I'm for you, Tab," cries I, "there's rope enough for each!"
So blubbered we, and bussed, and went to bed upon
The grace of Tab's good thought: by morning, all was gone!
We laughed – "What's life to him, a cripple of no account?"
Oh, waves increase around – I feel them mount and mount!
Hang us! Tomorrow brings Tom Bearward with his bears:
270 One new black-muzzled brute beats Sackerson, he swears:
(Sackerson, for my money!) And, baiting o'er, the Brawl
They lead on Turner's Patch, – lads, lasses, up tails all, –
I'm i' the thick o' the throng! That means the Iron Cage,
– Means the Lost Man inside! Where's hope for such as wage
War against light? Light's left, light's here, I hold light still,
So does Tab – make but haste to hang us both! You will?'

I promise, when he stopped you might have heard a mouse
Squeak, such a death-like hush sealed up the old Mote
        House.
But when the mass of man sank meek upon his knees,
280 While Tab, alongside, wheezed a hoarse 'Do hang us, please!'
Why, then the waters rose, no eye but ran with tears,

Hearts heaved, heads thumped, until, paying all past arrears
Of pity and sorrow, at last a regular scream outbroke
Of triumph, joy and praise.

                My Lord Chief Justice spoke,
First mopping brow and cheek, where still, for one that
   budged,
Another bead broke fresh: 'What Judge, that ever judged
Since first the world began, judged such a case as this?
Why, Master Bratts, long since, folk smelt you out, I wis!
I had my doubts, i' faith, each time you played the fox
Convicting geese of crime in yonder witness-box –   290
Yea, much did I misdoubt, the thief that stole her eggs
Was hardly goosey's self at Reynard's game, i' feggs!
Yet thus much was to praise – you spoke to point, direct –
Swore you heard, saw the theft: no jury could suspect –
Dared to suspect, – I'll say, – a spot in white so clear:
Goosey was throttled, true: but thereof godly fear
Came of example set, much as our laws intend;
And, though a fox confessed, you proved the Judge's friend.
What if I had my doubts? Suppose I gave them breath,
Brought you to bar: what work to do, ere "Guilty, Death," –   300
Had paid our pains! What heaps of witnesses to drag
From holes and corners, paid from out the County's bag!
Trial three dog-days long! *Amicus Curiae* – that's
Your title, no dispute – truth-telling Master Bratts!
Thank you, too, Mistress Tab! Why doubt one word you say?
Hanging you both deserve, hanged both shall be this day!
The tinker needs must be a proper man. I've heard
He lies in Gaol long since: if Quality's good word
Warrants me letting loose, – some householder, I mean –
Freeholder, better still, – I don't say but – between   310
Now and next Sessions . . . Well! Consider of his case,
I promise to, at least: we owe him so much grace.
Not that – no, God forbid! – I lean to think, as you,
The grace that such repent is any goal-bird's due:
I rather see the fruit of twelve years' pious reign –
Astraea Redux, Charles restored his rights again!

– Of which, another time! I somehow feel a peace
Stealing across the world. May deeds like this increase!
So, Master Sheriff, stay that sentence I pronounced
320 On those two dozen odd: deserving to be trounced
Soundly, and yet . . . well, well, at all events dispatch
This pair of – shall I say, sinner-saints? – ere we catch
Their gaol-distemper too. Stop tears, or I'll indite
All weeping Bedfordshire for turning Bunyanite!'

So, forms were galloped through. If Justice, on the spur,
Proved somewhat expeditious, would Quality demur?
And happily hanged were they, – why lengthen out my tale? –
Where Bunyan's Statue stands facing where stood his Jail.

Clive

I and Clive were friends – and why not? Friends! I think you
   laugh, my lad.
Clive it was gave England India, while your father gives – egad,
England nothing but the graceless boy who lures him on to
   speak –
'Well, Sir, you and Clive were comrades –' with a tongue
   thrust in your cheek!
Very true: in my eyes, your eyes, all the world's eyes, Clive was
   man,
I was, am and ever shall be – mouse, nay, mouse of all its clan
Sorriest sample, if you take the kitchen's estimate for fame;
While the man Clive – he fought Plassy, spoiled the clever
   foreign game,
Conquered and annexed and Englished!

                        Never mind! As o'er my punch
(You away) I sit of evenings, – silence, save for biscuit-crunch,   10
Black, unbroken, – thought grows busy, thrids each pathway of
   old years,
Notes this forthright, that meander, till the long-past life
   appears
Like an outspread map of country plodded through, each mile
   and rood,
Once, and well remembered still: I'm startled in my solitude
Ever and anon by – what's the sudden mocking light that
   breaks
On me as I slap the table till no rummer-glass but shakes
While I ask – aloud, I do believe, God help me! – 'Was it
   thus?
Can it be that so I faltered, stopped when just one step for
   us –'

(Us, – you were not born, I grant, but surely some day born
    would be)

20 '– One bold step had gained a province' (figurative talk, you
    see)

'Got no end of wealth and honour, – yet I stood stock still no
    less?'

– 'For I was not Clive,' you comment: but it needs no Clive to
    guess

Wealth were handy, honour ticklish, did no writing on the wall

Warn me 'Trespasser, 'ware man-traps!' Him who braves that
    notice – call

Hero! none of such heroics suit myself who read plain words,

Doff my hat, and leap no barrier. Scripture says the land's the
    Lord's:

Louts then – what avail the thousand, noisy in a smock-
    frocked ring,

All-agog to have me trespass, clear the fence, be Clive their
    king?

Higher warrant must you show me ere I set one foot before

30 T'other in that dark direction, though I stand for evermore

Poor as Job and meek as Moses. Evermore? No! By-and-by

Job grows rich and Moses valiant, Clive turns out less wise
    than I.

Don't object 'Why call him friend, then?' Power is power, my
    boy, and still

Marks a man, – God's gift magnific, exercised for good or
    ill.

You've your boot now on my hearth-rug, tread what was a
    tiger's skin:

Rarely such a royal monster as I lodged the bullet in!

True, he murdered half a village, so his own death came to
    pass;

Still, for size and beauty, cunning, courage – ah, the brute he
    was!

Why, that Clive, – that youth, that greenhorn, that quill-
    driving clerk, in fine, –

40 He sustained a siege in Arcot . . . But the world knows! Pass
    the wine.

Where did I break off at? How bring Clive in? Oh, you
    mentioned 'fear'!
Just so: and, said I, that minds me of a story you shall hear.

We were friends then, Clive and I: so, when the clouds, about
    the orb
Late supreme, encroaching slowly, surely, threatened to
    absorb
Ray by ray its noontide brilliance, – friendship might, with
    steadier eye
Drawing near, bear what had burned else, now no blaze – all
    majesty.
Too much bee's-wing floats my figure? Well, suppose a
    castle's new:
None presume to climb its ramparts, none find foothold sure
    for shoe
'Twixt those squares and squares of granite plating the
    impervious pile
As his scale-mail's warty iron cuirasses a crocodile.   50
Reels that castle thunder-smitten, storm-dismantled? From
    without
Scrambling up by crack and crevice, every cockney prates
    about
Towers – the heap he kicks now! turrets – just the measure of
    his cane!
Will that do? Observe moreover – (same similitude again) –
Such a castle seldom crumbles by sheer stress of cannonade:
'Tis when foes are foiled and fighting's finished that vile rains
    invade,
Grass o'ergrows, o'ergrows till night-birds congregating find
    no holes
Fit to build in like the topmost sockets made for banner-poles.
So Clive crumbled slow in London – crashed at last.

                            A week before,
Dining with him, – after trying churchyard-chat of days of   60
    yore, –
Both of us stopped, tired as tombstones, head-piece,
    foot-piece, when they lean

Each to other, drowsed in fog-smoke, o'er a coffined Past
    between.
As I saw his head sink heavy, guessed the soul's
    extinguishment
By the glazing eyeball, noticed how the furtive fingers went
Where a drug-box skulked behind the honest liquor, – 'One
    more throw
Try for Clive!' thought I: 'Let's venture some good rattling
    question!' So –
'Come, Clive, tell us' – out I blurted – 'what to tell in turn,
    years hence,
When my boy – suppose I have one – asks me on what
    evidence
I maintain my friend of Plassy proved a warrior every whit
70 Worth your Alexanders, Caesars, Marlboroughs and – what
    said Pitt? –
Frederick the Fierce himself! "Clive told me once" – I want to
    say –
"Which feat out of all those famous doings bore the bell away
– In his own calm estimation, mark you, not the mob's rough
    guess –
Which stood foremost as evincing what Clive called
    courageousness!"
Come! what moment of the minute, what speck-centre in the
    wide
Circle of the action saw your mortal fairly deified?
(Let alone that filthy sleep-stuff, swallow bold this wholesome
    Port!)
If a friend has leave to question, – when were you most brave,
    in short?'

Up he arched his brows o' the instant – formidably Clive again.
80 'When was I most brave? I'd answer, were the instance half as
    plain
As another instance that's a brain-lodged crystal – curse it! –
    here
Freezing when my memory touches – ugh! – the time I felt
    most fear.

Ugh! I cannot say for certain if I showed fear – anyhow,
Fear I felt, and, very likely, shuddered, since I shiver now.'

'Fear!' smiled I. 'Well, that's the rarer: that's a specimen to
   seek,
Ticket up in one's museum, *Mind-Freaks, Lord Clive's Fear,
   Unique!*'

Down his brows dropped. On the table painfully he pored as
   though
Tracing, in the stains and streaks there, thoughts encrusted
   long ago.
When he spoke 'twas like a lawyer reading word by word some
   will,
Some blind jungle of a statement, – beating on and on until   90
Out there leaps fierce life to fight with.

                        'This fell in my factor-days.
Desk-drudge, slaving at Saint David's, one must game, or
   drink, or craze.
I chose gaming: and, – because your high-flown gamesters
   hardly take
Umbrage at a factor's elbow if the factor pays his stake, –
I was winked at in a circle where the company was choice,
Captain This and Major That, men high of colour, loud of
   voice,
Yet indulgent, condescending to the modest juvenile
Who not merely risked but lost his hard-earned guineas with a
   smile.

'Down I sat to cards, one evening, – had for my antagonist
Somebody whose name's a secret – you'll know why – so, if   100
   you list,
Call him Cock o' the Walk, my scarlet son of Mars from head
   to heel!
Play commenced: and, whether Cocky fancied that a clerk
   must feel
Quite sufficient honour came of bending over one green baize,
I the scribe with him the warrior, – guessed no penman dared
   to raise

Shadow of objection should the honour stay but playing end
More or less abruptly, – whether disinclined he grew to spend
Practice strictly scientific on a booby born to stare
At – not ask of – lace-and-ruffles if the hand they hide plays
    fair, –
Anyhow, I marked a movement when he bade me "Cut!"

                                                'I rose.
110 "Such the new manoeuvre, Captain? I'm a novice: knowledge
        grows.
    What, you force a card, you cheat, Sir?"

                                'Never did a thunder-clap
Cause emotion, startle Thyrsis locked with Chloe in his lap,
As my word and gesture (down I flung my cards to join the
    pack)
Fired the man of arms, whose visage, simply red before,
    turned black.

'When he found his voice, he stammered "That expression
    once again!"

'"Well, you forced a card and cheated!"

                                '"Possibly a factor's brain,
Busied with his all-important balance of accounts, may deem
Weighing words superfluous trouble: *cheat* to clerkly ears may
    seem
Just the joke for friends to venture: but we are not friends, you
    see!
120 When a gentleman is joked with, – if he's good at repartee,
He rejoins, as do I – Sirrah, on your knees, withdraw in full!
Beg my pardon, or be sure a kindly bullet through your skull
Lets in light and teaches manners to what brain it finds!
    Choose quick –
Have your life snuffed out or, kneeling, pray me trim yon
    candle-wick!"

'"Well, you cheated!"

                'Then outbroke a howl from all the friends around.

276

To his feet sprang each in fury, fists were clenched and teeth
  were ground.
"End it! no time like the present! Captain, yours were our
  disgrace!
No delay, begin and finish! Stand back, leave the pair a space!
Let civilians be instructed: henceforth simply ply the pen,
Fly the sword! This clerk's no swordsman? Suit him with a   130
  pistol, then!
Even odds! A dozen paces 'twixt the most and least expert
Make a dwarf a giant's equal: nay, the dwarf, if he's alert,
Likelier hits the broader target!"

                                 'Up we stood accordingly.
As they handed me the weapon, such was my soul's thirst to
  try
Then and there conclusions with this bully, tread on and
  stamp out
Every spark of his existence, that, – crept close to, curled
  about
By that toying tempting teasing fool-forefinger's middle
  joint, –
Don't you guess? – the trigger yielded. Gone my chance! and
  at the point
Of such prime success moreover: scarce an inch above his
  head
Went my ball to hit the wainscot. He was living, I was dead.   140

'Up he marched in flaming triumph – 'twas his right, mind! –
  up, within
Just an arm's length. "Now, my clerkling," chuckled Cocky
  with a grin
As the levelled piece quite touched me, "Now, Sir Counting-
  House, repeat
That expression which I told you proved bad manners! Did I
  cheat?"

'"Cheat you did, you knew you cheated, and, this moment,
  know as well.
As for me, my homely breeding bids you – fire and go to Hell!"

277

'Twice the muzzle touched my forehead. Heavy barrel,
    flurried wrist,
Either spoils a steady lifting. Thrice: then, "Laugh at Hell who
    list,
I can't! God's no fable either. Did this boy's eye wink once?
    No!
150 There's no standing him and Hell and God all three against
    me, – so,
I did cheat!"

                'And down he threw the pistol, out rushed – by the
    door
Possibly, but, as for knowledge if by chimney, roof or floor,
He effected disappearance – I'll engage no glance was sent
That way by a single starer, such a blank astonishment
Swallowed up their senses: as for speaking – mute they stood
    as mice.

'Mute not long, though! Such reaction, such a hubbub in a
    trice!
"Rogue and rascal! Who'd have thought it? What's to be
    expected next,
When His Majesty's Commission serves a sharper as pretext
For . . . But where's the need of wasting time now? Naught
    requires delay:
160 Punishment the Service cries for: let disgrace be wiped away
Publicly, in good broad daylight! Resignation? No, indeed
Drum and fife must play the Rogue's March, rank and file be
    free to speed
Tardy marching on the rogue's part by appliance in the rear
– Kicks administered shall right this wronged civilian, – never
    fear,
Mister Clive, for – though a clerk – you bore yourself –
    suppose we say –
Just as would beseem a soldier!"

                '"Gentlemen, attention – pray!
First, one word!"

             'I passed each speaker severally in review.

When I had precise their number, names and styles, and fully
  knew
Over whom my supervision thenceforth must extend, – why,
  then –
''Some five minutes since, my life lay – as you all saw,   170
  gentlemen –
At the mercy of your friend there. Not a single voice was raised
In arrest of judgement, not one tongue – before my powder
  blazed –
Ventured 'Can it be the youngster blundered, really seemed to
  mark
Some irregular proceeding? We conjecture in the dark,
Guess at random, – still, for sake of fair play – what if for a
  freak,
In a fit of absence, – such things have been! – if our friend
  proved weak
– What's the phrase? – corrected fortune! Look into the case,
  at least!'
Who dared interpose between the altar's victim and the priest?
Yet he spared me! You eleven! Whosoever, all or each,
To the disadvantage of the man who spared me, utters speech   180
– To his face, behind his back, – that speaker has to do with
  me:
Me who promise, if positions change and mine the chance
  should be,
Not to imitate your friend and waive advantage!''

                              'Twenty-five
Years ago this matter happened: and 'tis certain,' added Clive,
'Never, to my knowledge, did Sir Cocky have a single breath
Breathed against him: lips were closed throughout his life, or
  since his death,
For if he be dead or living I can tell no more than you.
All I know is – Cocky had one chance more; how he used it, –
  grew
Out of such unlucky habits, or relapsed, and back again
Brought the late-ejected devil with a score more in his train, – 190
That's for you to judge. Reprieval I procured, at any rate.

Ugh – the memory of that minute's fear makes gooseflesh rise!
    Why prate
Longer? You've my story, there's your instance: fear I did, you
    see!'

'Well' – I hardly kept from laughing – 'if I see it, thanks must
    be
Wholly to your Lordship's candour. Not that – in a common
    case –
When a bully caught at cheating thrusts a pistol in one's face,
I should underrate, believe me, such a trial to the nerve!
'Tis no joke, at one-and-twenty, for a youth to stand nor
    swerve.
Fear I naturally look for – unless, of all men alive,
200 I am forced to make exception when I come to Robert Clive.
Since at Arcot, Plassy, elsewhere, he and death – the whole
    world knows –
Came to somewhat closer quarters.'

                                Quarters? Had we come to blows,
Clive and I, you had not wondered – up he sprang so, out he
    rapped
Such a round of oaths – no matter! I'll endeavour to adapt
To our modern usage words he – well, 'twas friendly licence –
    flung
At me like so many fire-balls, fast as he could wag his tongue.

'You – a soldier? You – at Plassy? Yours the faculty to nick
Instantaneously occasion when your foe, if lightning-quick,
– At his mercy, at his malice, – has you, through some stupid
    inch
210 Undefended in your bulwark? Thus laid open, – not to
    flinch
– That needs courage, you'll concede me. Then, look here!
    Suppose the man,
Checking his advance, his weapon still extended, not a span
Distant from my temple, – curse him! – quietly had bade me
    "There!
Keep your life, calumniator! – worthless life I freely spare:

Mine you freely would have taken – murdered me and my
    good fame
Both at once – and all the better! Go, and thank your own bad
    aim
Which permits me to forgive you!" What if, with such words as
    these,
He had cast away his weapon? How should I have borne me,
    please?
Nay, I'll spare you pains and tell you. This, and only this,
    remained –

Pick his weapon up and use it on myself. I so had gained   220
Sleep the earlier, leaving England probably to pay on still
Rent and taxes for half India, tenant at the Frenchman's will.'

'Such the turn,' said I, 'the matter takes with you? Then I
    abate
– No, by not one jot nor tittle, – of your act my estimate.
Fear – I wish I could detect there: courage fronts me, plain
    enough –
Call it desperation, madness – never mind! for here's in rough
Why, had mine been such a trial, fear had overcome disgrace.
True, disgrace were hard to bear: but such a rush against
    God's face
– None of that for me, Lord Plassy, since I go to church at
    times,
Say the creed my mother taught me! Many years in foreign   230
    climes
Rub some marks away – not all, though! We poor sinners
    reach life's brink,
Overlook what rolls beneath it, recklessly enough, but think
There's advantage in what's left us – ground to stand on, time
    to call
"Lord, have mercy!" ere we topple over – do not leap, that's
    all!'

Oh, he made no answer, – re-absorbed into his cloud. I caught
Something like 'Yes – courage: only fools will call it fear.'

                                     If aught

Comfort you, my great unhappy hero Clive, in that I heard,
Next week, how your own hand dealt you doom, and uttered
   just the word
'Fearfully courageous!' – this, be sure, and nothing else I
   groaned.
240 I'm no Clive, nor parson either: Clive's worst deed – we'll
   hope condoned.

[Wanting is – what?]

    Wanting is – what?
    Summer redundant,
    Blueness abundant,
    – Where is the blot?
Beamy the world, yet a blank all the same,
– Framework which waits for a picture to frame:
What of the leafage, what of the flower?
Roses embowering with naught they embower!
Come then, complete incompletion, O comer,
Pant through the blueness, perfect the summer!   10
    Breathe but one breath
    Rose-beauty above,
    And all that was death
    Grows life, grows love,
      Grows love!

Donald

'Will you hear my story also,
   – Huge Sport, brave adventure in plenty?'
The boys were a band from Oxford,
   The oldest of whom was twenty.

The bothy we held carouse in
   Was bright with fire and candle;
Tale followed tale like a merry-go-round
   Whereof Sport turned the handle.

In our eyes and noses – turf-smoke:
10   In our ears a tune from the trivet,
Whence 'Boiling, boiling,' the kettle sang,
   'And ready for fresh Glenlivet.'

So, feat capped feat, with a vengeance:
   Truths, though, – the lads were loyal:
'Grouse, five score brace to the bag!
   Deer, ten hours' stalk of the Royal!'

Of boasting, not one bit, boys!
   Only there seemed to settle
Somehow above your curly heads,
20   – Plain through the singing kettle,

Palpable through the cloud,
   As each new-puffed Havana
Rewarded the teller's well-told tale, –
   This vaunt 'To Sport – Hosanna!

'Hunt, fish, shoot,
   Would a man fulfil life's duty!
Not to the bodily frame alone
   Does Sport give strength and beauty,

'But character gains in – courage?
 Ay, Sir, and much beside it!   30
You don't sport, more's the pity:
 You soon would find, if you tried it,

'Good sportsman means good fellow,
 Sound-hearted he, to the centre;
Your mealy-mouthed mild milksops
 – There's where the rot can enter!

'There's where the dirt will breed,
 The shabbiness Sport would banish!
Oh no, Sir, no! In your honoured case
 All such objections vanish.   40

' 'Tis known how hard you studied:
 A Double-First – what, the jigger!
Give me but half your Latin and Greek,
 I'll never again touch trigger!

'Still, tastes are tastes, allow me!
 Allow, too, where there's keenness
For Sport, there's little likelihood
 Of a man's displaying meanness!'

So, put on my mettle, I interposed.
 'Will you hear my story?' quoth I. 50
'Never mind how long since it happed,
 I sat, as we sit, in a bothy;

'With as merry a band of mates, too,
 Undergrads all on a level:
(One's a Bishop, one's gone to the Bench,
 And one's gone – well, to the Devil.)

'When, lo, a scratching and tapping!
 In hobbled a ghastly visitor.
Listen to just what he told us himself
 – No need of our playing inquisitor!' 60

———————

Do you happen to know in Ross-shire
    Mount . . . Ben . . . but the name scarce matters:
Of the naked fact I am sure enough,
    Though I clothe it in rags and tatters.

You may recognize Ben by description;
    Behind him – a moor's immenseness:
Up goes the middle mount of a range,
    Fringed with its firs in denseness.

Rimming the edge, its fir-fringe, mind!
70   For an edge there is, though narrow;
From end to end of the range, a stripe
    Of path runs straight as an arrow.

And the mountaineer who takes that path
    Saves himself miles of journey
He has to plod if he crosses the moor
    Through heather, peat and burnie.

But a mountaineer he needs must be,
    For, look you, right in the middle
Projects bluff Ben – with an end in *ich* –
80   Why planted there, is a riddle:

Since all Ben's brothers little and big
    Keep rank, set shoulder to shoulder,
And only this burliest out must bulge
    Till it seems – to the beholder

From down in the gully, – as if Ben's breast,
    To a sudden spike diminished,
Would signify to the boldest foot
    'All further passage finished!'

Yet the mountaineer who sidles on
90   And on to the very bending,
Discovers, if heart and brain be proof,
    No necessary ending.

Foot up, foot down, to the turn abrupt
   Having trod, he, there arriving,
Finds – what he took for a point was breadth,
   A mercy of Nature's contriving.

So, he rounds what, when 'tis reached, proves straight,
   From one side gains the other:
The wee path widens – resume the march,
   And he foils you, Ben my brother!   100

But Donald – (that name, I hope, will do) –
   I wrong him if I call 'foiling'
The tramp of the callant, whistling the while
   As blithe as our kettle's boiling.

He had dared the danger from boyhood up,
   And now, – when perchance was waiting
A lass at the brig below, – 'twixt mount
   And moor would he stand debating?

Moreover this Donald was twenty-five,
   A glory of bone and muscle: 110
Did a fiend dispute the right of way,
   Donald would try a tussle.

Lightsomely marched he out of the broad
   On to the narrow and narrow;
A step more, rounding the angular rock,
   Reached the front straight as an arrow.

He stepped it, safe on the ledge he stood,
   When – whom found he full-facing?
What fellow in courage and wariness too,
   Had scouted ignoble pacing,   120

And left low safety to timid mates,
   And made for the dread dear danger,
And gained the height where – who could guess
   He could meet with a rival ranger?

'Twas a gold-red stag that stood and stared,
   Gigantic and magnific,
By the wonder – ay, and the peril – struck
   Intelligent and pacific:

For a red deer is no fallow deer
130   Grown cowardly through park-feeding;
He batters you like a thunderbolt
   If you brave his haunts unheeding.

I doubt he could hardly perform *volte-face*
   Had valour advised discretion:
You may walk on a rope, but to turn on a rope
   No Blondin makes profession.

Yet Donald must turn, would pride permit,
   Though pride ill brooks retiring:
Each eyed each – mute man, motionless beast –
140   Less fearing than admiring.

These are the moments when quite new sense,
   To meet some need as novel,
Springs up in the brain: it inspired resource:
   – 'Nor advance nor retreat but – grovel!'

And slowly, surely, never a whit
   Relaxing the steady tension
Of eye-stare which binds man to beast, –
   By an inch and inch declension,

Sank Donald sidewise down and down:
150   Till flat, breast upwards, lying
At his six-foot length, no corpse more still,
   – 'If he cross me! The trick's worth trying.'

Minutes were an eternity;
   But a new sense was created
In the stag's brain too; he resolves! Slow, sure,
   With eye-stare unabated,

Feelingly he extends a foot
   Which tastes the way ere it touches
Earth's solid and just escapes man's soft,
   Nor hold of the same unclutches   160

Till its fellow foot, light as a feather whisk,
   Lands itself no less finely:
So a mother removes a fly from the face
   Of her babe asleep supinely.

And now 'tis the haunch and hind foot's turn
   – That's hard: can the beast quite raise it?
Yes, traversing half the prostrate length,
   His hoof-tip does not graze it.

Just one more lift! But Donald, you see,
   Was sportsman first, man after: 170
A fancy lightened his caution through,
   – He well-nigh broke into laughter.

'It were nothing short of a miracle!
   Unrivalled, unexampled –
All sporting feats with this feat matched
   Were down and dead and trampled!'

The last of the legs as tenderly
   Follows the rest: or never
Or now is the time! His knife in reach,
   And his right-hand loose – how clever!   180

For this can stab up the stomach's soft,
   While the left-hand grasps the pastern.
A rise on the elbow, and – now's the time
   Or never: this turn's the last turn!

I shall dare to place myself by God
   Who scanned – for He does – each feature
Of the face thrown up in appeal to Him
   By the agonizing creature.

Nay, I hear plain words: 'Thy gift brings this!'
190   Up he sprang, back he staggered,
Over he fell, and with him our friend
    – At following game no laggard.

Yet he was not dead when they picked next day
    From the gully's depth the wreck of him;
His fall had been stayed by the stag beneath
    Who cushioned and saved the neck of him.

But the rest of his body – why, doctors said,
    Whatever could break was broken;
Legs, arms, ribs, all of him looked like a toast
200   In a tumbler of port-wine soaken.

'That your life is left you, thank the stag!'
    Said they when – the slow cure ended –
They opened the hospital door, and thence
    – Strapped, spliced, main fractures mended,

And minor damage left wisely alone, –
    Like an old shoe clouted and cobbled,
Out – what went in a Goliath well-nigh, –
    Some half of a David hobbled.

'You must ask an alms from house to house:
210   Sell the stag's head for a bracket,
With its grand twelve tines – I'd buy it myself –
    And use the skin for a jacket!'

He was wiser, made both head and hide
    His win-penny: hands and knees on,
Would manage to crawl – poor crab – by the roads
    In the misty stalking-season.

And if he discovered a bothy like this,
    Why, harvest was sure: folk listened.
He told his tale to the lovers of Sport:
220   Lips twitched, cheeks glowed, eyes glistened.

And when he had come to the close, and spread
    His spoils for the gazers' wonder,
With 'Gentlemen, here's the skull of the stag
    I was over, thank God, not under!' –

The company broke out in applause;
    'By Jingo, a lucky cripple!
Have a munch of grouse and a hunk of bread,
    And a tug, besides, at our tipple!'

And 'There's my pay for your pluck!' cried This,
    'And mine for your jolly story!'   230
Cried That, while T'other – but he was drunk –
    Hiccupped 'A trump, a Tory!'

I hope I gave twice as much as the rest;
    For, as Homer would say, 'within gate
Though teeth kept tongue,' my whole soul growled
    'Rightly rewarded, – Ingrate!'

Never the Time and the Place

Never the time and the place
    And the loved one all together!
This path – how soft to pace!
    This May – what magic weather!
Where is the loved one's face?
In a dream that loved one's face meets mine,
    But the house is narrow, the place is bleak
Where, outside, rain and wind combine
    With a furtive ear, if I strive to speak,
10   With a hostile eye at my flushing cheek,
With a malice that marks each word, each sign!
O enemy sly and serpentine,
    Uncoil thee from the waking man!
        Do I hold the Past
        Thus firm and fast
    Yet doubt if the Future hold I can?
    This path so soft to pace shall lead
    Through the magic of May to herself indeed!
Or narrow if needs the house must be,
20   Outside are the storms and strangers: we –
    Oh, close, safe, warm sleep I and she,
    – I and she!

The Names

Shakespeare! – to such name's sounding, what succeeds
   Fitly as silence? Falter forth the spell, –
   Act follows word, the speaker knows full well,
Nor tampers with its magic more than needs.
Two names there are: That which the Hebrew reads
   With his soul only; if from lips it fell,
   Echo, back thundered by earth, heaven and hell,
Would own 'Thou didst create us!' Naught impedes
We voice the other name, man's most of might,
   Awesomely, lovingly: let awe and love   10
Mutely await their working, leave to sight
   All of the issue as – below – above –
   Shakespeare's creation rises: one remove,
Though dread – this finite from that infinite.

Now

Out of your whole life give but a moment!
All of your life that has gone before,
All to come after it, – so you ignore,
So you make perfect the present, – condense,
In a rapture of rage, for perfection's endowment,
Thought and feeling and soul and sense –
Merged in a moment which gives me at last
You around me for once, you beneath me, above me –
Me – sure that despite of time future, time past, –
10 This tick of our life-time's one moment you love me!
How long such suspension may linger? Ah, Sweet –
The moment eternal – just that and no more –
When ecstasy's utmost we clutch at the core
While cheeks burn, arms open, eyes shut and lips meet!

Beatrice Signorini

This strange thing happened to a painter once:
Viterbo boasts the man among her sons
Of note, I seem to think: his ready tool
Picked up its precepts in Cortona's school –
That's Pietro Berretini, whom they call
Cortona, these Italians: greatish-small,
Our painter was his pupil, by repute
His match if not his master absolute,
Though whether he spoiled fresco more or less,
And what's its fortune, scarce repays your guess.   10
Still, for one circumstance, I save his name
– Francesco Romanelli: do the same!
He went to Rome and painted: there he knew
A wonder of a woman painting too –
For she, at least, was no Cortona's drudge:
Witness that ardent fancy-shape – I judge
A semblance of her soul – she called 'Desire'
With starry front for guide, where sits the fire
She left to brighten Buonarroti's house.
If you see Florence, pay that piece your vows,   20
Though blockhead Baldinucci's mind, imbued
With monkish morals, bade folk 'Drape the nude
And stop the scandal!' quoth the record prim
I borrow this of: hang his book and him!
At Rome, then, where these fated ones met first,
The blossom of his life had hardly burst
While hers was blooming at full beauty's stand:
No less Francesco – when half-ripe he scanned
Consummate Artemisia – grew one want
To have her his and make her ministrant   30
With every gift of body and of soul

295

To him. In vain. Her sphery self was whole –
Might only touch his orb at Art's sole point.
Suppose he could persuade her to enjoint
Her life – past, present, future – all in his
At Art's sole point by some explosive kiss
Of love through lips, would love's success defeat
Artistry's haunting curse – the Incomplete?
Artists no doubt they both were, – what beside
40   Was she? who, long had felt heart, soul spread wide
Her life out, knowing much and loving well,
On either side Art's narrow space where fell
Reflection from his own speck: but the germ
Of individual genius – what we term
The very self, the God-gift whence had grown
Heart's life and soul's life, – how make that his own?
Vainly his Art, reflected, smiled in small
On Art's one facet of her ampler ball;
The rest, touch-free, took in, gave back heaven, earth,
50   All where he was not. Hope, well-nigh ere birth
Came to Desire, died off all-unfulfilled.
'What though in Art I stand the abler-skilled,'
(So he conceited: mediocrity
Turns on itself the self-transforming eye)
'If only Art were suing, mine would plead
To purpose: man – by nature I exceed
Woman the bounded: but how much beside
She boasts, would sue in turn and be denied!
Love her? My own wife loves me in a sort
60   That suits us both: she takes the world's report
Of what my work is worth, and, for the rest,
Concedes that, while his consort keeps her nest,
The eagle soars a licensed vagrant, lives
A wide free life which she at least forgives –
Good Beatricé Signorini! Well
And wisely did I choose her. But the spell
To subjugate this Artemisia – where?
She passionless? – she resolute to care
Nowise beyond the plain sufficiency

Of fact that she is she and I am I   70
– Acknowledged arbitrator for us both
In her life as in mine which she were loth
Even to learn the laws of? No, and no,
Twenty times over! Ay, it must be so:
I for myself, alas!'
               Whereon, instead
Of the checked lover's-utterance – why, he said
– Leaning above her easel: 'Flesh is red'
(Or some such just remark) – 'by no means white
As Guido's practice teaches: you are right.'

Then came the better impulse: 'What if pride   80
Were wisely trampled on, whate'er betide?
If I grow hers, not mine – join lives, confuse
Bodies and spirits, gain not her but lose
Myself to Artemisia? That were love!
Of two souls – one must bend, one rule above:
If I crouch under proudly, lord turned slave,
Were it not worthier both than if she gave
Herself – in treason to herself – to me?'

And, all the while, he felt it could not be.
Such love were true love: love that way who can!   90
Someone that's born half woman not whole man:
For man, prescribed man better or man worse,
Why, whether microcosm or universe,
What law prevails alike through great and small,
The world and man – world's miniature we call?
Male is the master. 'That way' – smiled and sighed
Our true male estimator – 'puts her pride
My wife in making me the outlet whence
She learns all Heaven allows: 'tis my pretence
To paint: her lord should do what else but paint?   100
Do I break brushes, cloister me turned saint?
Then, best of all suits sanctity her spouse
Who acts for Heaven, allows and disallows
At pleasure, past appeal, the right, the wrong
In all things. That's my wife's way. But this strong

Confident Artemisia – an adept
In Art does she conceit herself? "Except
In just this instance," tell her, "no one draws
More rigidly observant of the laws
110 Of right design: yet here, – permit me hint, –
If the acromion had a deeper dint,
That shoulder were perfection." What surprise
– Nay scorn, shoots black fire from those startled eyes!
She to be lessoned in design forsooth!
I'm doomed and done for, since I spoke the truth.
Make my own work the subject of dispute –
Fails it of just perfection absolute
Somewhere? Those motors, flexors, – don't I know
Ser Santi, styled "Tirititototo
120 The pencil-prig," might blame them? Yet my wife –
Were he and his nicknamer brought to life,
Tito and Titian, to pronounce again –
Ask her who knows more – I or the great Twain
Our colourist and draughtsman!

       'I help her,
Not she helps me; and neither shall demur
Because my portion is – ' he chose to think –
'Quite other than a woman's: I may drink
At many waters, must repose by none –
Rather arise and fare forth, having done
130 Duty to one new excellence the more,
Abler thereby, though impotent before
So much was gained of knowledge. Best depart
From this last lady I have learned by heart!'

Thus he concluded of himself – resigned
To play the man and master: 'Man boasts mind:
Woman, man's sport calls mistress, to the same
Does body's suit and service. Would she claim
– My placid Beatricé-wife – pretence
Even to blame her lord if, going hence,
140 He wistfully regards one whom – did fate
Concede – he might accept queen, abdicate

298

Kingship because of? – one of no meek sort
But masterful as he: man's match in short?
Oh, there's no secret I were best conceal!
Bicé shall know; and should a stray tear steal
From out the blue eye, stain the rose cheek – bah!
A smile, a word's gay reassurance – ah,
With kissing interspersed, – shall make amends,
Turn pain to pleasure.'
              'What, in truth so ends
Abruptly, do you say, our intercourse?'   150
Next day, asked Artemisia: 'I'll divorce
Husband and wife no longer. Go your ways,
Leave Rome! Viterbo owns no equal, says
The byword, for fair women: you, no doubt,
May boast a paragon all specks without,
Using the painter's privilege to choose
Among what's rarest. Will your wife refuse
Acceptance from – no rival – of a gift?
You paint the human figure I make shift
Humbly to reproduce: but, in my hours   160
Of idlesse, what I fain would paint is – flowers.
Look now!'
          She twitched aside a veiling cloth.
'Here is my keepsake – frame and picture both:
For see, the frame is all of flowers festooned
About an empty space, – left thus, to wound
No natural susceptibility:
How can I guess? 'Tis you must fill, not I,
The central space with – her whom you like best!
That is your business, mine has been the rest.
But judge!'   170
         How judge them? Each of us, in flowers,
Chooses his love, allies it with past hours,
Old meetings, vanished forms and faces: no –
Here let each favourite unmolested blow
For one heart's homage, no tongue's banal praise,
Whether the rose appealingly bade 'Gaze
Your fill on me, sultana who dethrone

The gaudy tulip!' or 'twas 'Me alone
Rather do homage to, who lily am,
No unabashed rose!' 'Do I vainly cram
180 My cup with sweets, your jonquil?' 'Why forget
Vernal endearments with the violet?'
So they contested yet concerted, all
As one, to circle round about, enthral
Yet, self-forgetting, push to prominence
The midmost wonder, gained no matter whence.

There's a tale extant, in a book I conned
Long years ago, which treats of things beyond
The common, antique times and countries queer
And customs strange to match. ' 'Tis said, last year,'
190 (Recounts my author,) 'that the King had mind
To view his kingdom – guessed at from behind
A palace-window hitherto. Announced
No sooner was such purpose than 'twas pounced
Upon by all the ladies of the land –
Loyal but light of life: they formed a band
Of loveliest ones but lithest also, since
Proudly they all combined to bear their prince.
Backs joined to breasts, – arms, legs, – nay, ankles, wrists,
Hands, feet, I know not by what turns and twists,
200 So interwoven lay that you believed
'Twas one sole beast of burden which received
The monarch on its back, of breadth not scant,
Since fifty girls made one white elephant.
So with the fifty flowers which shapes and hues
Blent, as I tell, and made one fast yet loose
Mixture of beauties, composite, distinct
No less in each combining flower that linked
With flower to form a fit environment
For – whom might be the painter's heart's intent
210 Thus, in the midst enhaloed, to enshrine?
'This glory-guarded middle space – is mine?
For me to fill?'
                           'For you, my Friend! We part,

Never perchance to meet again. Your Art –
What if I mean it – so to speak – shall wed
My own, be witness of the life we led
When sometimes it has seemed our souls near found
Each one the other as its mate – unbound
Had yours been haply from the better choice
– Beautiful Bicé: 'tis the common voice,
The crowning verdict. Make whom you like best   220
Queen of the central space, and manifest
Your predilection for what flower beyond
All flowers finds favour with you. I am fond
Of – say – yon rose's rich predominance,
While you – what wonder? – more affect the glance
The gentler violet from its leafy screen
Ventures: so – choose your flower and paint your queen!'

Oh but the man was ready, head as hand,
Instructed and adroit. 'Just as you stand,
Stay and be made – would Nature but relent –   230
By Art immortal!'
           Every implement
In tempting reach – a palette primed, each squeeze
Of oil-paint in its proper patch – with these,
Brushes, a veritable sheaf to grasp!
He worked as he had never dared.
                'Unclasp
My Art from yours who can!' – he cried at length,
As down he threw the pencil – 'Grace from Strength
Dissociate, from your flowery fringe detach
My face of whom it frames, – the feat will match
With that of Time should Time from me extract   240
Your memory, Artemisia!' And in fact, –
What with the pricking impulse, sudden glow
Of soul – head, hand co-operated so
That face was worthy of its frame, 'tis said –
Perfect, suppose!
           They parted. Soon instead
Of Rome was home, – of Artemisia – well,

The placid-perfect wife. And it befell
That after the first incontestably
Blessedest of all blisses (– wherefore try
250   Your patience with embracings and the rest
Due from Calypso's all-unwilling guest
To his Penelope?) – there somehow came
The coolness which as duly follows flame.
So, one day, 'What if we inspect the gifts
My Art has gained us?'
                      Now the wife uplifts
A casket-lid, now tries a medal's chain
Round her own lithe neck, fits a ring in vain
– Too loose on the fine finger, – vows and swears
The jewel with two pendent pearls like pears
260   Betters a lady's bosom – witness else!
And so forth, while Ulysses smiles.
                           'Such spells
Subdue such natures – sex must worship toys
– Trinkets and trash: yet, ah, quite other joys
Must stir from sleep the passionate abyss
Of – such an one as her I know – not his
My gentle consort with the milk for blood!
Why, did it chance that in a careless mood
(In those old days, gone – never to return –
When we talked – she to teach and I to learn)
270   I dropped a word, a hint which might imply
Consorts exist – how quick flashed fire from eye,
Brow blackened, lip was pinched by furious lip!
I needed no reminder of my slip:
One warning taught me wisdom. Whereas here . . .
Aha, a sportive fancy! Eh, what fear
Of harm to follow? Just a whim indulged!

'My Beatricé, there's an undivulged
Surprise in store for you: the moment's fit
For letting loose a secret: out with it!
280   Tributes to worth, you rightly estimate
These gifts of Prince and Bishop, Church and State:

Yet, may I tell you? Tastes so disagree!
There's one gift, preciousest of all to me,
I doubt if you would value as well worth
The obvious sparkling gauds that men unearth
For toy-cult mainly of you womankind;
Such make you marvel, I concede: while blind
The sex proves to the greater marvel here
I veil to balk its envy. Be sincere!
Say, should you search creation far and wide,   290
Was ever face like this?'

               He drew aside
The veil, displayed the flower-framed portrait kept
For private delectation.

               No adept
In florist's lore more accurately named
And praised or, as appropriately, blamed
Specimen after specimen of skill,
Than Bicé. 'Rightly placed the daffodil –
Scarcely so right the blue germander. Grey
Good mouse-ear! Hardly your auricula
Is powdered white enough. It seems to me   300
Scarlet not crimson, that anemone:
But there's amends in the pink saxifrage.
O darling dear ones, let me disengage
You innocents from what your harmlessness
Clasps lovingly! Out thou from their caress,
Serpent!'

          Whereat forth-flashing from her coils
On coils of hair, the *spilla* in its toils
Of yellow wealth, the dagger-plaything kept
To pin its plaits together, life-like leapt
And – woe to all inside the coronal!   310
Stab followed stab, – cut, slash, she ruined all
The masterpiece. Alack for eyes and mouth
And dimples and endearment – North and South,
East, West, the tatters in a fury flew:
There yawned the circlet. What remained to do?

She flung the weapon, and, with folded arms
And mien defiant of such low alarms
As death and doom beyond death, Bicé stood
Passively statuesque, in quietude
320 Awaiting judgement.
             And out judgement burst
With frank unloading of love's laughter, first
Freed from its unsuspected source. Some throe
Must needs unlock love's prison-bars, let flow
The joyance.

          'Then you ever were, still are,
And henceforth shall be – no occulted star
But my resplendent Bicé, sun-revealed,
Full-rondure! Woman-glory unconcealed,
So front me, find and claim and take your own –
My soul and body yours and yours alone,
330 As you are mine, mine wholly! Heart's love, take –
Use your possession – stab or stay at will
Here – hating, saving – woman with the skill
To make man beast or god!'
              And so it proved:
For, as beseemed new godship, thus he loved,
Past power to change, until his dying-day, –
Good fellow! And I fain would hope – some say
Indeed for certain – that our painter's toils
At fresco-splashing, finer stroke in oils,
Were not so mediocre after all;
340 Perhaps the work appears unduly small
From having loomed too large in old esteem,
Patronized by late Papacy. I seem
Myself to have cast eyes on certain work
In sundry galleries, no judge needs shirk
From moderately praising. He designed
Correctly, nor in colour lagged behind
His age: but both in Florence and in Rome
The elder race so make themselves at home
That scarce we give a glance to ceilingfuls

Of such like as Francesco. Still, one culls   350
From out the heaped laudations of the time
The pretty incident I put in rhyme.

Spring Song

Dance, yellows and whites and reds, –
Lead your gay orgy, leaves, stalks, heads
Astir with the wind in the tulip-beds!

There's sunshine; scarcely a wind at all
Disturbs starved grass and daisies small
On a certain mound by a churchyard wall.

Daisies and grass be my heart's bedfellows
On the mound wind spares and sunshine mellows:
Dance you, reds and whites and yellows!

NOTES

Porphyria's Lover

Published January 1836 in W. J. Fox's liberal Unitarian journal, the *Monthly Repository*, with the title 'Porphyria'. Fox had praised and promoted *Pauline* (1833) and *Paracelsus* (1835). Immediately following 'Porphyria' was 'Johannes Agricola in Meditation', then called 'Johannes Agricola' (see below): these were the first dramatic monologues by Browning to appear in print. In *Dramatic Lyrics* (1842) the two poems lost their individual titles and became parts one and two of 'Madhouse Cells', with 'Johannes Agricola' now first in order. In *Poems* (1849) the two were given their final titles, though still linked as 'Madhouse Cells' I and II. In *Poetical Works* (1863) they were separated, and the 'Madhouse Cells' title was dropped; the two poems were placed in the section called 'Dramatic Romances'. Finally, in *Poetical Works* (1868), 'Johannes Agricola in Meditation' was placed in the section called 'Men and Women'.

Johannes Agricola in Meditation

For publication and title see above. The original publication in the *Monthly Repository* included an epigraph quoting (with minor errors) the entry on antinomianism in Defoe's *Dictionary of all Religions* (1704):

> Antinomians, so denominated for rejecting the Law as a thing of no use under the Gospel dispensation: they say, that good works do not further, nor evil works hinder salvation; that the child of God cannot sin, that God never chastiseth him, that murder, drunkenness, etc. are sins in the wicked but not in him, that the child of grace being once assured of salvation, afterwards never doubteth . . . that God doth not love any man for his holiness, that sanctification is no evidence of justification, etc. Potanus, in his Catalogue of Heresies, says John Agricola was the author of this sect, A.D. 1535.

The *Monthly Repository*, with its Unitarian tendency, would have been favourable to this satire on extreme Protestantism.

Song from *Pippa Passes* ('The year's at the spring')

Published 1841. *Pippa Passes* is a drama set in Asolo, a small town in north-east Italy which Browning visited in 1838. The concluding two lines express Pippa's innocence, not Browning's facile optimism, as the dramatic context makes clear (Pippa sings the song outside a room where, unknown to her, a woman and her lover are closeted together after killing the woman's husband).

Scene from *Pippa Passes* ('There goes a swallow to Venice . . .')

The speakers, according to the stage direction, are 'poor girls', i.e., prostitutes, whiling away the time before nightfall. **22.** *deuzans* Variety of apple said to keep two years (from French 'deux ans'); *junetings* jennetings, a variety of early apple; *leather-coats* russet apples with rough skins.

My Last Duchess

Published *Dramatic Lyrics*, 1842. The Duke of Ferrara is speaking to an envoy negotiating his next marriage. The characters and story are not historical, but meant to be typical of the period of the Italian Renaissance.

Soliloquy of the Spanish Cloister

Published *Dramatic Lyrics*, 1842. **10.** *Salve tibi* Latin greeting. **14.** *oak-galls* Growths on oak leaves, used in the manufacture of ink. **16.** *Swine's Snout* Botanically, the dandelion; insultingly, Brother Lawrence. **39.** *the Arian* Follower of Arius, fourth-century heretic who rejected the doctrine of the Trinity. **49.** *Galatians* St Paul's Epistle to the Galatians. The 'great text' is imaginary. **56.** *Manichee* Follower of the Manichean heresy, a dualist (believing that good and evil are of equal power in the universe). **60.** *Belial's gripe* Belial is one of the names of the Devil. 'Belial came next, than whom a spirit more lewd / Fell not from heaven, or more gross to love / Vice for itself' (Milton, *Paradise Lost* I 490–92). **64.** *sieve* Basket. **70.** *Hy, Zy, Hine* Opening words of a magic spell, interrupted by the bell for vespers. **71–2.** *Plena gratiâ / Ave, Virgo* 'Hail, Virgin [Mary] full of grace' (Latin).

The Pied Piper of Hamelin; *A Child's Story*

Published *Dramatic Lyrics*, 1842. 'W. M. the Younger' was the son of the actor-manager William Macready; Browning wrote the poem for him to illustrate while he was ill in bed. Line 10 is the second shortest in Browning's poetry. The shortest is the first line of *Pippa Passes*: 'Day!' **123–6.** Julius Caesar is said to have swum ashore after his ship was wrecked off Alexandria, carrying the manuscript of his history of the war with Gaul ('his commentary'). **136.** *by harp or by psaltery* Musical instruments associated with the Bible, e.g., Psalm 81:2, 'the pleasant harp with the psaltery'. **138.** *drysaltery* Shop selling oils, preserves, tinned meats etc. **139.** *nuncheon* Snack. **141.** *puncheon* Cask. **169.** *poke* Purse. **182.** *stiver* Coin of small value. **198,** *pitching and hustling* Also 'hustle-cap', a game in which coins are tossed at a mark, then gathered in a cap and shaken out: the one whose coin landed nearest takes all the coins that fall out heads; the process is repeated with the next nearest until all the coins are gone. **258.** *A text* Matthew 19:24. **279.** *tabor* Drum. **296.** *trepanned* Entrapped.

'How They Brought the Good News from Ghent to Aix'

Published *Dramatic Romances and Lyrics*, 1845. Aix is besieged; the 'good news' is of help on the way. The episode is not historical. All the places except Aix (Aix-la-Chapelle, now Aachen in West Germany) are in Belgium. **10.** *pique* 'The old-fashioned projection in front of the military saddle on the Continent' (Browning's gloss). **22.** *stout galloper* Stayer (as opposed to sprinter).

The Lost Leader

Published *Dramatic Romances and Lyrics*, 1845. The subject was Wordsworth's defection from the radical cause; the poem was probably written after he became Poet Laureate in 1843.

Meeting at Night

Published *Dramatic Romances and Lyrics*, 1845, with 'Parting at Morning', as a single poem in two parts, 'Night and Morning'. In 1849 the poems were separated and given their present titles, but continued to be published together.

Parting at Morning

See preceding note for publication. The speaker of the poem is the man, not, as many readers have assumed (including the present editor when he first read it), the woman. 'Him' in l.3 means the sun, as it does in l.20 of '"How They Brought the Good News from Ghent to Aix"'. Browning was asked in 1889 whether the fourth line was 'an expression by her of her sense of loss of him, or the despairing cry of a ruined woman?' He replied: 'Neither: it is *his* confession of how fleeting is the belief (implied in the first part) that such raptures are self-sufficient and enduring – as for the time they appear.'

Home-Thoughts, from Abroad .

Published *Dramatic Romances and Lyrics*, 1845.

The Bishop Orders His Tomb at Saint Praxed's Church

Published *Hood's Magazine and Comic Miscellany*, March 1845, with the title 'The Tomb at St. Praxed's'; then *Dramatic Romances and Lyrics*. The present title dates from *Poems*, 1849. Browning visited Rome in 1844 and saw the church of Santa Prassede, but both Bishop and tomb are imaginary (necessarily so in the latter case, since the Bishop's wishes are clearly not going to be fulfilled). Ruskin's praise in vol. IV of *Modern Painters* (1856) is notable: 'I know of no other piece of modern English, prose or poetry, in which there is so much told . . . of the Renaissance spirit, – its worldliness, inconsistency, pride, hypocrisy, ignorance of itself, love of art, of luxury, and of good Latin.' **1.** Ecclesiastes 1:2. 'Vanity' means 'futility'. **31.** *onion-stone* An inferior marble: 'the grey cipollino – good for pillars and the like, bad for finer work, thro' its being laid coat upon coat, onion-wise' (Browning's gloss). **41.** *frail* Basket made of rushes. **47–9.** Alluding to the monument of St Ignatius Loyola in the Gesu church in Rome, topped by a lapis lazuli globe; anachronistic, since it dates from 1690. **51–2.** Job 7:6 and 14:10. **54.** *antique-black* It. *antico-nero*, a high-quality black marble. **64.** *Child of my bowels* II Samuel 16:11 (David on the rebellion of his favourite son, Absalom). **66.** *travertine* Hard white stone used for ordinary building. **77–9.** *Tully* Cicero, a model of pure Latin style; *Ulpian* Domitius Ulpianus, lawyer and scholar of third century A.D. **89.** *mortcloth* Funeral pall. **95.** Santa Prassede is neither Christ nor male; 'the blunder about the sermon is the result of the dying man's haziness' (Browning's gloss). **99–100.** The Bishop correctly identifies 'elucescebat' (he was illustrious) as a post-Ciceronian form; Cicero would have had 'elucebat'. **101.** Genesis 47:9. **111.** *entablature* Marble block. **116.** *Gritstone* Coarse sandstone.

Love Among the Ruins

Published *Men and Women*, 1855. The unnamed landscape owes something to the Roman campagna, and something to Browning's reading about contemporary excavations of ancient cities; the draft title was 'Sicilian Pastoral'. **21.** Thebes in Egypt was known as 'Hecatompylos' on account of its hundred gates; Babylon also had one hundred gates. **73–8.** Lemprière's *Classical Dictionary* (ed. 1823) records of Thebes in Egypt: 'In the time of its splendour, it extended above twenty-three miles, and upon any emergency could send into the field by each of its hundred gates, 20,000 fighting men, and 200 chariots.'

A Lovers' Quarrel

Published *Men and Women*, 1855. Intense playful intimacy characterized the Brownings' first months together at Pisa, 1846–7; disagreements (about Napoleon III and spiritualism) came later, but are not the source of the 'quarrel' here: Browning's marriage therefore provided material for the poem but was not (in simple terms) its subject. **29–35.** *The Times* attacked the extravagance of Napoleon III's wedding, January 1853. **36.** *Pampas* The grasslands of Argentina. **43–9.** Elizabeth Barrett Browning reports such a seance, but not tête-à-tête with her sceptical husband. **90–91.** Proverbs 18:21. **123.** *minor third* The interval between the cuckoo's notes increases as spring progresses; the 'minor third' is an interval of one and a half tones. See also 'A Toccata of Galuppi's', l.19.

Up at a Villa – Down in the City

Published *Men and Women*, 1855. The setting is Tuscany. **42.** *Pulcinello-trumpet* Announcing a puppet show (Pulcinello is a Punch-figure). **44–6.** Tuscany at the time was ruled by the Grand Duke Leopold II, with Austrian support: the 'liberal thieves' are Italian nationalists (with whom Browning, as opposed to the Catholic Church hierarchy, sympathized), and the 'little new law' a reactionary measure.

Fra Lippo Lippi

Published *Men and Women*, 1855. Giorgio Vasari's *Lives of the Artists*, a favourite book, supplied most of the details for the career of the Florentine painter Filippo Lippi (c. 1406–69); the episode related by the poem is imaginary. Lippi's opinions coincide with Browning's at several, but by no means all points. **17–18.** Cosimo dei Medici (1389–1464) ruled Florence and was Lippi's patron; his 'house' reappears in 'The Statue and the Bust' (ll.33–9). **53–6.** Imitations of the *stornello*, a three-line Tuscan popular song beginning with the name of a flower. **121.** *the Eight* The magistrates of Florence. **130.** *antiphonary* Book of choral songs. **189.** *Giotto* Florentine painter and architect (1267–1337), praised in 'Old Pictures in Florence' (*Men and Women*; not in this edition). **196–7.** Matthew 14:1–12, confusing Herodias with her daughter Salome; Browning took the error from Vasari, probably deliberately (contrast ll.273–80): it exposes the Prior's ignorance or unease. **235–6.** Fra Angelico (1387–1455), a Dominican friar; Lorenzo Monaco (c. 1370–c. 1425), a Camaldolese: see ll.139–40. **273–80.** Tomasso Guidi (1401–28), called 'Masaccio' (clumsy), Lippi's teacher, not pupil; Browning misread a note in his edition of Vasari. **307.** *cullion* Rascal. **323.** *Saint Laurence* A deacon of Pope Sixtus II, martyred in 258 by being roasted on a gridiron. **327.** *phiz* Face. **347.** *They want a cast o' my office* They want an example of my work (with bawdy pun: they lack what I can give them). **348.** The painting described in the following lines is 'The Coronation of the Virgin', now in the Uffizi Gallery in Florence. **354.** Saint John the Baptist. **363.** In Browning's time this figure, kneeling in the right-hand bottom corner by a scroll reading 'is perfecit opus', was thought to be a self-portrait ('he made the work'); it is now known to be a portrait of the benefactor who commissioned the painting ('he made the work be'). Browning's 'Iste' (l.377) is an error. **375.** *camel-hair* Worn by John the Baptist (Matthew 3:4). **380.** *kirtles* Skirts or petticoats. **381.** *hot cockles* Lippi's bawdy joke depends on knowing that the real rustic game of hot cockles is one in which a blindfolded player has to guess who strikes him; it cannot, therefore, be played by only two people!

A Toccata of Galuppi's

Published *Men and Women*, 1855. In 1887 Browning commented: 'As for Galuppi, I had once in my possession two huge manuscript volumes almost exclusively made up of his "Toccata-pieces" – apparently a slighter form of the Sonata to be "touched" lightly off.' Browning's memory may be at fault; Baldassare Galuppi (1706–85) composed many keyboard pieces but no toccatas; in any event the piece here is imaginary. **1.** *Baldassaro* The spelling is Browning's error. **6.** Saint Mark's is the Cathedral of Venice; the Doges (chief magistrates in the days when Venice was a republic) performed an annual ceremony in which a ring was cast into the Adriatic to 'wed' the state to the sea, the source of its military and commercial power. **8.** *Shylock's bridge* The Rialto, 'where merchants most do congregate' (*Merchant of Venice* I iii 44). **11.** *masks* Probably meaning masquerades or masked balls (see l.17); but it may mean masques, dramatic entertainments. **14.** *bell-flower* Campanula **16.** *afford* 'Time' is understood; 'spare the time to listen to your music'. **18.** *clavichord* Galuppi was a harpsichordist and composed for this instrument, not the clavichord; P. Turner, in his edition of *Men and Women* (OUP, 1972) says that the clavichord's softer tone would be 'almost inaudible against the noise of general conversation', which may be why Browning substituted it; the lovers have to 'break talk off' to listen. **19-25.** The extent of Browning's musical knowledge, and the precise bearing of the terminology used here, are debatable; the general sense is clear, however: the speaker suggests a link between Galuppi's technique as a composer and the 'message' of his music, as interpreted both by his contemporary audience and (ll.34-43) by the speaker himself. **19.** *lesser thirds* Minor thirds, as in 'A Lovers' Quarrel', l.123. *sixths diminished* A diminished sixth is technically a minor sixth chromatically reduced by one semitone, and has 'little beyond a theoretical existence' (*Concise Oxford Dictionary of Music*); a commentator in 1887 remarked that 'mentioning diminished sixths in this off-hand way is rather like casually speaking of breakfasting off roc's egg as a matter of everyday occurrence'. J. Pettigrew and T. J. Collins (*Robert Browning: the Poems*, Harmondsworth, 1981) suggest that 'diminished' may be loosely used for 'minor'. **20.** *Those suspensions, those solutions* A suspension is the prolongation of a note from one chord into the following chord, producing a discord which is then resolved into a concord (the solution or resolution). **24-5.** *dominant's persistence . . . octave struck the answer* The dominant is the fifth note above the keynote; a chord formed on this note is normally resolved on to the chord of the keynote. 'Octave' presumably refers to the keynote struck in octaves 'to stress its finality' (Turner). **37-42.** Galuppi's music shakes the speaker's faith both in a hierarchy of 'souls' (whose progress beyond the material world is determined by the 'degree' of their spirituality) and in the place of his own rational, scientific soul in such a hierarchy. 'Butterflies' (l.39) may refer literally to the creatures themselves, or figuratively to the Venetians, or to both; the butterfly was a traditional emblem of the soul. 'Extinction' (l.39) refers not to death, but to there being nothing after it. According to Christ's teaching, those who are fulfilled on earth 'have their reward' (Matthew 6:2) and will not find salvation in the afterlife; here, it is not salvation that is at stake, but existence itself. 'Mirth and folly' (l.41) suggests Ecclesiastes 7:2-4: 'It is better to go to the house of mourning than to go to the house of feasting: for that is the end of all men; and the living will lay it to his heart . . . The heart of the wise is in the house of mourning; but the heart of fools is in the house of mirth.'

An Epistle Containing the Strange Medical Experience of Karshish, the Arab Physician

Published *Men and Women*, 1855. The story of Jesus' raising of Lazarus is in John 11:1-44; the form, as the title and opening suggest, is a secular counterpart to the New Testament Epistles, especially St Paul's (see also 'Cleon'). Karshish, Abib, and their 'lord the sage' are invented characters. **1.** The name 'Karshish' means 'gatherer' in Arabic. **28.** Vespasian commanded the Roman troops against the Jewish rebellion in A.D. 66, three years before he became Emperor; his son Titus carried on the war and destroyed Jerusalem in A.D. 70. **30.** *balls* Eyeballs. **42.** *viscid choler* Sticky bile. **43.** *tertians* Tertian fevers (which recur every other day). **44.** *falling-sickness* Epilepsy. **50.** *sublimate* A medicinal powder. **55.** *gum-tragacanth* A substance exuded from a shrub native to the Middle East, used in medicine as a vehicle for drugs. **82.** *exhibition* Administration. **117.** Matthew 18:2–3. **177.** *Greek fire* A primitive explosive compound, first used by the Greeks of Byzantium. **228.** *affects* Loves. **240.** *sublimed* Intensified. **248–59.** Karshish's garbled version of the crucifixion, Matthew 27. **247.** *leech* Physician.

Mesmerism

Published *Men and Women*, 1855. Mesmerism, founded on the teachings of the Austrian physician Franz Anton Mesmer (1734–1815), was a precursor of hypnotism, and was widely discussed in the 1840s and 1850s. Like spiritualism it was a topic of debate and disagreement between the Brownings. The term is used here loosely to indicate the exercise of occult power, though certain features (e.g. the use of the hands) are specifically associated with mesmerism. **44–5.** Calotypes were an early form of photograph. **75.** *tractile* Capable of being drawn out to a thread.

A Serenade at the Villa

Published *Men and Women*, 1855.

'Childe Roland to the Dark Tower Came'

Published *Men and Women*, 1855. 'I was conscious of no allegorical intention in writing it . . . Childe Roland came upon me as a kind of dream. I had to write it, then and there, and I finished it the same day, I believe. But it was simply that I had to do it. I did not know then what I meant beyond that, and I'm sure I don't know now. But I'm very fond of it' (Browning, 1887). A 'childe' is a young knight or candidate for knighthood. In the old Scottish ballad of Childe Roland, Roland, a son of King Arthur, rescues his sister from the castle of the King of Elfland. The subtitle refers to *King Lear* III iv 178–80, where Edgar, disguised as Poor Tom, quotes the ballad, along with the Giant's words in the tale of Jack the Giant-Killer: 'Child Rowland to the dark tower came, / His word was still "Fie, foh, and fum, / I smell the blood of a British man".' Browning carefully avoided ruling out an allegorical reading, only the conscious intention to write an allegory; readers who wish to try their hand should be warned that the enterprise strongly resembles carving a statue out of fog. **34.** *staves* Verses (of the funeral psalm). **48.** *estray* Legal term for stray animal. **66.** *Calcine* Burn to ashes, utterly consume, with the additional sense of refine, purge. **68.** *bents* Coarse grasses. **80.** *colloped* The usual sense ('having thick folds of flesh') contradicts 'gaunt'; perhaps 'raw-looking' (like a slice of meat). **106.** *howlet* Owl. **114.** *bespate* Bespattered (with suggestion of river 'in full spate'). **130.** *pad* Tread. **131.** *plash* Marshy pool. **133.** *fell cirque* Cruel, deadly amphitheatre (as in Roman circus). **141.** *brake* Machine (in several possible senses, e.g. a toothed instrument to crush flax, a heavy harrow); can also mean 'trap' or 'cage'. **143.** *Tophet* Biblical name for Hell. See also 'Ned Bratts', l.178n. **160.** *Apollyon* in Bunyan's *Pilgrim's Progress*, a 'foul fiend' with wings like a dragon ('dragon-penned'), named after the 'angel of the bottomless pit' in Revelation 9:11. **179.** *nonce* Moment. **182.** *blind as the fool's heart* Psalm 14:1: 'The fool hath said in his heart, There is no God.' **203.** *slug-horn* A horn used in battle or to sound a challenge (Browning's mistake, following Chatterton; the word is in fact a form of Anglo-Saxon 'slogan', battle-cry). The context recalls another Roland, the hero of Charlemagne's time and subsequent legend, who sounded his horn (too late) at Roncesvalles.

The Statue and the Bust

Published *Men and Women*, 1855. The statue is real; the bust imaginary; the story mostly the latter, according to Browning: 'the fiction in the poem . . . comprises everything but the (legendary) fact that the lady was shut up there by a jealous husband, and that the Duke commemorated his riding past her window by the statue's erection . . . There are niches in the palace wall where such a bust *might* have been placed, "and if not, why not?"' There is an analogy (though not a complete identification) with the story of Browning himself and Elizabeth Barrett; perhaps Browning also had in mind the twenty years waited by John Stuart Mill and Harriet Taylor until the death of her husband allowed them to marry in 1851. **1–2.** The equestrian statue of the Grand Duke Ferdinand de Medici (1549–1608) stands in the Piazza Annunziata, looking towards the Palazzo Antinori, a palace formerly owned by the Riccardi family (not, as Browning exasperatedly pointed out, the same as Duke Ferdinand's own palace, described in ll.33–9; this was the palace built by Cosimo dei Medici, Fra Lippo Lippi's patron, and from which the painter in Browning's poem plays truant). **21.** *coal-black tree* Ebony. **22.** *encolure* Mane (B.'s coinage, from Fr., neck of a horse). **23.** *dissemble* Imitate, match. **38–9.** Probably alluding to the Cosimo of 'Fra Lippo Lippi', in effect absolute ruler of Florence from 1434, though he preserved the forms of republican government, and the epithet 'cursed' applies more to his grandson Lorenzo than to his son Piero; P. Turner, in his edition of *Men and Women* (OUP, 1972), suggests instead Cosimo I (1519–74) and his son Francesco (1541–87). **57.** *catafalque* Hearse. **94.** *Arno* The river on which Florence stands. **95.** *Petraja* In the hills to the north of Florence; Ferdinand had a villa there. **159.** *serpent's tooth* Of time and self-frustration (but obliquely alluding to the origin of the phrase in *King Lear* I iv 288–9, in the sense that the embittered lady is the 'thankless child' of her past self). **169.** *Robbia's craft* If the allusion is specific, it must (anachronistically) be to the sculptor Luca della Robbia (1400–1482); it may however be to Robbia ware generally. The cornice in Browning's time was decorated in Robbia ware. **202.** *John of Douay* The sculptor Giovanni da Bologna (1524–1608) was born at Douai in northern France. **232–43.** Human integrity does not depend on the moral value of an action, but on the degree of conviction with which it is undertaken. In the metaphor, playing a game for real money ('pelf', 'coin') is equivalent to doing something virtuous; playing for 'a button', a 'counter' is equivalent to doing something wrong. Since the test is of integrity, not moral quality, it would be absurd ('an epigram') to demand the real coin of virtue when the 'button' of crime will do just as well. The 'stamp of the very Guelph' means British money; the royal family are Guelphs by descent. **247.** Luke 12:35, with Matthew 12:1–13 (the wise and foolish virgins). **250.** *De te, fabula!* 'The story is about you' (Horace, *Satires* I i 69–70).

How It Strikes a Contemporary

Published *Men and Women*, 1855. The title adapts that of a story by Jane Taylor (1783–1824), 'How It Strikes a Stranger', on which Browning drew much later for 'Rephan' (*Asolando*, 1889; not in this edition). Browning clearly used his own ideas, beliefs, and habits in the description of the poet here, but it is not simply a self-portrait. The real poet of the piece, after all, is the narrator who denies being one. **3.** *Valladolid* A city in north-west Spain, about 160 km from Madrid. Browning had not visited it. **90.** *Corregidor* Chief magistrate; the speaker goes on to identify him with the town crier, the point being that they metaphorically represent two kinds of poetry, one serious and authoritative ('The town's true master', l.40), the other frivolous and gaudy. **96.** *memorized* Memorialized. **115.** *Prado* Fashionable promenade.

The Patriot

Published *Men and Women*, 1855. The poem is associated with the Risorgimento, the struggle for Italian liberation from Austrian rule, with which Browning strongly sympathized, but the action, as the subtitle indicates, is universal and recurrent, not local and specific. L.26 originally read 'Thus I entered Brescia'; the revision removes any allusion to the twelfth-century revolutionary Arnold of Brescia. **19.** *Shambles' Gate* The place of execution.

Memorabilia

Published *Men and Women*, 1855. The poem is founded on an incident which took place when Browning was a boy, soon after his first passionate discovery of Shelley's poetry (recorded in *Pauline*, where Shelley is called 'sun-treader' – note the image of the eagle in the last two lines).

Andrea del Sarto

Published *Men and Women*, 1855. Said to have been written in response to a request by a friend for a copy of a painting in the Pitti Palace in Florence, believed at the time to be a self-portrait of Andrea (1486–1531) and his wife Lucrezia, and an expression of their unhappy relationship. The poem is set in 1525 (see l.105). As with Fra Lippo Lippi, Vasari was Browning's main historical source for details of Andrea's life and work: his marriage to the faithless and cold-hearted Lucrezia, who served as the model for many of his paintings, his return in 1519 at her instigation from the court of King Francis I where he had done some of his best work, his subsequent embezzlement of the King's commission money in order to build a house for himself and Lucrezia, his neglect of his parents, his supreme technical skill, his falling short of the highest genius. He was called 'del Sarto' because his father was a tailor, and 'Il Pittore senza Errori' because of his draughtsmanship. Vasari's accuracy is disputed by modern scholarship; however, his biography gave Browning materials not for another biography, but for a poem. **15**. *Fiesole* A town in the hills north-east of Florence. **76**. *Someone* Michelangelo (1475–1574); see ll.183–93. **93**. *Morello* Mountain to the north of Florence. **105**. Raphael, born at Urbino in 1483, died at Rome in 1520 (hence 'The Roman', l.178). Contrary to l.136, he did marry. **210**. *cue-owls* Anglicizing the Italian 'ciu', the call of the scops owl. **263**. *Leonard* Leonardo da Vinci (1452–1519).

In a Year

Published *Men and Women*, 1855.

Cleon

Published *Men and Women*, 1855. Set in the first century, during the apostleship of Paul, with whom Cleon, like Karshish in 'An Epistle', is implicitly compared, and who is mentioned by name at the end of the poem. The epigraph refers to a saying by the Greek poet Aratus (fourth century B.C.) quoted by St Paul in his address to the Athenians: 'as certain also of your own poets have said, For we are also his [God's] offspring' (Acts 17:28). Cleon and Protus are imaginary figures. **1**. *the sprinkled isles* The Sporades in the Aegean. **16**. *sea-wools* Dyed with purple from the murex. **41–2**. Zeus, in Greek mythology king of the Gods; the 'element of calm' is the Olympian detachment from human concerns enjoyed by the gods, but (since Cleon does not believe in an afterlife) also a euphemism for oblivion. **47**. Cleon's epic poem has been engraved on gold tablets. **51**. *phare* Lighthouse. **53**. *Poecile* Since Cleon is an invented figure, the reference is not to the historical 'stoa poikile', the painted colonnade at Athens, but to a similar (imagined) building. **60**. *moods* Modes (in ancient Greek music, scales differing in the sequence of intervals). **132**. *drupe* Stone-fruit; here, the wild plum. **140**. *Terpander* Musician and poet of seventh century B.C., credited with the invention of the seven-stringed lyre. **141**. *Phidias and his friend* Phidias, Athenian sculptor of fifth century B.C.; 'friend' in this context means 'fellow-artist', and may refer to the Athenian painter Polygnotus, roughly contemporary with Phidias, or to Apelles, who lived about a century later. **252**. *Naiad* Water-nymph. **258**. *what boots* 'How does it help'. **288**. *Phoebus* Apollo, god of the sun and of poetry, and the type of male beauty. **341**. *one with him* The same person; Cleon's notion of Christianity, like that of Karshish, is vague and confused. (In another sense, of which Cleon is unaware, Paul is indeed 'one with' Christ: e.g., Galatians 2:20: 'I am crucified with Christ: nevertheless I live; yet not I, but Christ liveth in me'.) **343**. *barbarian Jew* Cleon is mistaken as well as prejudiced; besides being a Jew, Paul was a Roman citizen, a fact he knew how to turn to his advantage (Acts 22:24–9).

Two in the Campagna

Published *Men and Women*, 1855. The 'Campagna' ('champaign', l.21) is the idyllic countryside around Rome, where the Brownings spent 'some exquisite hours' (with friends) in May 1854. The poem is not in any simple sense confessional, but the dramatic projection of a state of mind.

A Grammarian's Funeral

Published *Men and Women*, 1855. The 'grammarian' is a historical type; the 'revival of learning in Europe' (the Renaissance) began in the mid-fourteenth century in Italy. The grammarian's students are carrying his body from the rural lowlands to a cemetery in a mountaintop town, and the poem represents their funeral dirge. **86.** *Calculus* Stone (gall- or kidney-). **88.** *Tussis* Cough. **95.** *soul-hydroptic* Spiritually athirst (for knowledge). **124.** Matthew 7:7. **129–31.** *Hoti, Oun, enclitic De* The first two are Greek particles ('that', 'then'); the third a suffix meaning 'towards': 'That this is not to be confounded with the accentuated *De* meaning *but*, was the 'doctrine' which the Grammarian bequeathed to those capable of receiving it' (Browning's gloss).

James Lee's Wife

Published *Dramatis Personae*, 1864, with the title 'James Lee'. Section VI, ll.1–30, had been published May 1836 in the *Monthly Repository* (see above, note to 'Porphyria's Lover'). In *Poetical Works* (1868) the poem was given its final title. Section VIII was greatly expanded, with sixty-one new lines after l.26. Browning described the couple as 'people newly-married, trying to realize a dream of being sufficient to each other, in a foreign land (where you can try such an experiment) and finding it break up, – the man being tired first, – and tired precisely of the love'. The form and tone of the poem may owe something to Meredith's *Modern Love* (1862). Grief at his wife's death in 1861 may also have influenced Browning's tone and treatment, but once again it must be stressed that the poem is not directly autobiographical. The setting is Brittany, where Browning spent the summer in 1862 and 1863. **III, 72.** *bent* Stalk of coarse grass. **IV, 106.** *the Book* The Bible. The allusion is to the Promised Land, as in this passage from Deuteronomy 9:7–8: 'For the Lord thy God bringeth thee into a good land, a land of brooks of water, of fountains and depths . . . A land of wheat and barley, and vines, and fig trees, and pomegranates; a land of oil, olive and honey.' The phrase 'rivers of oil and wine' is not used in the Bible, but oil and wine are frequently linked, and the phrase 'rivers of oil' occurs in Job 29:6. **V, 137.** *barded and chanfroned* Armoured; bard = breastplate; chamfron (the usual form) = frontlet. **138.** *quixote-mage* Whimsical magician. **IX, 339.** *mutual flame* 'Here the anthem doth commence: / Love and constancy is dead; / Phoenix and the turtle fled / In a mutual flame from hence. // So they lov'd as love in twain / Had the essence but in one . . .' (Shakespeare, 'The Phoenix and the Turtle', ll.21–6).

Gold Hair: A Story of Pornic

Published *Dramatis Personae*, 1864. The story is founded on a real event which took place in the eighteenth century. The girl's 'boasted name' (l.4) is known, but l.5 asks for it not to be given. **16.** *flix* Fur of an animal; here implying softness and fleeciness. **84.** *pelf* Money, reward. **86–7.** *O cor / Humanum, pectora caeca* Lucretius, *De Rerum Natura* II 14 ('O human heart, and blind affections!'). **91–2.** *heard, / Marked, inwardly digested* Book of Common Prayer, Collect for Second Sunday in Advent: 'hear them [holy Scriptures], read, mark, learn, and inwardly digest them'. **99.** *for the nonce* For the purpose. **100.** The three following stanzas were added in the second edition of *Dramatis Personae* (also 1864) at the instigation of George Eliot, in order to clarify the girl's motive. **116.** *six times five* The precise figure is Browning's invention, allowing the allusion in stanza XXVI to the thirty pieces of silver for which Judas betrayed Christ. When Judas returned the money to the chief priests before hanging himself, they decided that since it was the 'price of blood' it could not be put in the Temple treasury; it was used to buy 'the potter's field, to bury strangers in' (Matthew 27:3–7). **124–5.** 'Lay not up for yourselves treasures upon earth . . . but lay up for yourselves treasures in heaven . . . for where your treasure is, there will your heart be also' (Matthew 6:19–21). **132.** *Watch and pray!* Christ's injunction to the disciples, Matthew 26:41 (in the garden at Gethsemane), Mark 13:33 (for the Second Coming). **141.** *The candid Impartial judges.* **143–5.** *Essays and Reviews*, a Broad Church collection edited by H. B. Wilson, and including Jowett's 'The interpretation of Scripture', was published in 1860, denounced for its liberalism by the Bishops in 1861, condemned in synod in 1864. John William Colenso (1814–83), Bishop of Natal, published commentaries on St Paul's Epistle to the Romans (1861) and the Pentateuch (vol. I, 1862) disputing the orthodox theology and historical authenticity of the Bible. **149–50.** *Original Sin, / The Corruption of Man's Heart* 'Original Sin . . . is the fault and corruption of the Nature of every man, that naturally is ingendered of the offspring of Adam; whereby man is very far gone from original righteousness, and is of his own nature inclined to evil, so that the flesh lusteth always contrary to the spirit; and therefore in every person born into this world, it deserveth God's wrath and damnation' (Article 9 of the Thirty-Nine Articles of Religion of the Church of England); 'The heart is deceitful above all things, and desperately wicked' (Jeremiah 17:9).

Dîs Aliter Visum; or, Le Byron de Nos Jours

Published *Dramatis Personae*, 1864. The Latin is a tag from Virgil, *Aeneid* ii 428, 'The gods thought otherwise', meaning that they intervened to frustrate human hopes; but the implication of the poem is that human beings themselves are responsible for the failure of their lives' fulfilment. The French means 'The Byron of our days': the man evoked in the poem is a poet who is lame (l.56) and 'Famous . . . for verse and worse' (l.57); like the Latin it is ironic, since the poet is old and, the poem suggests, a reduced version of his predecessor.

The setting is once again Brittany. When the poem opens, the man has just told the woman that he came near to proposing marriage to her ten years ago. The poem is her bitter response to this information. Much of it consists of her guesswork as to what was going through the man's mind on that occasion. She imagines him hesitating as to what to do, speculating about their respective thoughts if they were to marry, and deciding in the end not to take the risk. In ll.82–5 the woman 'quotes' the man 'quoting' her 'quoting' him, the most complex example in Browning's work of the nesting of voices within a dramatic monologue. **36.** Franz Schumann (1810–56). **38.** Jean-Marie Ingres (1780–1867), famous for his paintings of nudes. **40.** Heinrich Heine (1797–1856); translations of six of his love lyrics appeared in Elizabeth Barrett Browning's *Last Poems* (1862), which Browning edited. **42.** *votive frigate* Carved model hung from the beam of the church as an offering to the Virgin Mary from local fishermen. **58.** Sure of election to a vacant seat in the French Academy, which has forty members. **64.** *Three per Cents* Government stock yielding a low but safe income.

A Death in the Desert

Published *Dramatis Personae*, 1864. Browning's account of the deathbed testament of St John responds to the 'Higher Criticism' of the Bible, specifically to attacks on the historicity of the Gospels, the divinity of Jesus, and the authenticity of miracles in Renan's *Vie de Jésus* (1863) and Strauss's *Das Leben Jesu* (first publ. 1835–6; transl. George Eliot 1846; revised and re-issued 1864). Browning may also have drawn on Feuerbach's *Das Wesen des Christentums* (also transl. George Eliot, *The Essence of Religion*, 1854). St John, Browning's favourite Gospel, concludes with an assertion of historical accuracy: 'This is the disciple which testifieth of these things, and wrote these things: and we know that his testimony is true' (21:24). The poem accepts the traditional identification (challenged by the 'Higher Criticism') of the disciple John with the author of the Gospel, the three epistles of John, and Revelation, the final apocalyptic book of the New Testament (all these texts are extensively quoted in the poem). Browning was especially attracted by John's emphasis on love as the primary Christian value. According to tradition John died in extreme old age *c.* A.D. 100 near Ephesus in Asia Minor; however, no exact indications of place or time are given in the poem, and all the circumstances and characters (apart from those mentioned in the Bible, and the heretic Cerinthus) are imaginary. **1–12.** The sections in square brackets at the beginning and end of the poem, and at ll.82–104, contain the comments of the owner of the manuscript, who is presumably making a copy of it for someone else or for posterity. **1.** *Antiochene* There were two Antiochs, one in Syria and one in Asia Minor; it is not clear which Pamphylax was from. The manuscript is supposed to be 'of' Pamphylax but not 'by' him, since, as we learn later (ll.651–3), the actual scribe was not Pamphylax himself, but Phoebas, to whom Pamphylax related the story before his martyrdom. **4.** The Greek letters, the fifth and twelfth in the alphabet, stand for the writer's name (see l.9), and are also numbers, here indicating sections of the manuscript (from 5 to 40); since the poem opens in the midst of the story, the first four sections are presumably missing. 5. *Chosen Chest* A chest in which the writer keeps documents relating to the 'chosen' (i.e., the elect, the members of the early Christian sect to which he belongs). 6. *juice of terebinth* Turpentine. 7. *Xi* Fourteenth Greek letter. 14. *plantain-leaf* Mentioned (comically) as a restorative in *Romeo and Juliet* I ii 51–2. The plantain is a low herb with broad flat leaves. 18. *a brother* Not literal; 'comrade'. 23. *the decree* A decree of persecution against the Christians by Trajan (Roman Emperor A.D. 98–117). 36. *Bactrian* Bactria was an ancient country of central Asia, lying between the Hindu-Kush and the Oxus. 39. *quitch* A coarse grass. 50. *nard* Spikenard, an aromatic balsam or ointment. Mary Magdalene anoints the feet of Jesus with 'ointment of spikenard', John 12:3. 64. John 11:25. 69. F. B. Pinion, in his edition of *Dramatis Personae* (London and Glasgow: Collins, 1969) suggests that this is the griffon falcon, 'which has a distinctive white ruff of projecting feathers'. 73. *James and Peter* Fellow disciples of John (see ll.114–15). 82–104. Adapting and expanding two passages, one from John 1:13, which speaks of believers 'born, not of blood, nor of the will of the flesh, nor of the will of man, but of God' and the other from I John 5:7: 'there are three that bear witness in earth, the spirit, and the water, and the blood: and these three agree in one'. 104. *glossa* Gloss, explanation. 114–15. *it is long . . . death* James was martyred c. A.D. 43 (Acts 12:2); Peter was crucified c. A.D. 67 in Rome (foretold in John 21:18–19). 121. *He* Christ; the following two lines allude to John's vision of him in Revelation 11:14–16. 131–2. I John 1:1. 140. *Patmos* In the Aegean; scene of John's vision in Revelation. 141. *take a book and write* Revelation 1:11. 148–51. Note (among many other passages in St John's Gospel and Epistles) I John 4:7–8: 'Beloved, let us love one another: for love is of God . . . He that loveth not knoweth not God; for God is love.' 158. 'And every spirit that confesseth not that Jesus Christ is come in the flesh is not of God: and this is that spirit of antichrist, whereof ye have heard that it should come; and even now already is it in the world' (I John 4:3). 163–5. Jesus rebukes James and John for suggesting 'that we command fire to come down from heaven' and destroy their enemies (Luke 9:51–6); he gives his followers 'power to tread on serpents and scorpions' (Luke 10:19; see also Mark 16:18). 177. 'Where is the promise of His coming?' II Peter 3:4, attributed not, as here, to the impatient young, but to 'scoffers' in the 'last days'. 186–7. 'And we know that we are of God, and the whole world lieth in wickedness. And we know that the Son of God is come, and hath given us an understanding, that we may know him that is true, and we are in him that is true, even in his Son Jesus Christ. This is the true God, and eternal life' (I John 5:19–20). 212. Following this line, in the first and second editions of *Dramatis Personae*, Browning wrote: 'Closed with and cast and conquered, crucified'. Whether by accident or design, the deletion of this line in *Poetical Works* (1868) and subsequent editions removed a numerological pun from l.666 (see below). 216. *the right hand of the throne* After the Resurrection and his appearance to his disciples, Jesus 'was received up into heaven, and sat on the right hand of God' (Mark 16:19). 222. *Resume* Regain, re-assume control of. **226.** *the children* John in his first epistle calls his readers 'little children'. **231–2.** *insubordinate . . . once* Objects too close to the eye resist its ordering glance and require the assistance of the artificer's 'optic glass'. **241.** *dispart, dispread* Part asunder and spread out. **254.** *emprise* Enterprise. **283.** *sophist* Philosopher (implying a modern, sophisticated sceptic). **284–6.** The Prometheus trilogy attributed to Aeschylus tells of the Titan Prometheus's theft of fire from Olympus and gift of it to mankind, and of his punishment and eventual release by Zeus (Jove or Jupiter). Only the second play of the trilogy, *Prometheus Bound*, survives today; the 'satyrs' come from a fragment assigned to the lost first play, *Prometheus Firebearer*, which Browning represents as still extant in John's time. There is a further allusion to this play in ll.530–33. **304–10.** John, James and Peter see Jesus transfigured, Luke 9:28–36; Jesus walks on the sea of Galilee, John 6:15–21, and raises Lazarus from the dead, John 11; John and the other disciples forsake Jesus at his arrest in the garden of Gethsemane, Mark 14:50. **329.** *Ebion* Apocryphal founder of the Ebionites, an early Christian sect who denied the divinity of Jesus. *Cerinthus* A theologian of the first century, said to have lived in Ephesus at the same time as John; like the Ebionites he denied the divinity of Jesus, and introduced elements of Gnosticism and Judaism into his teaching. See also below. **355–65.** This vision of future doubt is influenced by doubts recorded in the Gospels themselves, e.g., (noting 'portico', l.357) John 10:22–4: 'And it was at Jerusalem the feast of the dedication, and it was winter. And Jesus walked in the temple in Solomon's porch. Then came the Jews round about him, and said, How long dost thou make us to doubt? If thou be the Christ, tell us plainly.' **364.** *any of His lives* Any of the Gospel stories. **365.** Corresponding to the Trinity of Father, Son, and Holy Spirit. **368.** *it cannot pass* 'Heaven and earth shall pass away, but my words shall not pass away' (Jesus in Matthew 24:35). **372.** *Wonders* Miracles. **390.** *Certes* Certainly (archaic). **405.** *stood still* As in Joshua 10:12–14. **439.** *virtues* Qualities (what the herb is good for). **532.** *ephemerals'* Mortals, i.e, mankind. **533.** In the legend, Prometheus carries a live coal from Olympus inside a stalk of giant fennel. **565.** *Atlas* The Atlas mountains are in north-west Africa; the name derives from one of the Titans who in legend held up the sky on his shoulders. **577.** *that* That which. **608.** *statuary* Sculptor. **623.** *at a jet* In a single act (of will and execution combined); from French 'd'un seul jet'. **625.** *The pattern on the Mount* The original stone tables on which the Ten Commandments were inscribed, given to Moses on Mount Sinai (Exodus 32:15–16). **652.** *fight the beasts* Pamphylax is to be martyred; cf. St Paul, I Corinthians 15:32: 'If after the manner of men I have fought with beasts at Ephesus, what advantageth it me, if the dead rise not? let us eat and drink; for tomorrow we die'. **657–8.** When the risen Jesus appears to the disciples at the end of St John's Gospel, Peter asks him what 'the disciple whom Jesus loved' (i.e., John himself) is to do: 'Jesus saith unto him, If I will that he tarry till I come, what is that to thee? follow thou me. Then went this saying abroad among the brethren, that that disciple should not die: yet Jesus said not unto him, He shall not die; but, If I will that he tarry till I come, what is that to thee?' (21:22–3). John is denying that Jesus promised him that he would be alive to witness the Second

Coming (see above, l.11, and below, ll.677-8). **659.** *this speech* The deathbed speech recorded in the poem. **664.** *breast to breast with God* John leans on Jesus's breast at the Last Supper (John 13:23-5). **665-87.** The owner of the document resumes here, transcribing a comment addressed to Cerinthus (see l.329 above) by an unnamed person who holds the orthodox doctrine that Christ was, indeed, the son of God. For the doctrine of incorporation, see John 17:20-23; for the metaphor of Christ as the bridegroom, see (among others) John 3:29 and II Corinthians 11:2: 'I have espoused you to one husband, that I may present you as a chaste virgin to Christ'. Cerinthus had apparently studied the manuscript without altering his opinion that Jesus was 'Mere man', going against John's specific injunction that the 'acknowledgment of God in Christ' was the way of salvation (ll.474-81). The owner of the manuscript, in the last words of the poem, pronounces on Cerinthus the judgement of spiritual death which John described (ll.482-513). In the first and second editions of the poem, which have an extra line (see above, l.212), Cerinthus is named at l.666, not 665; 'Six Hundred threescore and six' is the 'number of the beast' in Revelation 13:18.

Caliban upon Setebos; or, Natural Theology in the Island

Published *Dramatis Personae*, 1864. The epigraph is from Psalm 50:21; the context of the surrounding verses is also relevant: 'Offer unto God thanksgiving; and pay thy vows unto the most High: and call upon me in the day of trouble: I will deliver thee, and thou shalt glorify me. But unto the wicked God saith, What hast thou to do to declare my statutes, or that thou shouldest take my covenant in thy mouth? . . . Thou givest thy mouth to evil, and thy tongue frameth deceit. Thou sittest and speakest against thy brother; thou slanderest thine own mother's son. These things hast thou done, and I kept silence; thou thoughtest I was altogether such an one as thyself: but I will reprove thee, and set them in order before thine eyes. Now consider this, ye that forget God, lest I tear you in pieces, and there be none to deliver. Whoso offereth praise glorifieth me: and to him that ordereth his conversation aright will I shew the salvation of God.' Browning's Caliban, who is represented in the poem at a time before the action of *The Tempest* begins, resembles Shakespeare's creation in being both monstrous and sensitive, especially in his close observation of the natural world. See e.g., *The Tempest* II ii 157-62: 'I prithee let me bring thee where crabs grow; / And I with my long nails will dig thee pig-nuts; / Show thee a jay's nest, and instruct thee how / To snare the nimble marmoset; I'll bring thee / To clust'ring filberts, and sometimes I'll get thee / Young scammels from the rock.' Caliban mentions Setebos, the god worshipped by his 'dam' (mother), the witch Sycorax, at I ii 372-3, but does not speculate about his nature; the 'Quiet', the divinity above Setebos, is Browning's invention. The poem's intellectual sources are those of contemporary debates about evolution and the 'missing link' (Darwin, *Origin of Species*, 1859) and, as the title suggests, of older attempts to prove the existence or benevolence of God by reference to the design of the natural world (William Paley, *Natural*

Theology, 1802; see also the note on the 'Bridgewater Treatises' in 'Mr Sludge, "The Medium"', l.1140). Caliban, by contrast, deduces a cruel, jealous and capricious God from his own experience and observation; his notion of Setebos combines pagan and Old Testament ideas of sacrifice and propitiation with Calvinist ideas about predestination and God's arbitrary selection of saved and damned. Caliban refers to himself in the third person in some parts of the poem (often eliding the pronoun and putting an apostrophe before the verb, so that ''Will' in l.1 means 'He will', ''Thinketh' in l.25 means 'He thinketh' etc.). As in *The Tempest*, the plants and creatures described in the poem are an eclectic mixture of English and exotic species (as befits an imaginary and magical landscape). **7.** *pompion-plant* Pumpkin. **20–21.** Prospero, magician and ruler of the island in *The Tempest*; Miranda, his daughter. Caliban, who inherited the island from Sycorax, is now Prospero's 'slave': 'he does make our fire, / Fetch in our wood, and serves in offices / That profit us' (I ii 308, 311–13). Caliban says of Prospero, ''tis a custom with him / I' th' afternoon to sleep' (III iii 83–4). **22–3.** *gibe . . . speech* '[Caliban] You taught me language, and my profit on't / Is, I know how to curse' (I ii 363–4). **50.** *pie* Woodpecker. **51.** *oakwarts* Oak-apple galls, growths produced on oak-trees by the larvae of a species of gall wasp. **83.** *grigs* Crickets. **92.** *mankin* Puny creature; 'manakin' is also the name of a small, brightly coloured tropical species of bird. **142.** The cuttlefish, a cephalopod, has eight arms and two longer tentacles. **156.** *oncelot* Ocelot, a leopard-like cat, grey with fawn spots edged with black. **157.** *ounce* Lynx. **160.** In *The Tempest*, Caliban attempted to rape Miranda; it was after this that Prospero enslaved him (I ii 344–50). **161.** *Ariel* The spirit who carries out Prospero's magic commands in *The Tempest*. **163–6.** Caliban in *The Tempest* is compared to a fish (II ii 18f.), and kept in a hole in a rock (I ii 342–3). **177.** *orc* The killer whale; but Caliban probably means an unspecified sea-monster (so used by Browning in *The Ring and the Book* ix 970). **211.** *ball* Meteorite. **214–15.** The allusion is to a fossil. **229.** *urchin* Hedgehog. **258.** *films* Membranes.

Confessions

Published *Dramatis Personae*, 1864. **1.** *buzzing in my ears* Marlowe, *Doctor Faustus* II i 12–14: '[Good Angel] Faustus, repent. Yet God will pity thee. [Evil Angel] Thou art a spirit. God cannot pity thee. [Faustus] Who buzzeth in my ears I am a spirit?' **3.** *vale of tears* Book of Common Prayer, Psalm 84:6 ('vale of misery').

Youth and Art

Published *Dramatis Personae*, 1864. In Rome in the winter of 1859–60 Browning did a lot of modelling in clay, and the sculptor John Gibson (1790–1866), mentioned in l.8, was an admired friend. 'Smith' the sculptor and 'Kate Brown' the singer, are, as their names suggest, invented characters. **12.** *Grisi* Giulia Grisi (1811–69), Italian soprano. **31.** *shook upon E* in alt Trilled a high E (above the treble stave); trilling or 'shaking' a note is a technical term and does not imply poor control. **32.** *chromatic scale* A musical scale which uses nothing but semitones (as distinct from the diatonic scales). **34.** *gave guesses* Gossiped about who was in love with whom. **57.** The 'Prince' may be Queen Victoria's consort, Prince Albert (d. 1861), or the Prince of Wales, the future Edward VII whom Browning met in Rome in 1859. The 'Board' may be that of a grand dinner (e.g., the Royal Academy Dinner of 1851, attended by Prince Albert), or the Board of a public or charitable institution; in either case, this mark of social success and public importance, like his knighthood and membership of the Royal Academy (l.60), denotes Smith's sacrifice of his youthful ambition to be a great artist, as does Kate Brown's mercenary marriage. **58.** *bals-paré* Full-dress evening balls.

A Likeness

Published *Dramatis Personae*, 1864. **10.** *John's corns ail.* The insensitive comments of his wife and her cousin make John wince. **14.** *masks, gloves and foils* Equipment for fencing. **16.** A tandem is a two-wheeled carriage with two horses harnessed one before the other, hence the need for the long whip. **18.** *the Tipton Slasher* William Perry, from Tipton in Staffordshire, English boxing champion 1850–57; he lost the title to Tom Sayers (see below). **21** *Chablais* A district in the French Alps, east of Geneva. **22.** *Rarey drumming on Cruiser* In John S. Rarey's *Art of Taming Horses*, which Browning bought in 1858, there is a picture of Rarey whipping his horse, Cruiser. **23.** Tom Sayers was English boxing champion, 1857–60. See 'Mr Sludge, "The Medium"', l.1269n. **34.** *mezzotint* Engraving by a method in which part of a roughened plate is scraped to give lights and half lights, the rest left to give shadows. **49.** *pencil and lyre* Art and music. **54.** *Marc Antonios* Marcantonio Raimondi, early-sixteenth century engraver, famous for his prints from Raphael. **55.** *Festina lentè!* 'Hasten slowly!', a tag from the Roman historian Suetonius. **61.** *Volpato's* Giovanni Volpato (1733–1803), renowned engraver.

Mr Sludge, 'The Medium'

Published *Dramatis Personae*, 1864. A craze for spiritualism swept England and America in the 1850s; Elizabeth Barrett strongly believed in it, while Browning was a resolute sceptic. Sludge is modelled on the American medium Daniel Dunglass Home (1833–86) whom Browning had denounced after attending a seance in London in 1855, later claiming that he had detected Home in the act of cheating. In a letter of 1863 Browning referred to Home as a 'dung-ball'. After the publication of the poem, Home retaliated by claiming that Browning was jealous of the fact that the 'spirits' had crowned his wife with a wreath during the seance and passed him over; Browning mentions this in a letter of 1871, adding: 'If I ever cross the fellow's path I shall probably be silly enough to soil my shoe by kicking him . . . Indeed, I have got to consider such a beast as the proper associate and punishment of those who choose to shut their eyes and open their arms to bestiality incarnate.' The character of Sludge's patron,

Hiram H. Horsefall, is imaginary. The setting of the poem in Boston reflects the fact that New England was the centre of American intellectual life and in particular of Transcendentalist philosophy, many of whose adherents were also believers in spiritualism. Sludge is Browning's only American monologuist; though neither of the Brownings ever visited America, they had many American friends in Italy. **9**. *Catawba* A light sparkling wine, from a variety of grape named after the Catawba River in South Carolina where it was first discovered. Browning may have taken it from Longfellow's poem 'Catawba Wine' (publ. 1858); see l.1440. **31**. *undeveloped* Spiritualist jargon: the spirit has not passed through the stages of purification and refinement in the afterlife. **35–7**. Benjamin Franklin (1706–90), first Postmaster-General of the new United States, which, with his reputation for practical business sense and his association with electricity, makes him a suitable figure for Sludge to call on. American spiritualist circles claimed Franklin as head of the 'College of Spirits', a posthumous reversal of his rationalism and scepticism about supernatural phenomena during his lifetime. Thomas Paine (1737–1809), radical and rationalist, author of *The Rights of Man* and *The Age of Reason*; Franklin helped him to settle in America in 1774. **54**. *Greeley's newspaper* Horace Greeley (1811–72) founded the *New-York Tribune* in 1841 and was editor until his death. **65**. *Vs* Five-dollar bills; see l.100, 'V-notes'. **81**. In his essay 'Of Vicissitude of Things', Bacon reports the opinion that were it not for the constancy of the fixed stars and the earth's diurnal motion, 'no individual would last one moment; certain it is, that the matter is in a perpetual flux, and never at a stay'. 'Bacon came' may refer to his historical existence, or to his 'appearance' at one of Sludge's seances. **121–2**. *rare philosophers / In plaguy books* Browning's father's library contained many such books on alchemy and the occult, on which Browning drew extensively for *Paracelsus* (1835). **132**. *signs and wonders* A Biblical, and especially New Testament tag, e.g., Jesus's words in John 4:48: 'Except ye see signs and wonders, ye will not believe.' **133**. *scouts* Scorns. **136**. Samuel Johnson (1709–84); John Wesley (1703–91), founder of Methodism. 'Talking of ghosts, he [Johnson] said, "It is wonderful that five thousand years have now elapsed since the creation of the world, and still it is undecided whether or not there has ever been an instance of the spirit of any person appearing after death. All argument is against it; but all belief is for it"' (Boswell, *Life of Johnson*, Tue. 31 Mar. 1778). Immediately following this entry there is a reference to Wesley. Browning probably read in Southey's *Life of Wesley* of the episode of the poltergeist in Wesley's father's parsonage. **158**. Hamlet to the sceptical Horatio, *Hamlet* I v 166–7: 'There are more things in heaven and earth, Horatio, / Than are dreamt of in your philosophy.' Sludge quotes twice more from this play (ll.246–7, 461) as well as from another Shakespeare play with a supernatural element, *Macbeth* (see l.654n.). **168**. *Porson*. Richard Porson (1759–1808), Regius Professor of Greek at Cambridge and one of the greatest classical scholars of his time. **218**. *the stranger in your gates* A visitor who is not a family member; from Exodus 20:10, 'thy stranger that is within thy gates'. **220**. *guest without the wedding-garb* Expelled from the feast in Jesus's parable, Matthew 22:11–14. **221**. *doubting Thomas*

The apostle Thomas doubted the reality of Jesus's resurrection until convinced by touching his wounds, John 20:24–9. **233.** *Mexican War* Between Mexico and the United States, 1846–8. **234.** *free of* Free to enjoy ('given the freedom of'). **246–7.** *gulling you / To the top o' your bent Hamlet* III ii 374–5: 'They fool me to the top of my bent.' **265.** *canvas-backs* A variety of North American duck, famous for its flavour. **280.** Pennsylvania was one of the early centres of the spiritualist movement in America, with reports of congregations speaking in tongues; see also below, l.417. **286.** *Horseshoe* The Horseshoe Falls, the Canadian Falls at Niagara. **303–46.** Sludge's satirical account is close to Browning's own opinion, written shortly after his encounter with Home, of the results of 'a voluntary prostration of the intelligence before what is assumed to transcend all intelligence': 'Once arrived at this point, no trick is too gross; absurdities are referred to as "low spirits", falsehoods to "personating spirits" – and the One, terribly apparent spirit – the father of lies – has it all his own way.' **309–12.** The correct version should be that Francis Bacon (1561–1626), on his elevation to the peerage took the title of Baron Verulam; he was born not at York but at York House in London, and died at St Albans, not Wales; the rule (not 'reign') of Oliver Cromwell (1599–1658) as Lord Protector during the Interregnum began in 1653, long after Bacon's death. **328.** *Tread on their neighbour's kibes* Treat their neighbours unfeelingly ('kibes' are chilblains). **330.** *Barnum* P. T. Barnum (1810–91), the American showman. **343.** *a Thirty-third Sonata* For the piano, of which Beethoven wrote thirty-two. **345.** The United Society of Believers in Christ's Second Coming, founded by an Englishwoman, Ann Lee, who emigrated to America in 1774, were called 'Shakers' because of their physical response to spiritual influences in their services. *G, with a natural F* A musical impossibility; the scale of G demands F sharp. **346.** *the 'Stars and Stripes'* Probably 'The Star-Spangled Banner', the song by Francis Scott Key which became the American national anthem. If it were 'set to consecutive fourths' it would sound discordant. **353.** *gamboge* Gum resin used as a yellow pigment. **387.** *cockered* Pampered. **393** *kennel* Gutter. **431–3.** Sludge compares his slide into cheating with that of an alcoholic who begins by putting a dash of brandy in his tea ('souchong') and ends up drinking brandy straight. **461.** *Very like a whale* Polonius, mocked by Hamlet in *Hamlet* III ii 372. **480.** *Saul and Jonathan* The King of Israel before David, and his son, whom he attempts to kill at one point (I Samuel 18f.). **481.** *Pompey and Caesar* Rivals for power in the last Roman republic; Pompey was Caesar's son-in-law. **500.** *blow of blacks* Coal-smuts blown by the wind, an image of gossip. **526.** *their Broadway* Perhaps the Corso in Rome. **528.** *lapstone* The stone that cobblers lay in their laps to beat leather upon. **576.** *prairie-dog* A slip by Browning; the prairie-dog is a rodent, not, as intended, a wild dog. **589.** *Milton composing baby-rhymes* A double irony: it would be absurd to imagine Milton writing 'baby-rhymes', yet Sludge (or Browning) may also be alluding to Milton's 'Hymn on the Morning of Christ's Nativity', with its celebration of the infant Jesus. **589–90.** *Locke / Reasoning in gibberish* The philosopher John Locke (1632–1704), whose major work was the *Essay concerning Human Understanding*. **591–2.** *Asaph setting psalms / To crotchet and quaver* Another musical impossibility: Asaph, Biblical musician and singer in the time of King David, could not set his psalms in a musical notation developed centuries later. **595.** *pothooks* Curved strokes in handwriting, associated with a learner's hand. **654.** *strut and fret his hour Macbeth* V v 24–5: 'Life's but a walking shadow, a poor player / That struts and frets his hour upon the stage.' **655.** *spawl* Spit copiously; *target* Shield. **659–60.** Sludge has been forced to act a part, speaking the fustian lines and wearing the humiliating make-up imposed on him by his patrons. **667.** *Swedenborg* Emanuel Swedenborg (1688–1772), Swedish mystic whose visionary writings had a strong attraction for spiritualists (among them, as Browning was aware, Elizabeth Barrett). **678.** Rahab was the prostitute who helped Joshua's spies in Jericho (Joshua 2); 'Miss Stokes' stands for the respectable spiritualist who 'prostitutes' herself by telling lies in a good cause. **683.** *a live coal from the altar* Isaiah 6:6–7: 'Then flew one of the seraphims unto me, having a live coal in his hand, which he had taken with the tongs from off the altar: and he laid it upon my mouth, and said, Lo, this hath touched thy lips; and thine iniquity is taken away, and thy sin purged.' **690–93.** This famous anecdote is told of Nelson at the Battle of Copenhagen, 1801. **694:** *a real love of a lie* Bacon, in his essay 'Of Truth', speaks of 'a natural though corrupt love of the lie itself'. **706–7.** *marching on / To the promised land* A phrase from the hymn 'Through the night of doubt and sorrow' (number 274, *Hymns Ancient and Modern*). **740–45.** Alluding to the episode in Acts 17, in which the frivolous Athenians invite Paul to preach to them on 'Mars' hill', the Areopagus: 'For all the Athenians and strangers which were there spent their time in nothing else, but either to tell, or to hear some new thing.' **775.** *fribble* Trifler. **784.** The 'greenhorn' is the prostitute's inexperienced young client; the 'bully' her 'protector'. **788.** *Pasiphae* In Greek myth, wife of Minos, King of Crete, whose union with a bull produced the Minotaur. **802.** *sympathetic ink* Invisible ink. **803.** *odic lights* Supposed to be emanations of a spiritual force called Od, 'discovered' by the German chemist Karl von Reichenbach in 1845. **805–6.** *though it seem to set / The crooked straight again* In defiance of Ecclesiastes 1:15: 'That which is crooked cannot be made straight.' **832.** *delf* Glazed earthenware, from Delft or Delf in Holland. **846.** *Samuel's ghost appeared to Saul* Conjured up by the help of a medium, I Samuel 28:7–25. **910.** *raree-show* A show carried in a box, such a peep-show or puppet-show, exhibited at markets and fairs. **919.** *The Bible says so* Genesis 1:14: 'And God said, Let there be lights in the firmament of heaven . . . and let them be for signs, and for seasons, and for days, and years.' **921.** *Charles's Wain* The constellation of the Great Bear, or Big Dipper. **929.** *powder-plots prevented* Referring to the thwarting of the Gunpowder Plot to blow up the Houses of Parliament in 1605. **995–1004.** The informal 'knocking' represents the unorthodox summons to belief conveyed by intimations from the spirit-world, in contrast to the 'bell' of human reason, natural theology, or the 'traditional peal' of church bells, i.e., orthodox Christianity. **1035.** *canthus* Corner of the eye, where the lids meet. **1074.** *the "Great and Terrible Name"* Psalm 99:1–3: 'The Lord reigneth; let the people tremble: he sitteth between the cherubims; let the earth be moved. The Lord is great in Zion; and he is high above all the people. Let them praise thy great and terrible name; for it is holy.' Further on (l.1086f.) Sludge alludes to the refusal of orthodox Jews to pronounce the name of Jahweh (Jehovah). **1117.** *stomach-cyst* Apparently Browning's coinage, meaning a minute primitive organism, such as the one described in the following lines. **1128–40.** For the 'natural theology' outlined here, see note to 'Caliban upon Setebos' above. **1137.** *We are His children* St Paul's words to the Athenians (see ll.740–5n.), Acts 17:28, though the context is the reverse of the one Sludge alludes to here (that 'all things minister / To man'): 'in him [God] we live, and move, and have our being; as certain also of your own poets have said, For we are also his offspring.' See note to 'Cleon' above. **1140.** *the Bridgewater book* The Reverend Francis, Earl of Bridgewater (1758–1829), left money in his will for the writing of essays 'On the Power, Wisdom, and Goodness of God, as Manifested in the Creation'. The 'Bridgewater Treatises' were published 1833–40; the first, by Thomas Chalmers (1780–1847), was called 'The Adaptation of External Nature to the Moral and Intellectual Constitution of Man'. See note to 'Caliban upon Setebos', above. **1170.** *boblink* Usually 'bobolink', a North American songbird. **1187.** *that same personage* Sludge, who is using the metaphor of himself as 'heir' (see ll.1140ff.), invokes the analogy of the literal heir to the English throne, the Prince of Wales (future Edward VII), whose entourage during his visit to America caused much comment in the American press. **1225.** *'Time' with the foil in carte* A technical term in fencing, meaning to judge the correct moment to parry an opponent's thrust. **1227.** *Make the red hazard* Pocket the red ball in billiards. **1268.** *the President* At the time of publication, Lincoln. *Jenny Lind* The celebrated soprano (1820–87), known as the 'Swedish Nightingale'. **1269.** *Emerson* Ralph Waldo Emerson (1803–82), poet, essayist, philosopher, and by this time the pre-eminent American man of letters. Browning had never met him, but knew and admired his work. *the Benicia Boy* The American boxing champion, John Heenan (from his birthplace, Benicia in California). On 17 April 1860 he fought a celebrated drawn bout with the English champion, John Sayers (see 'A Likeness', l.23n.); in her letters of the time Elizabeth Barrett referred several times to the interest aroused by the contest. **1299.** *Beacon Street* One of the principal streets in Boston. **1331–7.** Sludge's 'hazy notion' of a passage in the Greek (not Roman) historian Herodotus (fifth century B.C.); in book I of his *History*, Herodotus recounts that women in Babylon (not Egypt) prostituted themselves once in their lifetime at the temple of Aphrodite. **1381.** *cresset* Fire-basket. **1392.** *harlequin's pasteboard sceptre* In traditional pantomime, a magic wand used by Harlequin against his rival, the Clown. **1439–41.** *Lowell, Longfellow, Hawthorne* Prominent American writers, the first and third of whom were also personal friends of Browning's: James Russell Lowell (1819–91), poet, essayist and critic; Henry Wadsworth Longfellow (1807–82), poet; Nathaniel Hawthorne (1804–64), writer of fiction. **1450.** *the Lizard Age* A book about dinosaurs. **1451.** *the Old Country War* The American War of Independence, 1775–83. **1452.** *Jerome Napoleon* Youngest brother of Napoleon Bonaparte (1784–1860). **1454.** *life in stones* By the study of fossils. **1455.** *Fire into fog* Probably alluding to the 'fire-mist', the primeval state of the universe in some contemporary theories; the term was coined by Robert Chambers in *Vestiges of the Natural History of Creation* (1844). **1465**. The book is imaginary. Thebes, in Egypt, was fabled for wealth and power; it may have been one of the models for the city in 'Love Among the Ruins' (see ll.21n., 73–8n.). **1472–4**. Both Lady Jane Grey, executed in 1553 by Mary Tudor after an abortive attempt to make her Queen, and Elizabeth I were Protestant heroines and enemies of the Catholic Mary; Sludge's fantasy of them together in heaven would be calculated to please the (presumably Protestant) Horsefall. It is not clear whether this is the actual fraud whose detection precedes the opening of the poem, or whether Sludge is using it as an illustration. **1479**. *arnica* Mountain tobacco (*Arnica montana*) is used in a tincture for relieving swelling and bruises. **1523**. *herring-pond* The Atlantic (*OED* first records this colloquialism in 1686).

Apparent Failure

Published *Dramatis Personae*, 1864. The morgue was not in fact demolished, and still stands, but is closed to the public. **1–8**. The Brownings were in Paris from October 1855 to June 1856. The two events referred to – the 'baptism' and the 'Congress' – did not take place at the same time. The Imperial Congress to end the Crimean War opened in Paris on 25 February 1856 and peace was concluded a month later. At this Congress Count Camillo Benso Cavour successfully pleaded for the recognition of Piedmont as an independent state after its aid to the British and French in the war; Prince Alexander Gortschakoff and Count Karl Ferdinand Buol-Schauenstein represented Russia and Austria respectively. Prince Louis Napoleon, the only son of the Emperor Napoleon III, was baptized in June 1856. **10**. *Doric* Originally the earliest of the three 'orders' of Greek architecture; here meaning a plain, strong style of building. **12**. The Italian poet and humanist Petrarch (1304–74) lived for much of his life in Provence; Fontaine-de-Vaucluse, near Avignon, source of the river Sorgue, was a favourite retreat. The Brownings visited it on their journey to Italy after their marriage in 1846. **39**. *Tuileries* The palace where French sovereigns resided. **43–4**. *Does the Empire . . . missed?* Napoleon III made himself Emperor in 1852, ending the Second Republic. **46–7**. *red in vain / Or black* Socialist or reactionary; with a pun on the gambling game 'rouge et noir' (see next lines). **58–63**. Browning's opposition to the doctrine of eternal punishment is re-stated in several other poems, notably 'Ixion' (*Jocoseria*, 1883). **60**. Revelation 1:11: 'I am Alpha and Omega, the first and the last'.

Epilogue [to *Dramatis Personae*]

Published *Dramatis Personae*, 1864. In the first edition the first and second speakers were not identified. King David, ancestor and highest type of Christ in the Old Testament, represents the certainties of traditional religion; Ernest Renan (1823–92), author of the controversial *Vie de Jésus* (1863), represents contemporary scepticism about the authenticity of the Gospel narratives and despair at the loss of faith in the central Christian truth of the Incarnation. The third speaker, unnamed in all editions, voices Browning's view that faith is not dependent on a particular doctrine or mode of worship, and that the Incarnation takes place not in the historical figure of Jesus, but in the universe whose shifting play of circumstances defines each human being's unique identity, and which reciprocally manifests the full range of human experience ('feels and knows'). 1–21. The source is II Chronicles 5:11–14, describing the dedication of the Temple at Jerusalem, when Solomon brought the Ark of the Covenant into the sanctuary: 'And it came to pass, when the priests were come out of the holy place (. . . also the Levites, which were the singers . . . being arrayed in white linen, having cymbals and psalteries and harps, stood at the east end of the altar, and with them an hundred and twenty priests sounding with trumpets:) it came even to pass, as the trumpeters and singers were as one, to make one sound to be heard in praising and thanking the Lord; and when they lifted up their voice with the trumpets and cymbals and instruments of musick, and praised the Lord, saying, For he is good; for his mercy endureth for ever: that then the house was filled with a cloud, even the house of the Lord; so that the priests could not stand to minister by reason of the cloud: for the glory of the Lord had filled the house of God.' 11. *lift* Past tense, 'lifted' (an allowed form). 24–5. *that star / Which came, stood, opened once* The star which guided the Magi to Bethlehem, and 'came and stood over where the young child was' (Matthew 2:9): an emblem of the Incarnation of God in Man. 36–7. *When a first shadow . . . motion* When the first doubts arose about the authenticity of the Gospels and therefore the truth of the Incarnation. 46. *lesser lights* The moon and stars (Genesis 1:16); the 'greater light', the sun ('son', Jesus) is gone. The speaker goes on to say that each star may be, as science suggests, a sun to its own world, but that is no comfort to us. 57. *serene* Serene brightness.

House

Published *Pacchiarotto and How He Worked in Distemper: with Other Poems*, 1876. It is the plainest statement of Browning's lifelong disavowal of autobiographical or confessional poetry (there are of course many exceptions in passages and whole poems, including, by a necessary irony, 'House' itself; for a good example of the principle in action, see the next poem, 'Saint Martin's Summer'). The poem revives the young Browning's dislike of Wordsworth (see note to 'The Lost Leader') in its rebuttal of Wordsworth's 'Scorn not the Sonnet', which opens: 'Scorn not the Sonnet; Critic, you have frowned, / Mindless of its just honours; with this key / Shakespeare unlocked his heart.' In his essay on Shelley (1852), Browning on the contrary praises Shakespeare as the type of the 'objective' (non-confessional) poet. Browning himself wrote notably few sonnets and published none in volume form; one of the few is a sonnet in praise of Shakespeare, 'The Names' (see p. 293). 3. *pelf* Possessions. 29. *goodman* Householder or husband.

Saint Martin's Summer

Published *Pacchiarotto and How He Worked in Distemper: with Other Poems*,

1876. Saint Martin's Summer', or 'Indian Summer', refers to the period of fine weather thought to occur often in mid-autumn (Saint Martin's day is 11 November); in the poem it stands for the second flowering of love. The poem may have been influenced by the break between Browning and Louisa, Lady Ashburton, in 1869, after he refused her proposal of marriage, but it is not directly autobiographical. 1. *protesting* In the sense of 'protestations' (of love); also l.67. 7–8. *mansion . . . bower* Metaphors (elaborated in the following lines) for commitment to a stable and would-be permanent relationship as against a more transient affair. 71–2. *Penelope, Ulysses* Types of wisdom and prudence in Homer's *Odyssey*.

Ned Bratts

Published *Dramatic Idyls*, 1879. The poem, based on the story of 'Old Tod' in John Bunyan's *Life and Death of Mr. Badman* (1680), is also a portrait of Bunyan himself, whom Browning regarded with 'utmost admiration and reverence'; Browning freely changed the circumstances of Bunyan's life and work in order to bring him personally into the story. 5. *bibbing* Tippling. 12. *tag-rag and bobtail* Rabble, riff-raff. *a-bowsing* Boozing. 17. *Of a reek* Reeking (with sweat). 18. *forbye* Besides. 20. *they* The 'gentry'. 28. *boggled* Took fright. 29. *Tom Styles . . . Jack Nokes* Conventional names (like 'John Doe'); Brewer's *Dictionary of Phrase and Fable* differentiates between Tom as 'the honest dullard' and Jack as 'the sharp, shrewd, active fellow', which fits the context here, where Tom is being hanged for Jack's crime. 32. *frizzles* Curls (of the judge's wig). 33. *fleered* Rejoiced (at getting off 'scot-free'); to 'fleer' in this context is to laugh coarsely. 35. *rank puritans caught at prayer* Worship outside the Church of England was forbidden under the Act of Uniformity, 1662, in force until the Toleration Act of 1689. 'Puritans' is here a catch-all term of abuse for any Nonconformist or Dissenting church. 43. *Serjeant* Judge; until 1873 common law judges were always chosen from barristers who had attained the degree of serjeant-at-law. 52. *Publican* Besides the literal meaning, recalling the biblical sense of 'tax-gatherer' and its associations ('publicans and sinners', Mark 2:16; 'an heathen man and a publican', Matthew 18:17). 64. *javelineers* Sheriff's officers who provided the escort for judges at the assizes. 67. *Dropped the baby down the well* Killed an unwanted illegitimate child; *left the tithesman in the lurch* Evaded paying tax ('tithes') due to the Church. 71. *in our Public* 'In our public house', with a play on 'in public, openly': while the court meets to decide the fate of comparatively minor offenders, Ned Bratts and his wife have been carrying on their dual activities as criminals and informers with impunity. 78. *quean* Hussy. 79. *pedlar* Here, euphemism for 'thief'; *noggin* Mug (of ale). 82. *midden* Dunghill. 83. *billet* Wooden club. 86. *(I've baulked a d—)* By saying 'lily-livered' instead of 'damned', Ned Bratts avoids the sin of swearing. See also ll.92, 100, 104, 243. 89. *not a stoppage to travel has chanced* 'Not a hold-up (by a highwayman) has occurred'. 92. *Od's* 'God's' (this oath has slipped by Ned's guard). 96. *He danced the jig that needs no floor* One of many similar euphemisms for hanging. 97. *'Twas Scroggs that houghed the mare!* Smouch was hanged not for the theft of which he failed to give Ned Bratts and Tab their cut, but for an offence he did not commit, 'houghing' or hamstringing a horse. **98.** Psalm 37:36 (Book of Common Prayer): 'I myself have seen the ungodly in great power: and flourishing like a green bay-tree.' **100.** *Zounds* 'God's wounds'. **102.** *the Book* Bunyan's *Pilgrim's Progress* (see l.111n.). **104.** *'Sdeath* 'God's death'. **111.** *Who wrote it in the Jail* Bunyan was imprisoned in Bedford Jail for preaching without a licence, 1660–72, during which time he wrote most of *Pilgrim's Progress* (not published however until 1678). **114.** *Gammer* 'Old woman'; the male equivalent is 'Gaffer' (l.119). **114–15.** *bobbing like a crab / On Yule-tide bowl* Alluding to the traditional Christmas game where players with their hands tied duck for crab-apples floating in a bowl. **117.** *fuddling-cap* To 'fuddle one's cap' is to get drunk; 'cap' in this and cognate phrases means 'head', so Browning's use of 'fuddling-cap' as an article of clothing is an error. **126.** *pad on, my prate-apace* 'Keep on talking, loudmouth.' **129.** Bunyan was a tinker by profession; in prison he made lace to support himself and his family. His blind daughter sold the lace (l.135 below). **130.** *twelve years ago* Bunyan was arrested in 1660 (see l.111n.); this, and l.315, therefore fix the date of the action as 1672; Bunyan was in fact released from prison in June of that year, a fact foreshadowed in ll.307–12. **156–7.** *a Dives . . . Charles* 'Dives' in Latin means rich man, and is the name conventionally given to the rich man in the parable in Luke 16:19–31, who is damned while the beggar Lazarus is saved. 'Charles' is Charles II, who came to the throne at the restoration in 1660 (see ll.315–16); 'Charles's Wain [Wagon]' is a name for the constellation of the Great Bear. **160.** *lump of leavened sin* I Corinthians 5:6–8: 'Know ye not that a little leaven leaveneth the whole lump? . . . Therefore let us keep the feast, not with old leaven, neither with the leaven of malice and wickedness; but with the unleavened bread of sincerity and truth.' **161.** *"'Down on my marrow-bones!'* 'I went down on my knees (to ask forgiveness).' **164–70.** A variant of the parable in Luke 13:7–9: 'Then said he unto the dresser of his vineyard, Behold, these three years I come seeking fruit on this fig tree, and find none; cut it down; why cumbereth it the ground? And he answering said unto him, Lord, let it alone this year also, till I shall dig about it, and dung it: and if it bear fruit, well: and if not, then after that thou shalt cut it down.' **166.** *dreriment* Dreariness or dismalness; Browning probably found this archaic form in Spenser, who coined it. **168.** *cloister* In the (original, now obsolete) sense of an enclosed space; but the anti-Catholic Bunyan may also be punning on the word's religious connotations. **172.** *stag-horns* Bare upper branches; this nonce-use was probably influenced by the stag-horn beetle. **174.** *marle* Soil; Milton's 'burning marl' (*Paradise Lost* i 296) had associated the word with hell, and Browning may also have come across the phrase in George Eliot's *Daniel Deronda* (1876). **178.** *Tophet* Biblical name for Hell; used by Bunyan in *Pilgrim's Progress* (see l.203n. below; also 'Childe Roland to the Dark Tower Came', ll.143n. and 160n. **179.** *'Look unto me and be ye saved!'* Isaiah 45:22. **180.** Alluding to Moses striking water from the rock in the wilderness (Exodus 17:6 and Numbers 20:11). *outstreats* out flows. In a footnote in the first edition, Browning cited Donne's use of this word in 'The Progress of the Soul', a poem also alluded to admiringly in *The Two Poets of Croisic* (1878). **181–2.** Isaiah 1:18: 'Come now, and let us reason together, saith the Lord: though your sins be as scarlet, they shall be as white as snow; though they be red like crimson, they shall be as wool.' **201.** *a just-lugged bear* A bear that has just been tormented by having its fur pulled. **202.** *You had* 'You could have'. **203.** *Christmas* Ned Bratts's error for Christian, the hero of *Pilgrim's Progress*. From this point the poem is saturated with specific allusions to famous episodes and characters from *Pilgrim's Progress*: Christian's flight from the City of Destruction, abandoning his wife and children, the 'burden' (of original sin) from which he is released by grace, his entry through the 'wicket-gate' to the way of salvation, the Slough of Despond, the encounter with the fiend Apollyon, the martyrdom of Faithful in Vanity Fair, etc. **204–5.** *Joseph's sack . . . which held the cup* Ned Bratts's confused recollection of Genesis 44, in which Joseph, sending his brothers back to Canaan with sacks of food, conceals his silver cup in the sack of his youngest brother, Benjamin, and then makes believe to accuse them of theft. **206.** *chine* Backbone. **207.** *you pitched me as I flung* 'You gave as good as you got.' **221.** *I had* 'I would have.' **225.** Compare the angel with his sickle in Revelation 14:19. **229.** *thrid* Thread, follow the course of. **231.** The Delectable Mountains come into view towards the end of Christian's journey; Faithful had taken 'death's short cut' by his martyrdom. **243.** *Odds my life* A minced oath, as at l.92. **246.** Ned Bratts, wishing to flatter the judge's wisdom, first addresses him as Master Worldly-Wiseman, and then, remembering that he is one of the villains of *Pilgrim's Progress*, revises this to the genuinely wise Interpreter who helps Christian. **263.** *peach* Inform. **270.** *Sackerson* A celebrated Elizabethan bear, mentioned in *Merry Wives of Windsor* I i 269; Ned Bratts however speaks as though the bear were still alive. **271.** *Brawl* Dance. **274–5.** *Where's hope . . . light?* John 3:20: 'every one that doeth evil hateth the light'. The man in the iron cage (of despair) in *Pilgrim's Progress* is said to have 'sinned against the light of the word'. **288.** *I wis* Or 'iwis', archaic term meaning 'assuredly, indeed'. **289–90.** 'A Fox should not be of the Jury at a Goose's trial' (Thomas Fuller, *Gnomologia*, 116). **292.** *i'feggs* A variant of 'i'faith'. **298.** *though a fox confessed* 'Though you were an acknowledged villain'. **303.** *Amicus Curiae* 'Friend of the Court' (a joke on the legal term, which is not literally applicable to Ned Bratts). **315–16.** The restoration of the monarchy after the Civil War and the Interregnum took place with the accession of Charles II in 1660, celebrated in Dryden's poem *Astraea Redux*. Astraea was the Roman goddess of Justice. **320.** *those two dozen odd* The 'rank Puritans' of ll. 35–8. **325–6.** These lines were not in the first edition. **328.** *Bunyan's Statue* By Sir Joseph Boehm (1834–90), given to the town in 1874.

Clive

Published *Dramatic Idyls, Second Series*, 1880. Robert Clive, later Baron Clive of Plassey (1725–74), one of the principal architects of British rule in India, did fight a duel in his youth, but Browning's version of the story (which he recalled hearing over thirty years before he wrote the poem) differs considerably from the original, notably in the confession of Clive's opponent that he did indeed cheat at cards, and Clive's explanation that he was afraid, not that his opponent would kill him, but that he would contemptuously spare his life. The framing narrative of the father reminiscing to his son is Browning's invention. Clive had been accused of corruption on his return from India in 1767; the story told by the poem's narrator is set a week before his suicide in 1774. 8. *Plassy* The battle in 1757 which secured British control of north-east India. 11. *thrids* Threads. 12. *this forthright, that meander* Straight and crooked paths; from *The Tempest* III iii 3. 13. *rood* A measure of 5½ yards. 16. *rummer-glass* A large drinking glass. 26. *Scripture says* John 10:1 is nearest: 'He that entereth not by the door into the sheepfold, but climbeth up some other way, the same is a thief and a robber.' Browning may also recall Milton's Satan leaping over the wall of Paradise, *Paradise Lost* iv 178–83. 31. *Poor as Job and meek as Moses* Proverbial expressions, qualified in the following line: Job, made poor by his afflictions, is subsequently restored to prosperity: 'So the Lord blessed the latter end of Job more than his beginning' (Job 42:12); Moses, the meekest of all men (Numbers 12:3), nevertheless confronts Pharaoh and leads the Children of Israel out of bondage. 39–40. Clive was eighteen when he went to India in 1743 as a clerk with the East India Company; soon after he entered the army, and was a colonel when he took the city of Arcot in 1751. 47. *Too much bee's-wing floats my figure?* 'Is my metaphor too complicated?' Bee's-wing is the crust that forms on old port wine. The sense of the 'figure' in the preceding lines, as of the one in the lines which follow, is that the narrator was better able to befriend Clive in his decline than when he was at the height of his fame. 65. *drug-box* Opium, to which Clive was addicted. 70. *Pitt* William Pitt the Elder (1708–78). 71. *Frederick the Fierce* Frederick the Great (1712–86), King of Prussia. 72. *bore the bell away* Carried off the prize. 76. *mortal* Mortal nature. 91. *factor-days* Days as a clerk. 92. *Saint David's* A fort near Madras. 112. *Thyrsis . . . Chloe* Conventional names for pastoral lovers in classical and neo-classical literature. 183–4. *Twenty-five / Years ago* An approximation; actually twenty-eight. 190. Luke 11:24–6: 'When the unclean spirit is gone out of a man, he walketh through dry places, seeking rest; and finding none, he saith, I will return unto my house whence I came out. And when he cometh, he findeth it swept and garnished. Then goeth he, and taketh to him seven other spirits more wicked than himself; and they enter in, and dwell there: and the last state of that man is worse than the first.'

['Wanting is – what?']

Published *Jocoseria*, 1883, untitled.

Donald

Published *Jocoseria*, 1883. The poem, an attack on the philistinism and moral blindness of the advocates of blood-sports, is also a rebuke to Browning's son Pen, a keen hunter; he and his friends at Oxford are almost certainly the models for the hearty, unthinking young men at the beginning of the poem.

However, ll.41–4 distance the narrator from too close an identification with Browning himself, since they state that the narrator, too, went to Oxford and is a distinguished classical scholar (see Introduction). 5. *bothy* Hut, cottage. 12. *Glenlivet* A variety of Scotch whisky. 62. *Mount . . . Ben . . .* Ben is Scottish for 'mount'; the narrator cannot remember the name which should follow. 76. *burnie* Small burn or stream. 79. *an end in* ich Characteristic of Gaelic names. 100. *foils* In the archaic sense of 'treads, tramples on'. 103. *callant* Youth. 107. *brig* Bridge. 120. *scouted* Scorned. 136. *Blondin* Jules Blondin, French tightrope artist (1829–97), famous for his crossing of Niagara Falls in 1859. 182. *pastern* The part of the deer's foot above the hoof. 206. *clouted* Patched up. 210. *bracket* To hang on the wall (as an ornamental lamp-holder, for example). 234–5. *'within gate / Though teeth kept tongue'* 'Although I kept quiet' (as Browning remarks, a phrase adapted from Homer).

Never the Time and the Place

Published *Jocoseria*, 1883. 7. *the house is narrow* The grave, as in 'The Statue and the Bust', l.216, 'the narrow room'. 12–13. The enemy is the devil, who in the lover's dream suggests that the death of the 'loved one' means final separation, a suggestion the 'waking man' repudiates.

The Names

Published 1884 in a booklet printed for the 'Shakespearean Show' at the Albert Hall, in aid of charity; not collected by Browning, who rarely wrote sonnets and never included them in his collections (see note to 'House'). The poem alludes to the saying by Alexandre Dumas (the younger), 'After God, Shakespeare has created most.' 5–6. *That which the Hebrew reads / With his soul only* In orthodox Judaism it is forbidden to pronounce the name of God, Jahweh.

Now

Published *Asolando*, 1889.

Beatrice Signorini

Published *Asolando*, 1889. Founded on an anecdote in a source Browning frequently used, Filippo Baldinucci's twenty-volume *Notizie de' Professori del Disegno* (Florence, 1681–1728), concerning two seventeenth-century Italian painters, one a major figure, Artemisia Gentileschi (1597–c. 1652), the other a minor artist, Francesco Romanelli (1617–62). Browning treated the material with his usual freedom (e.g., in Baldinucci the relationship between Francesco and Artemisia is 'an innocent friendship'; the initiative for the joint painting is Francesco's; Artemisia knows from the beginning that she is to be the subject of the central portrait; her border is of fruit, not flowers; Beatrice destroys the portrait in her husband's absence, not to his face), and the psychology is very much his own. The poem is Browning's last on the theme of painting, and the only one to refer to a woman painter. 2. *Viterbo* About forty miles north-west of

Rome. **4-5.** *Cortona's school . . . Berretini* Pietro Berrettini [sic] da Cortona (1596-1669); Cortona is about thirty-five miles east of Siena. **16-24.** Artemisia painted *Desire* (a nude figure) in honour of Michelangelo's memory, and gave the painting to his family ('Buonarotti's house'); on Baldinucci's advice the nudity was covered up. Browning's scorn for Baldinucci's prudishness and religious bigotry is also evident in two other poems (not in this edition): 'Filippo Baldinucci on the Privilege of Burial' (*Pacchiarotto*, 1876) and 'Parleying with Francis Furini' (*Parleyings*, 1887). **32.** *sphery* Like the spheres, the heavenly bodies in ancient cosmology. **34.** *enjoint* Embed. **79.** *Guido's* The painter Guido Reni (1575-1642). **111.** *acromion* The outer extremity of the shoulder-blade. **118.** *motors, flexors* Muscles of motion and bending. **119-20.** *Ser Santi . . . pencil-prig* 'The painter Santi di Tito (1536-1603), renowned for the precision of his drawing, was given his nickname by Titian. **145.** *Bicè* Diminutive of Beatrice. **161.** *idlesse* Leisure. **251-2.** *Calypso's . . . Penelope* At the start of Homer's *Odyssey*, Odysseus is 'prevented from returning to the home and wife he longed for by that powerful goddess, the Nymph Calypso, who wished him to marry her, and kept him in her vaulted cave.' **261-76.** '*Such spells . . . indulged* Francesco's internal monologue; he speaks aloud from l.277. **262.** *sex* The female sex. **298-9.** *Grey / Good mouse-ear* 'Mouse-ear' is a name given to several plants; the nearest to 'grey' in colour would be chickweed, which has delicate white flowers. **299.** *auricula* A species of primula; 'formerly a great favourite with flower-fanciers . . . the corollas often powdered with white or grey' (*OED*). **307.** *spilla* Italian 'pin'; glossed in the next line as the 'dagger-plaything' with which Beatrice pins her hair. **325.** *occulted star* A star hidden from view by another passing in front of it. **348.** *the elder race* Renaissance painters such as Michelangelo or Raphael.

Spring Song

Published 1886 in *The New Amphion* ('The Book of the Edinburgh University Union Fancy Fair'); then incorporated (without the title) as the concluding lines of 'Parleying with Gerard de Lairesse' (*Parleyings*, 1887), introduced as follows:

> Here's rhyme
> Such as one makes now, – say, when Spring repeats
> That miracle the Greek Bard sadly greets:
> 'Spring for the tree and herb – no Spring for us!'
> Let Spring come: why, a man salutes her thus:

The lyric has been placed out of chronological sequence in order to end the volume. It undoubtedly refers in some sense to Elizabeth Barrett, but not in specific detail: she is buried at Florence under a marble monument, not under a 'mound' in what is clearly an English churchyard. In a letter to Browning during their courtship Elizabeth Barrett referred to an untitled draft of 'Home-Thoughts, from Abroad' as Browning's 'spring-song'. Browning is known to have re-read the courtship letters late in life.

Index of Titles

Index of First Lines

CHRONOLOGY

1812 Born 7 May in Camberwell, son of Robert Browning, clerk in Bank of England, and Sarah Anna Wiedemann.

1812 Birth of Sarianna, RB's only sibling.

1820–26 Weekly boarder at Revd Thomas Ready's school in Peckham.

1823–4 Becomes friends with Eliza and Sarah Flower, wards of W. J. Fox, Unitarian minister, political radical and editor of the *Monthly Repository*, which will publish early poems by RB in the mid 1830s.

1826–8 Privately educated at home; writes a volume called *Incondita* (= trifles) but destroys it; two poems ('The Dance of Death' and 'The First-Born of Egypt') survive in copies made by Sarah Flower, who says RB was fourteen when he wrote them.

1828 Attends courses in Latin, Greek and German at London University (founded 1827, now University College London) but leaves May 1829.

1830 Contributes to the *Trifler*, an amateur literary magazine.

1832 Sees the famous actor Edmund Kean in one of his last performances as Richard III, and conceives a 'foolish plan' to 'assume & realise I know not how many different characters' (poet, novelist, composer, etc.); writes *Pauline*, supposedly the first product of this plan.

1833 *Pauline* published anonymously (Saunders & Otley), paid for by RB's aunt Mrs Silverthorne; reviewed favourably in *Monthly Repository*; a copy sent by Fox to John Stuart Mill for a review which never appeared eventually finds its way back to RB, who responds to Mill's comments with copious annotations of his own. Not a single copy of the poem is sold, and RB does not acknowledge his authorship until the threat of pirate publication forces him to include *Pauline* in the *Poetical Works* of 1868.

1834 *March–June*: Travels to Russia as unpaid secretary on diplomatic mission.

Begins writing *Sordello*, but lays it aside when a friend suggests the Renaissance physician and alchemist Paracelsus as subject for a poem.

September: Begins work on *Paracelsus*.

1835 Publication of *Paracelsus* (Effingham Wilson); RB's father funds this and all his son's volumes, except *Strafford*, until 1846. The poem has considerable critical success, notably with the actor-manager W. C. Macready, who persuades RB to write for the stage.

1836 Helps the critic John Forster complete his prose *Life of Strafford* and again lays *Sordello* aside to write his own tragedy, *Strafford*.

1837 *Strafford* published (Longman) and produced at Covent Garden on 1 May, with Macready in title role; closes after five performances.

1838 Travels by sea to Trieste, then Venice and nearby 'delicious Asolo', together with other locations mentioned in Sordello.

1839 Macready rejects RB's second play, *King Victor and King Charles*.

1840 *Sordello* published (Moxon, RB's publisher until after 1846); received with near-universal derision. Macready rejects *The Return of the Druses*, despite RB's strenuous efforts to make it acceptable. Browning family moves from Camberwell to New Cross, Hatcham, in Surrey.

1841 Publication of *Pippa Passes*, first in series of cheap, paper-bound pamphlets with series title *Bells and Pomegranates* (RB later explained that these terms derived from a passage in the Bible and were intended to symbolize an alternation or mixture of 'grave and gay, singing and sermonizing'). Macready reluctantly accepts *A Blot in the 'Scutcheon* for the stage.

1842 *March*: Publication of *King Victor and King Charles*, no. 2 of *Bells and Pomegranates*.

July: RB reviews a biography of Tasso in the *Foreign Quarterly Review* but turns the review into an essay defending the eighteenth-century poet and forger Thomas Chatterton; this 'Essay on Chatterton' is RB's only formal piece of prose criticism apart from the 'Essay on Shelley' published ten years later.

November: Publication of *Dramatic Lyrics*, no. 3 of *Bells and*

Pomegranates, RB's first collection of shorter poems, including 'My Last Duchess' and 'The Pied Piper of Hamelin'.

1843 *January*: Publication of *The Return of the Druses*, no. 4 of *Bells and Pomegranates*.

February: Publication of *A Blot in the 'Scutcheon*, no. 5 of *Bells and Pomegranates*; the play is finally produced at Drury Lane but closes after three performances and ends RB's friendship with Macready.

1844 Offers *Colombe's Birthday* to Charles Kean, son of Edmund Kean and Macready's leading rival, but negotiations break down and RB publishes the play as no. 6 of *Bells and Pomegranates*; he never attempts to write for the stage again (his last two plays, published in 1846, were not offered to a theatre).

July: Travels by sea to Naples, and also visits Rome and Florence for the first time.

December: Returns to find flattering reference to his poetry in Elizabeth Barrett's recently published *Poems*. EB, six years older, financially independent though living under her father's roof, and far better known as a poet, was a reclusive invalid, but RB was already an admirer of her work and their mutual friend John Kenyon encouraged him to write to her.

1845 *10 January*: Writes to Elizabeth Barrett: 'Dear Miss Barrett, I love your poems with all my heart . . . and I love you too.' The correspondence develops into a courtship, with letters and meetings (beginning on 20 May) increasing in frequency and intimacy, the latter carefully kept from EB's domineering father, Edward Moulton Barrett, who had a deep aversion to the thought of any of his children (of either sex) marrying.

November: RB publishes his second collection of shorter poems, *Dramatic Romances and Lyrics*, no. 7 of *Bells and Pomegranates*, including 'How They Brought the Good News from Ghent to Aix', 'The Lost Leader' and 'Home-Thoughts, from Abroad'.

1846 *February*: Publication of *Luria* and *A Soul's Tragedy*, two plays which together make up no. 8 of *Bells and Pomegranates*, the last in the series.

10 September: EB's father announces that the family is moving out of their London residence in Wimpole Street while it is repainted; alarmed at the thought of being separated, RB and EB

343

decide on an immediate clandestine marriage, which takes place on 12 September at St Marylebone Church; a week later they leave for Italy, arriving at Pisa on 14 October. Mr Barrett renounces his daughter, refuses to answer her letters or acknowledge the birth of his grandson, and dies unreconciled to her in 1857.

1847 RB and EB move to Florence, eventually settling in Casa Guidi on the south bank of the Arno, their home until EB's death except for visits to England and Paris in 1851–2, 1855–6 and 1858.

1849 Publication of RB's *Poems* in two volumes, RB's first collected edition, though omitting *Strafford* and *Sordello*; issued by Chapman & Hall, EB's publishers, who continue to publish RB until 1868, except for a volume of selections issued by Moxon in 1865.

8 March: Birth of the Brownings' only child, Robert Wiedemann Barrett Browning (nicknamed 'Penini', then 'Pen'); ten days later RB's mother dies.

EB shows RB the sonnets she wrote during their courtship, eventually published as *Sonnets from the Portuguese* (title suggested by RB).

1850 Publication of EB's collected *Poems* including *Sonnets from the Portuguese*, and of RB's *Christmas-Eve and Easter Day*.

1851 Publication of EB's *Casa Guidi Windows*, a reflection of her (and RB's) support for the Italian movement for unity and independence, the 'Risorgimento'. RB's father becomes embroiled in a breach-of-promise suit.

1852 RB's father is forced to leave England to avoid paying damages and settles with Sarianna in Paris. RB writes introduction to a volume of Shelley's letters (all but two of which turn out to be forged); now known as the 'Essay on Shelley', RB's second and last formal piece of prose criticism.

1855 Publication of *Men and Women*, consisting of fifty-one poems including 'Love Among the Ruins', 'Fra Lippo Lippi', 'Childe Roland to the Dark Tower Came', 'Bishop Blougram's Apology', 'Andrea del Sarto', 'A Grammarian's Funeral' and the dedication to EB, 'One Word More'. RB had counted on the volume restoring his reputation; the disappointing reviews (and sales) plunge him into a deep depression.

1856 Publication of EB's *Aurora Leigh*, a critical (and commercial) success. A legacy from John Kenyon gives the Brownings financial security.

1857 Death of EB's father.

1860 Publication of EB's *Poems before Congress*.

1861 *29 June*: EB dies at Casa Guidi. A month later RB leaves Florence with Pen; he settles in London, with holidays in Scotland, France, Switzerland and, in later years, Italy again, though never Florence.

1862 Publication of EB's *Last Poems*, selected and edited by RB.

1863 Publication of *Selections from the Poetical Works*, chosen by RB's friends John Forster and B. W. Procter, and of *Poetical Works* (3 vols.), including *Strafford* and *Sordello*. Further volumes of selections are published in 1865 (Moxon), 1872 and 1880 (Smith, Elder).

1864 Publication of *Dramatis Personae*, including 'Rabbi Ben Ezra', 'A Death in the Desert', 'Caliban upon Setebos' and 'Mr Sludge, "The Medium"'. For the first time in RB's career, a second edition is called for. Starts work on *The Ring and the Book*.

1866 Death of RB's father in Paris; Sarianna moves to London and lives with RB.

1867 Awarded honorary MA by Oxford University and honorary fellowship by Balliol. The Master of Balliol, Benjamin Jowett, is a friend, and RB wants Pen to enter Balliol, but Pen fails the examination and eventually matriculates at Christ Church (1869); from 1874 he studies painting and sculpture and pursues a minor artistic career until his father's death.

1868 Publication of *Poetical Works* (6 vols., Smith, Elder, RB's publishers for the remainder of his career).

1868–9 *November–February*: Publication of *The Ring and the Book* in four instalments, each volume containing three books of the poem; RB at last achieves critical acclaim and a measure of commercial success.

1869 A friendship with Louisa, Lady Ashburton, leads to her proposing that they marry; RB refuses ('my heart [is] buried at Florence'), after which Lady Ashburton lets it be known that *she* refused *him*, the version accepted by RB's biographers until the mid 1980s.

1871 Publication of *Balaustion's Adventure*, a narrative poem incorporating a 'transcript' (RB's preferred term for 'translation') of Euripides' *Alcestis*; reaches several editions. Publication of *Prince Hohenstiel-Schwangau, Saviour of Society*, a long dramatic monologue spoken by the Prince, a thinly disguised portrait of the recently abdicated Emperor Napoleon III.

1872 Publication of *Fifine at the Fair*, a long dramatic monologue spoken by Don Juan; RB calls it his 'most metaphysical and boldest' poem since *Sordello*. Second edition of *The Ring and the Book* published.

1873 Publication of *Red Cotton Night-Cap Country*, a narrative poem based on a recent sensational court-case in Normandy.

1875 Publication of *Aristophanes' Apology*, a long dramatic monologue spoken by the heroine of *Balaustion's Adventure* but containing lengthy interpolations by Aristophanes and incorporating another 'transcript' of Euripides, this time the *Heracles*. Publication of *The Inn Album*, a narrative poem set in England with a melodramatic plot.

1876 Publication of *Pacchiarotto, and How He Worked in Distemper: with Other Poems*, a collection of shorter poems; the title poem is a satire on RB's critics.

1877 Publication of *The Agamemnon of Aeschylus*, with a preface in which RB defends the extreme literalness of his translation.

1878 Publication in one volume of *La Saisiaz* and *The Two Poets of Croisic*, the first a philosophical elegy in memory of RB's friend Annie Egerton Smith, who had died suddenly while on holiday in the Alps with RB and Sarianna, the second a comic poem about the literary pretensions of two figures from a village in Brittany.

1879 Publication of *Dramatic Idyls*, a collection of shorter poems including 'Martin Relph', 'Iphan Ivànovitch' (founded on a legend about a woman who threw her own children to the wolves pursuing her sleigh, which RB had heard in Russia forty-five years before) and 'Ned Bratts'.

1880 Publication of *Dramatic Idyls, Second Series* (prompted by critical and commercial success of previous volume), including 'Clive' and 'Pan and Luna'.

1881 Browning Society founded.

1882 Awarded honorary degree of DCL by Oxford University.

1883 Publication of *Jocoseria*, a collection of shorter poems including

'Ixion' (an attack on the doctrine of eternal punishment) and 'Never the Time and the Place'.

1884 Awarded honorary degree of LLD by Edinburgh University. Publication of *Ferishtah's Fancies*, philosophical and religious poems spoken by the Persian sage Ferishtah alternating with shorter lyrics; the volume is one of RB's most successful and goes into several editions.

1887 Publication of *Parleyings with Certain People of Importance in Their Day*, comprising an indirect autobiography in which the poet 'parleys' with obscure figures from the past who were important not just in their day but in his own childhood and early youth, among them the poet Christopher Smart, the painter Francesco Furini and the musician Charles Avison.

1888–9 Publication of *Poetical Works*, 16 vols.

1889 *12 December*: Browning dies in Venice, on the publication day of his final volume *Asolando*. Difficulties about burying him in EB's grave in Florence (the cemetery is officially closed) could probably have been overcome, but Pen accepts instead an offer of a grave in Poets' Corner in Westminster Abbey.

FURTHER READING

For a broader survey, see the chapter on 'Studying Browning' in John Woolford and Daniel Karlin, *Robert Browning*, London, 1996 (Longman Studies in Eighteenth- and Nineteenth-Century Literature).

1. EDITIONS

The Ring and the Book, ed. R. D. Altick, Harmondsworth, 1971 (Penguin English Poets)

The Poems of Browning, ed. J. Pettigrew and T. J. Collins, 2 vols., Harmondsworth, 1981 (Penguin English Poets)

Poetical Works of Robert Browning, general editor I. Jack, Oxford, 1981– (in progress) (Oxford English Texts)

Robert Browning: The Poems, ed. J. Woolford and D. Karlin, London, 1991– (in progress) (Longman Annotated English Poets)

Robert Browning: An Edition of the Major Works, ed. A. Roberts, Oxford, 1999 (Oxford Authors)

2. CORRESPONDENCE

The Brownings' Correspondence, ed. P. Kelley, R. Hudson and S. Lewis, Winfield (Kansas), 1984– (in progress; vols. 1–15 so far issued, to 1847)

The Letters of Elizabeth Barrett Browning, ed. F. G. Kenyon, 2 vols., London, 1897

Elizabeth Barrett Browning: Letters to Her Sister, ed. L. Huxley, London, 1929

Letters of Robert Browning, ed. T. L. Hood, London, 1933

Robert Browning and Julia Wedgwood: A Broken Friendship as Revealed in their Letters, London, 1937

Dearest Isa: Robert Browning's Letters to Isabella Blagden, ed. E. C. McAleer, Austin (Texas), 1951

New Letters of Robert Browning, ed. W. C. DeVane and K. L. Knickerbocker, London, 1951

Letters of the Brownings to George Barrett, ed. P. Landis, Urbana (Illinois), 1958

Browning to His American Friends, ed. G. R. Hudson, London, 1965

The Letters of Robert Browning and Elizabeth Barrett Barrett, 1845–1846, ed. E. Kintner, Cambridge (Mass.), 1969

Learned Lady: Letters from Robert Browning to Mrs Thomas Fitzgerald 1876–1889, ed. E. C. McAleer, Cambridge (Mass.), 1969

Elizabeth Barrett Browning's Letters to Mrs David Ogilvy 1849–1861, ed. P. Heydon and P. Kelley, London, 1974

Browning's Trumpeter: The Correspondence of Robert Browning and Frederick J. Furnivall 1872–1889, ed. W. S. Peterson, Washington D.C., 1979

More Than Friend: The Letters of Robert Browning to Katherine de Kay Bronson, ed. M. Meredith, Waco (Texas) and Winfield (Kansas), 1985

Robert Browning and Elizabeth Barrett: A Selection from the Courtship Correspondence, ed. D. Karlin, Oxford, 1989

Elizabeth Barrett Browning's Letters to Her Sister Arabella, ed. S. Lewis, Winfield (Kansas), 2002

3. BIOGRAPHY

Mrs (Alexandra Sutherland) Orr, *Life and Letters of Robert Browning*, London, 1891

W. H. Griffin and H. C. Minchin, *The Life of Robert Browning*, London, 1910; 2nd edn, 1938

Betty Miller, *Robert Browning: A Portrait*, London, 1952

Maisie Ward, *Robert Browning and His World*, 2 vols., London, 1967–9

William Irvine and Park Honan, *The Book, the Ring, and the Poet*, New Haven (Conn.), 1974

John Maynard, *Browning's Youth*, Cambridge (Mass.), 1977

Daniel Karlin, *The Courtship of Robert Browning and Elizabeth Barrett*, Oxford, 1985

Clyde de L. Ryals, *The Life of Robert Browning: A Critical Biography*, Oxford, 1993

Sarah Wood, *Robert Browning: A Literary Life*, London, 2001

4. CRITICISM AND WORKS OF REFERENCE

Mrs (Alexandra Sutherland) Orr, *A Handbook to the Works of Robert Browning*, London, 1885; revised and updated in successive edns to 1896

G. K. Chesterton, *Robert Browning*, London, 1903

W. C. DeVane, *A Browning Handbook*, 2nd edn, New York, 1955 (first publ. 1937)

Robert Langbaum, *The Poetry of Experience*, New York, 1957

Park Honan, *Browning's Characters: A Study in Poetic Technique*, New Haven, 1961

Robert Browning: The Critical Heritage, ed. B. Litzinger and D. Smalley, London, 1968

W. David Shaw, *The Dialectical Temper: The Rhetorical Art of Robert Browning*, Ithaca, 1968

Harold Bloom, *A Map of Misreading*, Oxford, 1975

Herbert F. Tucker, *Browning's Beginnings: The Art of Disclosure*, Minneapolis, 1980

E. Warwick Slinn, *Browning and the Fictions of Identity*, London, 1982

Philip Kelley and Betty Coley, *The Browning Collections: A Reconstruction*, Winfield (Kansas), 1984

Loy D. Martin, *Browning's Dramatic Monologues and the Post-Romantic Subject*, Baltimore, 1985

John Woolford, *Browning the Revisionary*, London, 1988

Daniel Karlin, *Browning's Hatreds*, Oxford, 1993

A Concordance to the Poems and Plays of Robert Browning, compiled by R. J. Shroyer and T. J. Collins, New York, 1996

Donald S. Hair, *Robert Browning's Language*, Toronto, 1999